AUTHORSHIP PUZZLES IN THE HISTORY OF ECONOMICS

Literary and historical detective work which attempts to penetrate the anonymity of authors has a perennial fascination. Yet it is often tantalisingly inconclusive in its results. This book shows, through six case-studies, that a simple and robust statistical technique may be employed to add to the body of available evidence, and to indicate the likely author of an anonymous publication. The statistical technique used is simple and the numerical characteristics of an author's style which provide the basic raw material upon which the method works are themselves easy to understand.

The book also shows how such an approach may throw light on a situation in which, far from there being no obvious candidate for authorship, there is a variety of competing claimants to an unsigned work. The cases studied here range from seventeenth-century economic pamphlets to a mysterious volume of essays which has been attributed to an illustrious nineteenth-century statesman. The results of the investigation should be of interest to economists, historians, and to a wide public interested in the history of ideas, as well as to those who find fascination in the very idea of an author's 'fingerprints'.

D. P. O'Brien is Professor of Economics at the University of Durham. He was previously Reader in Economics at Queen's University, Belfast. His previous works are: *Information Agreements, Competition and Efficiency* (with D. Swann); *J. R. McCulloch: A Study in Classical Economics*; *The Correspondence of Lord Overstone* (3 vols); *J. R. McCulloch: Treatise on Taxation* (editor); *Competition in British Industry* (with D. Swann and others); *Competition in British Industry: Case Studies* (with D. Swann and others); *The Classical Economists*; *Competition Policy, Profitability and Growth* (with W. S. Howe and others); *Pioneers of Modern Economics in Britain* (editor, with J. R. Presley).

A. C. Darnell is Lecturer in Economics at the University of Durham. His research interests are econometrics and the history of economic thought.

Other books by D. P. O'Brien

INFORMATION AGREEMENTS, COMPETITION AND EFFICIENCY (*with D. Swann*)
J. R. McCULLOCH: A Study in Classical Economics
THE CORRESPONDENCE OF LORD OVERSTONE (*3 vols*)
J. R. McCULLOCH: Treatise on Taxation (*editor*)
COMPETITION IN BRITISH INDUSTRY (*with D. Swann and others*)
COMPETITION IN BRITISH INDUSTRY: Case Studies (*with D. Swann and others*)
THE CLASSICAL ECONOMISTS
COMPETITION POLICY, PROFITABILITY AND GROWTH (*with W. S. Howe, D. M. Wright and R. J. O'Brien*)
PIONEERS OF MODERN ECONOMICS IN BRITAIN (*editor, with J. R. Presley*)

Authorship Puzzles in the History of Economics

A Statistical Approach

D. P. O'Brien
Professor of Economics
University of Durham

and

A. C. Darnell
Lecturer in Economics
University of Durham

First published 1982 by
THE MACMILLAN PRESS LTD
London and Basingstoke
Companies and representatives throughout the world

ISBN 0 333 30078 5

Printed in Hong Kong

Contents

List of Figures

List of Tables

Preface

Our thanks are due to a number of people not all of whom may be aware that they have helped us. In particular we owe a debt to Professor W. O. Thweatt whose efforts to prove that McCulloch wrote material previously attributed to Torrens stimulated us to search for an alternative approach to the problem. We also owe a debt, as indicated in Chapter 1, to the Rev. A. Q. Morton and his associates; our attempts to interpret their use of collocations were fundamental to the development of our method. We must also thank a number of those connected with the NUMAC computing service, especially the ladies who tirelessly punched our text onto computer cards. We also owe a special debt to the designers of the program COCOA (Count and Concordance generation on Atlas), G. L. M. Berry-Rogghe and T. D. Crawford, without whom none of this work would have been possible; and at an early stage in our work we had valuable assistance in the operation of this program from Camilla Boldyreff of NUMAC. Another member of the NUMAC staff, Nigel Hall, also provided valuable help by writing a program which enabled us to investigate word position in relation to sentence length as a means of discriminating between authors.

We must also thank the staff of a number of libraries and record offices, especially those of Edinburgh University Library, the Goldsmith Library, University of London, the staff of Somerville College Library, Oxford, and of the British Library, as well as those of Kent County Record Office at Maidstone. We are particularly indebted to Lord Congleton, who very kindly gave us access to the papers of Sir Henry Parnell. We received a good deal of cooperation from librarians in the work which led to Chapter 5 and we are very grateful to those named in the notes to that chapter. Of course, a work of this kind involves special demands upon the 'home' library and we are appreciative of the help which we received from the Inter-Library Loan section of Durham University Library. We are also grateful for the comments we received from individual academics; Professor Barry Gordon was particularly helpful and made most valuable suggestions of possible authors of the works discussed in Chapters 5 and 8.

We have also to thank Duke University Press as the publishers of *History of Political Economy*, for permission to reproduce, in Chapter 4, material which originally appeared in that journal.

Special thanks are due to Ann Hillier who typed (several times) the whole of the text and virtually all the tables, and who even managed to read (as distinct from merely transcribe) what she typed, while showing a fine disregard for demarcation by typing not only the text of the book but also some of the text which we subjected to analysis, putting it straight into computer file for us via a terminal keyboard.

D. P. O'B.
A. C. D.

1 Introduction

I. AUTHORSHIP DISPUTES

Authorship puzzles are hardly a new problem. The various fears, pressures, and literary conventions, which have induced authors, particularly in earlier centuries, to withhold their names from publications, have resulted in a series of problems of authorship attribution which have exercised scholars for generations.

Such problems have concerned ancient Classical literature, mediaeval Latin literature, and English literature from at least the 17th century onwards. Since neither of us has any pretensions to Classical scholarship however, the discussion will concentrate on literature in English, although, as two important methodological discussions relate respectively to Greek and mediaeval Latin,[1] we shall refer to two non-English examples below.

The most celebrated (and, in our opinion, insoluble) of the problems which have preoccupied workers in this field is the question of whether the actor William Shakespeare wrote the plays attributed to him. In particular, a case has been presented for the attribution of the plays to Christopher Marlowe; and, as we shall see, the Marlowe attribution received support from what was probably the first systematic attempt to apply statistical analysis to problems of authorship.[2] This is perhaps ironic; our own experience in 17th century literature would suggest that, far from being a suitable place to *start* the development of this kind of technique, it is probably the last. For, whichever statistical variables are chosen – even the variable word-length which was used in this case[3] – they are all to a greater or lesser extent at the mercy of the printer (and, in the case of Shakespeare, of the shorthand writer). Printers seem to have had a particularly free hand in the 17th century. In addition, the use of dialogue, and of particular forms of dialogue to portray particular characters, poses problems which affect both plays and novels severely.[4]

Another celebrated problem is the authorship of the *Junius Letters*.[5] These were a series of political pamphlets written in the years 1769–72. The author went to considerable pains to conceal his identity, not only from the public, but also from the printer; and although there is, by common consent, one leading candidate for authorship (Sir Philip Francis), at least 40 other people have been suggested as possible authors.

A problem familiar to American historians is that of the *Federalist Papers*.[6] These papers were written in 1787–8. The known authors are Alexander Hamilton, John Jay and James Maddison. Their object was to persuade the citizens of New York State to ratify the Constitution. The authorship of twelve of these is a matter for dispute, since either Hamilton or Maddison may have written them, while three others may possibly be the work of Maddison using material supplied by Hamilton.

More recently the Rev. A. Q. Morton – perhaps best-known to newspaper readers for his work on the Pauline Epistles – has, with his colleagues, dealt with a number of intriguing literary problems.[7] These include: the question of whether 'another lady' who completed the novel *Sanditon* by Jane Austen was a successful imitator of her literary style; the problem of whether Sir Walter Scott's literary style remained constant over all the vicissitudes in health and fortune which afflicted him in the years 1816–31; the consistency in style of different parts of the work of Henry James; the consistency in different parts of the work of John Fowles; the recent attempts by Utechin and Mitchelson to imitate Conan Doyle and whether these can be distinguished from the original; the authentication of some work by Mrs Gaskell; and the internal consistency of the Shakespeare play *Pericles*, part of which, it has been suggested, is by some other author.

In economic literature – with which we are concerned since one author is an economist and the other an econometrician – there are a number of outstanding puzzles, most of which have received fairly extensive discussion, and we deal in the following chapters with six cases. Of those we discuss, the most celebrated are undoubtedly the vexed question of whether Sir Josiah Child was 'Philopatris', the authorship of the *Westminster Review* attack on Samuel Bailey, and the authorship of the October 1819 *Edinburgh Review* article on Owen. But the question of Bailey's own involvement in other pamphlets has also received a good deal of attention; Professor Tucker's work on the authorship of the 1830 *Essays on Political Economy* is of great interest; and the question of whether McCulloch or Parnell wrote several *Edinburgh Review* articles on Ireland has posed unsolved problems for researchers, especially those involved in the magnificent *Wellesley Index*.[8] The list is by no means exhaustive; we found that the computing problems posed even by the texts we have analysed were formidable, and we feel that we have covered a reasonable selection of the known problems. We have confined ourselves to English; and, with the exception of the problem of Sir Josiah Child, we have confined ourselves to the 19th century. But we have carefully indicated our method; and because it works well in the six cases discussed here, we hope that others may take over where we have left off and apply the method (further developing it as they go along, as we have done) to other outstanding issues.

II. THE PRIMARY APPROACH – LITERARY AND HISTORICAL DETECTION

The primary approach to authorship problems must surely be literary and historical detection. These come in two forms; the use of evidence internal to the work under discussion, and the investigation of external historical evidence.

Both of these have an important role to play but neither is satisfactory on its own. The use of internal evidence is mainly important as a method of suggesting what external historical evidence should be sought. On its own it is entirely unreliable as a method of *discrimination*, because it puts subjective selection in the forefront of the picture. It is, of course, the sort of evidence used to 'prove' that the works of Shakespeare were written by some other Elizabethan; but the same text will usually yield a variety of such 'proofs', each establishing the responsibility of a different putative author. But as a method of suggesting the historical clues to be looked for (a sort of Popperian hypotheses formation prior to testing by looking for historical clues) it is invaluable; and a classic example is provided by Tucker who, after reading the 19th century essays attributed to one 'Geo. Robertson' made a list of the author's attributes, which led in turn to William Huskisson. Again, in the case of the *Junius Letters*, historical research has proved of primary importance in highlighting the possibility that the author was Sir Philip Francis and thus in justifying the concentration upon him of the statistical analysis conducted by Ellegard.

Literary and historical detection can sometimes, by turning up vital clues, almost complete the task of identifying an author. Mr Sraffa's Ricardo edition contains a number of remarkable examples of this, including material concerning the identity of an 'ingenious calculator' referred to in Ricardo's *Economical and Secure Currency* and in his *Plan for a National Bank*; and 'Mr – of the Bullion Report' is identified as the

British merchant, banker, and secret agent, John Parish. Yet even in these cases the evidence remains circumstantial.[9]

But, in any case, detection as successful as this is very much the exception. More often, literary and historical detection can come to a dead end. A classic case of this is outlined in our discussion of the authorship of the October 1819 *Edinburgh Review* article, in Chapter 4. For all the historical evidence appeared to point one way; and virtually all commentators agreed that Torrens was the author. But then an ingeniously argued case was published, which sought to establish, in the face of this evidence, that McCulloch was the author. Again, one may have, as in the case of the *Edinburgh Review* articles on Ireland discussed in Chapter 7, flatly contradictory claims to authorship by different writers. Faced with a situation like this, one looks for some way of easing the log-jam by approaching the problem from an entirely different angle; and we believe, as others have done before us, that statistical analysis of the numerical attributes of the text can provide just such a way.

III. THE STATISTICAL ANALYSIS

Statistical analysis only comes on the scene, then, once the background literary and historical research has been done. It is not a substitute for it; rather it is a (we believe, vital) complement to it, once the short-listing has been done. Although our statistical procedures provide discrimination rather than fingerprints, there is still something to be learnt from a parallel with police procedure in a serious crime investigation. For the police do not fingerprint an entire population; they confine fingerprinting to a list of 'possibles'. Similarly, we cannot test for discrimination between the work of hundreds of authors; we need a short list of 'suspects'. *The statistical procedure then seeks to select variables which have the power to discriminate between the known works of possible authors, while failing to discriminate between different works (or parts of the same work) of a given author or disputed text; and then uses the same variables to attempt discrimination between the work of these known authors and the disputed text. Where the variables which were successful in discriminating between the known authors succeed in discriminating the disputed text from the work of all but one of the candidates for authorship, a presumptive case to support the claims of that author's advocates has been established.*

The earliest attempts to use this kind of approach, of which we know, were by T. C. Mendenhall, following a suggestion by Augustus de

Morgan.[10] De Morgan had suggested *average* word length as a means of discrimination; Mendenhall, however, possibly because of scientific interest in spectroscopic analysis,[11] sought to analyse the frequency distributions of word lengths in samples of text. Although the analysis established that the distributions for Marlowe and Shakespeare were virtually identical, and that the one for Bacon was markedly different, the chosen variable possessed little genuine power of discrimination; and indeed the distributions for Thackeray and Dickens proved hard to distinguish. The tests employed to distinguish different distributions were not based upon a foundation of statistical theory but were what are known jocularly as 'eyeball statistics', i.e. looking at the distributions and attempting to distinguish them by visual characteristics.

Since Mendenhall's pioneering efforts, a number of other researchers have worked on statistical analysis of authorship. We are not attempting here any exhaustive history of these attempts; but it may be of interest if we indicate some of the earlier attempts which we ourselves have found particularly interesting and helpful.

In the 1930s, Dr C. B. Williams attempted to use word length as a discriminatory variable – again without success.[12] He abandoned his efforts; but his interest in the subject was re-awakened by a remarkable article published in 1938 by G. Udney Yule.[13] Yule was exercised by two particular problems: the authorship of the Latin *De Imitatione Christi*; and the question whether the *Observations upon the Bills of Mortality* was really the work of Sir William Petty rather than that of John Graunt, to whom it has been attributed. Yule's variable was sentence length; and he produced tables of sentence length giving the mean, median, first and third quartiles, the interquartile range, and the ninth decile.

The sentence length discrimination worked quite well with the Latin text and did seem to establish that Thomas à Kempis, and not Gerson, wrote the *Imitatione*. It worked less well with the English text – there was some overlap between the different authors, on the measures of dispersion suggested – but indicated that Petty was probably not the author of the *Observations*. But no formal statistical tests were employed and, throughout most of the discussion, Yule appears to have regarded them as unsuitable.[14]

His article is still extremely well worth reading today. There are three particular points of interest. Firstly, Yule provided a detailed and intriguing discussion of the difficulties of defining sentence length – difficulties which were particularly acute in 17th century texts.[15] Secondly, he raised a number of difficulties about word length, which might not occur to the casual reader, particularly the occurrence of words like 'anywhere' which could be one or two words; and he quoted the following verse:

> Forever; 'tis a single word!
> Our rude forefathers deemed it two:
> Can you imagine so absurd
> A view?[16]

Thirdly, and perhaps most importantly, Yule, who had explored sampling techniques in his study, discussed the validity of these techniques in a literary context, and concluded that they were invalid for the following reasons. Firstly, because it is preferable to *select* samples which deal with the same subject matter, as far as possible, in case the discriminatory variable should be affected by choice of subject matter; secondly because there is a danger in random sampling due to the risk of bias 'arising from the varying lengths of sentences and the fact that the series of sentence-lengths, in order as they occur, is not a random one. To take a simple but extreme example, suppose our book consisted of equal numbers of pages containing respectively 30 sentences of 15 words each, and 15 sentences of 30 words each. Actually then the book would contain two sentences of 15 words to one of 30 words. But if we proceeded by the method used for obtaining "random passages" from Petty, taking only a sample of 10 sentences from each page determined by Tippett's [random] numbers, we would tend to get a sample containing equal numbers of sentences of the two lengths: the number of long sentences would be over-weighted.'[17] These seem to us important and valid reasons, and they are the ones we would advance for our use of continuous and lengthy sections of text, particularly as, although we do not use sentence length as a discriminatory variable, we do use First Word, and the number of First Word occurrences is directly related to the sentence lengths.

As noted above, Yule's work re-awakened the interest of C. B. Williams, who argued that the heavily-skewed distributions of sentence length could be transformed into log-normal distributions.[18] Unlike Yule, he showed little hesitation in using formal statistical tests of significance; but here he encountered a difficulty. For he produced his own data on sentence length from samples of the work of Chesterton, Wells and Shaw, and, although he found that the log means were significantly different between Shaw and Wells, the difference of means for Shaw and Chesterton was barely significant. This was serious because he had to fall back on the standard deviations to discriminate between Shaw and Chesterton. This, in turn, meant that the method was not really applicable to cases of disputed authorship, for there was always the possibility that failure to discriminate between the means of disputed and known texts could simply be the result of failure of the method; and a significant difference between the means for one author and a disputed text, and between the variance for another author and a disputed text, would simply leave the whole matter unresolved. Although there have been subsequent attempts to revive sentence length as the key variable,[19] it does not seem to us to be as fruitful a way forward as the non-parametric methods subsequently developed.

A major attempt to apply statistical analysis to authorship disputes was made by Ellegard in connection with the authorship of the *Junius Letters*.[20] He found that sentence length worked poorly with English prose[21] and he chose, as the key variables, the frequency of unusual words, following Yule's work on vocabulary in his *Statistical Study of Literary Vocabulary* of 1944.[22] Yule had developed a vocabulary constant *K* which varied inversely with vocabulary size. This, however, proved to have poor discriminatory power within the context of 18th century English prose.[23] Ellegard proceeded by selecting a list of distinctive words – distinctive in the sense that some of them were peculiar to 'Junius' and that others of them were particularly unusual in his writings. These he memorised, and then counted the frequency of their occurrence by hand. This was a remarkable feat of scholarly tenacity, and it enabled him, using the dispersions of relative frequencies of unusual words within a multivariate normal distribution, to discriminate between texts and to conclude that Sir Philip Francis wrote the *Junius Letters*. Without wishing to detract in any way from this splendid effort, we did not feel that this would be a satisfactory way to proceed for our purposes. It involves very large samples (because of the use of special words) for it to be reliable; and it is also extremely laborious, even with the aid of a computer, if words are to be selected as characterstic of a writer on any other basis than crude numerical frequency.

The study of English prose which set new standards in a number of respects was that by Mosteller and Wallace, who attempted to establish whether Maddison or Hamilton was the author of a number of the *Federalist Papers*.[24] They found that the frequency of *common* words was the most effective tool of discrimination, and they used what they called 'filler' words (but avoiding contextual words like 'war'). They tried the fit of both Poisson and negative-binomial distributions. They found that Poisson did not fit the occurrence of a number of words, notably 'may' and 'his' although it was quite a good fit for the frequency of 'an', 'any', and 'upon'.

Their approach was very laborious. To avoid contextual words they chose filler words from a list compiled by Miller, Newman and Friedman, choosing the 70 highest frequency words and a random set of 20 low frequency words. They also obtained a vocabulary of 6,700 words from samples of 35,000 words of Hamilton and 35,000 words of Maddison. They eliminated a number of low frequency and contextual words[25] and the remainder were tested for their ability to discriminate by plotting both the Hamilton and Maddison distributions on binomial probability paper. They kept those for which the authors' rates differed by at least three standard deviations. This provided them with 103 words. They also obtained 28 low frequency words collected from four successive sets of papers from each author.

Their first approach was to estimate linear discriminant functions on half the material of known authorship and then to test the functions on the other half. After this they applied the functions to the disputed papers. They also used a Bayesian procedure. There are a number of obvious difficulties with this but we reserve discussion of them until Chapter 2.

The choice of discriminatory variable had thus progressed from average word length (de Morgan) to frequency distribution of word length (Mendenhall), to sentence length (Yule), to rare vocabulary (Ellegard), to common vocabulary (Mosteller and Wallace). The statistical methodology had also progressed significantly from 'eyeball statistics' to simple calculations of measures of central tendency and dispersion, then to simple tests of significance of differences, then to use of the multivariate-normal distribution, and finally to the supplementation of this by the negative-binomial distribution, and the use of linear discriminant functions.

However, developments which were to prove perhaps more important in English prose had begun earlier in dealing with problems of Greek prose. This was in the work of W. C. Wake, dating from 1948.[26] Wake's fundamental perception is summarised by two of the authors who have done much to develop techniques stemming from this perception: 'Wake was soon able to show that what is most characteristic of an author is not his few personal idiosyncrasies but the rate at which he performs the operations which he shares with all his colleagues.'[27] Wake does not appear to be referred to in the study by Mosteller and Wallace, although in their emphasis upon common words they had something of the same perception.

Building upon Wake's work, Michaelson, Morton and Hamilton-Smith developed a Greek stylometry which was apparently converted to a stylometry of English under the pressure of circumstances in 1974.[28] This involved using variables derived from three concepts: collocations, positional stylometry and proportional pairs. Collocations are the conjunctions of pairs of words. Thus the relative frequency with which 'be' is preceded by different words, is often found to differ significantly between authors. 'Positional stylometry' relates to the position in sentences of particular words. This has proved particularly powerful in dealing with Greek prose. An example of its use in English would be 'the' as first word, expressed as *a proportion of* the total number of occurrences of 'the' in a sample. It is also possible to discriminate between texts by using the relative frequency of different words as first words of sentences. The concept of proportional pairs relates to such pairs of words as 'no, not' or 'with, without'. The basic procedure is that the observation is the occurrence of both parts of the pair in one sentence as a proportion of the total number of occurrences of both words.

IV. METHOD OF THE PRESENT STUDY

In the present study we have followed the path laid down by Morton and his associates, but developed it in a number of respects. We have, first of all, prepared the text by removal of a number of characteristics which blur comparisons. Thus all quotations from other authors are removed, together with footnotes and tables. All extraneous full stops after expressions such as 'cent', 'viz', and '£sd' are also removed as these mislead the computer when it is selecting first words of sentences. Textual preparation is important and it is rarely discussed, although Yule was an important exception to this.[29] The case for this kind of editing is clear enough; it is particularly important to remove long sequences of words which come from other authors if we are not to obscure clear differences in the literary habits of particular writers.

The text thus prepared has been fed into the IBM 370 NUMAC computer, which (fortunately for us) has a large memory capacity. Using a programme called COCOA we have then selected the literary habits which we have found fulfil the double requirement of indicating uniformity within the work of one writer while discriminating between writers. We found that choice of first word and collocations with 'the' and 'be' were the most powerful discriminating characteristics.

The collocations selected may be case-and-sample-specific; but, so long as the *same* collocations show uniformity within one author and discrimination between different authors, this is not a serious cause for concern.

The use of chi-squared as a test of independence is particularly satisfactory because this is a non-parametric technique. Some statisticians have argued that, because fixed distributions often do not fit literary variables very well, it may be necessary to develop new ones. To us, the poor fit of fixed distributions suggests, rather, that it is preferable to use 'distribution-free' tests. In using chi-squared, we went considerably beyond the use made by Michaelson, Morton and Hamilton-Smith, although discussion of the technicalities of this is reserved for Chapter 2. However, some general points may be made here. Firstly, the power of the tests can be considerably increased by using contingency tables which include all the possible collocations with one particular word, with as many disaggregated rows as possible, rather than a 2×2 table of the kind used by Morton and his associates. Secondly, we have tried, at least as far as possible, to amalgamate cells in a way which makes literary sense. Thus in collocations with 'be' it makes literary sense to amalgamate 'may be' and 'might be' but it does not make literary sense to amalgamate collocations such as these with 'must be'. As far as is possible, we have avoided such amalgamations. Although limited by the rule concerning chi-squared which is in general acceptance (not more than 20 per cent of cells should have an expected value of less than 5), we have tried to use tables with as many rows as possible as, through the change in the degrees of freedom, this produces a more powerful test. The details of this are explained in Chapter 2.

We have also taken large samples in an effort to avoid the clustering of occurrences of one particular habit which quite clearly does take place in literary samples. We still found that it could occasionally be a problem, particularly in one piece of work by Torrens. But large samples help to avoid this difficulty, which was particularly noted by Yule,[30] as well as helping to reduce the need to amalgamate cells.

The occurrence of 'clumping' is one reason why the method cannot be applied mechanically without an intelligent appreciation of what is going on. Another reason is that surprising words turn out to be contextual. For instance, one sample of the work of Sir Henry Parnell, which we used in the tests reported in Chapter 7, came from his *Penal Laws*.[31] But it turns out that the word 'by' is contextual in this work because many sentences, dealing with a particular form of legislation, start with 'By the Act of . . .'.

There is a very real danger in this form of testing – that it will lead one to select the collocations which provide the discrimination one requires. To guard against this it is *vital* that the *same* collocations should show homogeneity between texts which are known to be by the same author. It follows from this that we prefer to have several samples of the work of each author who is a candidate for authorship of the disputed piece although, given one very large, and attested, sample it is probably reasonable to split this into two or more parts to test for homogeneity between the parts. Thus we split Huskisson's 1810 pamphlet into two parts and found homogeneity between the parts. (We also split the disputed piece attributed to Huskisson into two parts and found it to be homogeneous.)

Of course it is possible (although, in view of the labour in which we have been involved, it seems rather unlikely) that somebody will wish to attempt to replicate some of our results for himself. With this in mind, we have carefully indicated samples, editions, and sample sizes in each chapter following.

Of course, it is possible to raise fastidious objections to the procedures employed. Statisticians may be particularly worried over the problem of the independence of observations. But, in the last resort, the proof of the pudding is in the eating. If the method works – and it seems that it does – then over-scrupulous objections seem rather otiose. This point was correctly perceived by Ellegard in his earlier study.[32] What we (and others) have done is to take the applicability of statistical assumptions as a working hypothesis and then see if they succeed in discriminating. Indeed, literary use of statistical procedures has one possible advantage over normal use: we *start* with the knowledge that the material comes from two different authors (populations) and we then see whether the tests will discriminate *between populations*, whereas normally we do not know whether the observations come from the same population, and that is what we are testing.

It may be as well to say a brief word about the practical difficulties which anyone attempting a study of this kind encounters, although with the rapid developments of micro-processors it is possible that technological advances may sweep away many of the difficulties we have met. Firstly, there is the problem of input. If this is via punched cards, the quantities required are very large indeed. Thus for the 5,800 words of the sample from Parnell's *Penal Law Reform* referred to above, we needed 726 cards. It is possible to get a typist to work directly at a computer terminal and to type in text; but our experience is that this requires a high-quality professional typist (preferably familiar with the peculiarities of computer terminals), or else the rate of error is rather high and a great deal of editing of text is required. It may be that this problem will disappear if scanning develops beyond its present primitive state, with the micro-processor revolution.

The process of reading literary text into file involves heavy calls upon CPU time. Thus in order to read the cards and create the file to store the sample from *Penal Law Reform* involved more than three seconds of CPU time so that anyone working with a computer where CPU usage is severely rationed would be in difficulties. Once the machine has read the cards, the problem of file space arises. Despite the generous allowances, per individual computer number, of file space made available under NUMAC, together with extra file space made available to us, we found this a considerable constraint.

Those who are principally accustomed to using a computer for regression analysis may like a simple comparison. To read a file containing 15 time series variables, each having 660 observations (monthly data over 55 years) and to run a simple bivariate regression for each variable on a linear time trend involves marginally less CPU time than simply reading the cards containing our *Penal Law* sample – and the latter was only about half the size of many of the extracts which we used.

These are in the nature of external limitations to statistical analysis of authorship which may well disappear in the course of time. There will, however, remain one internal limitation – but one taking a variety of forms – which we see no way of solving. This is the limitation that, in order to compare texts with different known authors, we have to establish homogeneity in both the texts of known authors and the disputed texts. If bits and pieces have been inserted or altered by an editor, a printer, or a committee (such as the Court of Directors of the East India Company, a possibility discussed in Chapter 3), and if these are statistically insignificant, we cannot detect this. The text may appear to be internally homogeneous and all the product of one hand even though a particular paragraph has been inserted by another hand. This has serious implications for the history of ideas. However, the situation is not as desperate as it looks. If we avoid matters over which the caprices of generations of printers have been particularly in evidence – spelling, punctuation, particularly within a sentence, and the use of capital letters and italics – then outside insertions are not likely to be very important. Moreover, as we show in Chapter 7, if a disputed text is divided into clear sections, we can certainly test whether the sections are homogeneous. It is indeed one great merit of employing chi-squared that it can be used on both large and small samples. Nevertheless, the problem does remain. However, we do not consider it to be very serious (at least beyond the 17th century) and we would certainly regard it as insignificant by comparison with what can certainly be achieved using the methods we have employed in this study.

2 Statistical Background

I. INTRODUCTION

There are three broad statistical approaches capable, in principle, of analysing literary problems, namely the Classical parametric, the Bayesian, and the non-parametric. The early developments all used Classical parametric techniques which, while showing promise in dealing with problems arising from Greek prose, have, generally speaking, not performed satisfactorily in applications to English prose, as noted in Chapter 1. Indeed, of all parametric approaches, by far the most successful application was within the realm of Bayesian analysis but, as indicated below, we are a little uneasy about the use of Bayesian statistics within the field. By contrast, techniques derived from non-parametric statistics, are, in our opinion, particularly well suited not only to the very questions of literary puzzles but also to the data generated by literary samples.

The purpose of this chapter, then, is to give a brief description of the principles and requirements of the three classes of technique and to give a full statement of the use of a non-parametric χ^2 test which we employ in subsequent chapters.

II. PARAMETRIC APPROACHES

Statistical analysis of literary text starts with given texts and a number of named authors. Parametric techniques then typically identify a particular characteristic of the authors in question and analyse the distribution of measures of that characteristic throughout the works of those authors. One characteristic often used in such studies is choice of sentence length, measured by the number of words. Parametric techniques proceed on the basis of an attempt to describe the observed distribution by a theoretical distribution characterised and determined by a set of parameters which we shall denote here by θ. Suppose we have two contending authors, A and B, and suppose further that from their known works we estimate the values of θ relevant to each as $\hat{\theta}_A$ and $\hat{\theta}_B$. Suppose also that from analysis of the anonymously written work we estimate a value $\hat{\theta}_Q$.

The questions we need to ask may be formulated as below:

Using the sample statistics $\hat{\theta}_A$, $\hat{\theta}_B$ and $\hat{\theta}_Q$, can we make inferences regarding their true population counterparts θ_A, θ_B and θ_Q? In particular, can we say whether:

(i) θ_A is significantly different from θ_B; whether
(ii) θ_A is significantly different from θ_Q; and whether
(iii) θ_B is significantly different from θ_Q?

Clearly if we are able to answer 'yes', 'yes' and 'no' respectively, we have support for the hypothesis that the unknown hand was author B and not author A. However, let us consider the information required to enable us to answer such questions.

Because the questions are directed towards differences between parameters, it is necessary that we know the sampling distribution of the parameter estimators; we may then formulate a test statistic which is based on known sample quantities. These necessary conditions invariably lead the investigator to assume a particular sampling distribution which is completely described by a small number of population parameters. Unfortunately, common and familiar distributions such as the Binomial, Negative-Binomial, Poisson, Normal and Log-Normal do not seem to fit literary variables at all well, and this view is certainly supported by our investigations.[1] This has led to the suggestion[2] that new distributions need to be formulated in order that a parametric approach may be adopted to handle literary problems.

However, simply because we cannot attack a given problem using the available tools within a parametric technique does not necessarily imply that we require additions to the tool kit; it may well imply that the inappropriate tool bag has been picked up. An alternative bag contains non-parametric techniques. They are concerned not with parameters and fixed distributions but with answering questions formulated in different ways; and, as we demonstrate below, questions of disputed authorship are particularly amenable to analysis by non-parametric methods. The advantages of non-parametric methods are that: (i) the assumptions are usually few and easily met; (ii) the calculations are usually straightforward and quickly performed; (iii) the range of applicability is wide; (iv) in most cases the associated probability statements are exact; and (v) data from small samples and those measured on a weak ordinal scale may be analysed.[3]

For these reasons, we have employed a non-parametric application of the χ^2 distribution which is explained below; the analysis has proved to be successful and is much simpler to use than any existing parametric method. However, it was noted above that a Bayesian approach has been used effectively in dealing with literary problems; and before dealing with our non-parametric technique it is desirable to say something about the Bayesian work.

III. BAYESIAN ANALYSIS AND TESTS OF AUTHORSHIP

Mosteller and Wallace,[4] in analysing the authorship of *The Federalist Papers*, make use of a Bayesian approach. The essential feature of such an approach is the estimation of 'posterior odds'. 'Posterior odds' describe the analyst's belief, based on prior information and sample information, that one author and not another was responsible for having written a particular anonymous work. Prior information is encapsulated by the analyst's setting of the 'prior odds'. Thus, if we lack prior information, the odds are set at '50–50', while if we have prior information and believe that author A, not author B, was responsible, we set the prior odds accordingly, at say 100 to 1 in favour of A. The sample information is described unambiguously by the so-called 'likelihood ratio' which is a statistic measuring the extent to which the data support the one hypothesis *vis à vis* the other. Bayes' Theorem tells us that the posterior odds are equal to the product of the prior odds and the likelihood ratio.

To use Bayes' Theorem, then, we need to specify the prior odds, calculate the likelihood ratio from the sample, and multiply the two together to obtain the posterior odds upon which we will make our decision as regards the authorship of the work in question.

There are two major problems with this approach in the study of authorship puzzles. In the first place, it is necessary to specify a particular distribution of the characteristic in question. Thus, if we are analysing, for example, usage of a particular word, we must specify the form of distribution which describes the frequency with which each author uses that word. We have indicated above that there are particular difficulties in the identification of a suitable distribution. We believe, as will be argued below, that problems of authorship may be tackled using much simpler techniques and, furthermore, we believe that Bayes' Theorem is not the best device to use in these studies.

The latter remark is made in light of the second major problem which arises with Bayes' Theorem. In order to calculate posterior odds, one requires the specification of prior odds. Thus any two investigators faced with identical samples may arrive at different decisions simply because they differ in the specification of the subjective prior odds. How do we arrive at our prior odds? Mosteller and Wallace, whose use of Bayesian techniques in this field is the leading exemplar, state that: 'if you are an historian with knowledge of the problem you may have quite strong beliefs that lead to the assignment of large odds in one or the other direction.'[5] However, this view springs from a conception of the role of statistical techniques in dealing with literary problems which is rather different from our own. In our view, the aim of such techniques should be to *supplement* the (inevitably) ambiguous historical and textual arguments. We prefer to keep the literary and historical evidence distinct and not to blend it directly into the statistical analysis. Ideally, we seek a statistical procedure which is *independent* of (prior) historical and textual arguments. For this reason we prefer not to use Bayes' Theorem in such studies. The use of the Theorem is justified by Mosteller and Wallace on the grounds that 'Prior distributions are not of major importance.'[6] While we would not dispute the very high standard of the work done by Mosteller and Wallace, such a statement seems capable of being interpreted as saying that the sample information is itself dominating the prior information. If this is the case, then one might suggest the use of classical likelihood ratio techniques or non-parametric methods as being better suited to the problem. But, more fundamentally, our hesitations stem from the use of priors which indicate the investigator's desire to blend non-sample information with sample information. We prefer to present the two sorts of evidence as separate entities and draw our conclusions accordingly. In not one of the studies described in later chapters do *we* find contradictions between the two sorts of evidence, but this is nothing more than a comment on the priors which we hold. Were we to take a Bayesian approach we would, therefore, arrive at similar conclusions to those which we have reached, but, having incorporated the historical evidence in a formal way, we might regard the results as being stronger and more conclusive then we feel can be obtained from statistical analysis in this context.

The above is not to be seen as a general critique of Bayesian methods. On the contrary, the present authors have great sympathy with such methods. The question is one of the relative usefulness of applying them in a literary context. In decision-making problems where the costs of making the wrong decision may be identified, the Bayesian approach has much to offer. However, since we seek evidence complementary to, and independent of, the historical and textual evidence, we prefer not to use them in approaching questions of disputed authorship.

IV. THE NON-PARAMETRIC APPROACH

The approach which we have chosen to employ is a non-parametric method. One of the major advantages of such a method is its reliance on a very small set of assumptions; a second major advantage is consequent upon it being non-parametric, namely that one has no parameters to estimate. The latter has important implications, as we shall see below, for the amount of computation necessary to apply the method to a given problem of authorship, and the former advantage indicates that we have adopted a method which conforms with the precept known as 'Occam's Razor', i.e. we have used the simplest effective means. The principle we adopt is extremely simple; yet it is, as subsequent chapters indicate, very powerful. The germ of the principle may be found in a letter written by Augustus de Morgan in 1851 to an old Cambridge friend, the Rev. W. Heald: 'I should expect to find that one man writing on two different subjects agrees more nearly with himself than two different men writing on the same subject.'[7] De Morgan was, in this case, referring to an author's usage of *word length* and his hypothesis was that authors may be distinguished by the average length of individual words used by them. This itself has not proved a fruitful line of inquiry, as indicated in Chapter 1. However, the two crucial elements of his suggestion were, first, his concern with examination of habits common to *all* authors and, secondly, his suggestion that one would expect to find 'the slight differences between one writer and another to be well maintained against each other, and very well agreeing with themselves'.[8]

Thus, what de Morgan, some 130 years ago, was suggesting was that in order to address ourselves to questions of authorship we should concentrate on habits which are common to all authors, used consistently by each individual author under consideration, and are used distinctly (yet consistently) by different authors; i.e. what distinguishes one author from another is the way in which he distinctly and consistently uses a habit which is itself in common usage across authors. This principle is, quite clearly, at variance with those methods which stress an author's idiosyncracies. One of the major disadvantages of this latter approach is its very large data requirement. Suppose, for example, that author A uses a particular word, peculiar to himself, once every thousand words, on average. Suppose further that the anonymous piece in question is only some two thousand words long. Both events, the occurrence of the word (possibly multiple occurrences) and its non-occurrence, are compatible with the hypothesis of the piece having been written by author A. A much larger section of anonymously written work would be required before such a technique could be capable of yielding strong evidence but in all cases we are faced with a finite, and frequently small, anonymous piece. Any method which relies on the search for idiosyncratic behaviour is, therefore, one limited to those cases where large samples of text are available. The method which we present below is capable of dealing most satisfactorily with both small and large samples. On these grounds, then, it is to be preferred.

The important questions are, thus, what high-frequency habits are to be used and how can we operationalise the concepts of 'consistent usage' and 'distinguishing usage'?

(a) The choice of suitable habits

Two broad classes of literary characteristics have been examined in these studies, namely usage of particular words in particular positions within sentences and usage of particular collocations; a collocation is an ordered pair of words such as 'and the' or 'would be' which are, respectively, collocations of 'the' and 'be'.

Attention was drawn to the potentialities of the systematic study of word position and word mobility in a most interesting paper by Michaelson and Morton.[9] In their study, the authors introduce the terms 'isotropic' and 'anisotropic'. An 'anisotropic word' is one which is 'bound' in the sense that it occurs only in a range of preferred positions within a sentence. Thus, for example, a word which is most typically used as the first word of a sentence is anisotropic; equally a word used most typically as the penultimate word of a sentence is anisotropic. A word which is not 'bound', and which is thus completely mobile, is categorised as isotropic. The aim of the method of categorising words as anisotropic or isotropic is to obtain the statistics of the forward and backward positions of each word. The forward position of a word is simply its position number in the sentence. Thus if the word is the first word its position is '1', if the second word then '2' and so on. The backward position of each word is simply obtained by counting backwards from the last word. Thus, if the word occurs as a first word, its backward position is the number of words in that sentence. Clearly, a mobile (isotropic) word is expected, on average, to occur at the mid-point of a sentence. Therefore the means of the forward and backward counts will exhibit only random sampling differences.

There are two important objections to the use of such a categorisation as a means of discriminating between the works of various authors. First, as Michaelson and Morton themselves recognise,[10] the statistics are not independent of sentence length. Thus data derived from word position is incorporating data of another kind, that derived from sentence length, in a disguised form. Secondly, and much more significantly, any test of whether or not an observed difference between the means of forward and backward statistics is due to random sampling differences requires the analyst to be specific about the sampling distribution of the relevant statistics. It is a little difficult to be sure exactly how Michaelson and Morton carried out their statistical tests, for they are not explicit about their assumptions nor do they appear to explain upon what grounds their test statistics are distributed as χ^2. Indeed, they themselves were markedly wary of claiming that they had answered any questions of stylometry; rather they offered their work as simply providing some additional questions.[11]

We have ourselves experimented with positional stylometry, though we modified the suggestions of Michaelson and Morton. In order to produce statistics independent of sentence length, we expressed the foward and backward counts as a percentage of the relevant sentence length. This would, we hoped, enhance the chances of the technique's success with English where, as has been noted above, sentence lengths themselves are particularly poor discriminators (in apparent contrast to their use in Greek which was the context of the Michaelson and Morton study). We examined the positional behaviour of some thirteen words[12] using the material relevant to Chapter 8 (in which the authors examined are W. Huskisson, J. D. Hume and W. Jacob) but we had no success whatsoever. What we discovered was something about the structure of the English language *per se* rather than something about any individual author. For we found that each of the words considered was isotropic for each author whose work was examined. No discrimination at all was possible. No author's work exhibited positional habits unique to him. Our precise results were that for each word and each author the positional distributions were uniform; thus, for example, we found that, by breaking sentences into deciles, one tenth of the total occurrences of each word occurred in each decile, and this was the positional distribution of each word within the work of all authors. This line of research, then, proved to be of no use at all in discriminating between the work of authors writing in English. On reflection this is, perhaps, not surprising. Written English is of a very flexible structure. A sentence is typically constructed of a number of clauses, and English does not operate within a rigid format within which many positional 'rules' must be obeyed. There are no formal grammatical constraints upon the position of main verbs or main clauses; there are equally no constraints on the position or number of subordinate clauses. Hence we should expect to find individual words to be highly mobile, and this is, indeed, exactly what we discovered. Furthermore, sentence length is a variable which usually fails to discriminate between pieces of English prose written by different authors although it is apparently successful in Greek. As was noted above, the statistics suggested by Michaelson and Morton are themselves dependent on sentence length; without going too deeply into this question, it seems possible that the success they achieved with Greek prose was either a result of their positional statistics acting as proxies for sentence length or of the more formal structure of classical Greek prose when compared with English prose. Whatever the cause of their success, we must report that in English the technique was a failure. We thus felt obliged to turn to a different aspect of positional behaviour.

Authors writing in English seem to choose the first word of a sentence from a quite limited subset of their vocabulary, so that, for example, it is quite typical to observe only one hundred different first words being used in a piece of some five hundred sentences. Furthermore, of the one hundred first words, a large proportion are used only once, leaving a small set of no more than a dozen frequently used first words.[13] Their analysis has proved particularly powerful in our studies of authorship puzzles, but we shall postpone a detailed discussion of the way in which we utilise the habit of first word usage until the next section of this chapter. This is, however, a suitable point at which to remark that in order to identify a word as the first word of a sentence we must be able to identify a 'sentence'. As has been noted above, the concept is not without ambiguity; but we have experienced difficulty in identifying sentences only when working with 17th century literature.[14] The 19th century material has presented no serious problems in this respect.

The other major class of literary habit we have employed is that of an author's usage of collocations. While it is clear from the above discussion that we cannot discriminate between writers in English by their absolute positioning of particular words within the sentence of occurrence,[15] it remains for us to examine whether we may discriminate by the positioning of particular words relative to other particular words.

Since we focus our interest upon high frequency vocabulary, it is useful at this point to examine some of the basic elements of the structure of written English, and to identify the set of high frequency words. The words most frequently used by writers in English are the definite and indefinite articles, particular prepositions, conjunctions and pronouns and the verb 'be'. Indeed, to be specific, the most frequently used word in all the material we have studied is the definite article 'the', followed by the prepositions and conjunctions 'of', 'to', 'and', 'in', 'that', 'which', 'as', 'for', 'from', 'with' and 'by'; the pronouns 'it' and 'this' are also most frequent, as is the indefinite article 'a' and the verb 'be'.

By way of example, we present in Table 2.1 the frequency profile of data derived from Huskisson's Speech on the Resumption of Cash Payments.[16] It is most interesting to note that the sixteen words mentioned above represent less than 1 per cent of the vocabulary used in this piece (the vocabulary total is 1930 words), yet they account for more than 33 per cent of the total number of words used. (These words account for 3,626 of the total of 10,712 words.) Furthermore, a mere 10 per cent of the vocabulary accounts for 70 per cent of the total words, while the words used once only account for less than 10 per cent of the total words yet represent more than 50 per cent of the vocabulary! The data may be presented graphically in a variety of ways. If we use the terminology that n_i words are used x_i times, then clearly the sum of the n_i yields the vocabulary total, V, and the sum of the products $n_i x_i$ yields the word total, W. It is possible, then, to plot the vocabulary proportions (n_i/V) against the word proportions (x_i/W) so as to describe the distribution. This would yield a shape having a long right-hand tail, but some detail would be blurred since, for example, using the data in Table 2.1, the horizontal axis needs a range from 1/10,712 to 899/10,712 while the range of the vertical axis would run from 1/1930 to 1036/1930.

TABLE 2.1 Huskisson's vocabulary data

*Word count**	*Number such*	*Vocabulary total*	*Word total*	*Cumulative % of vocab.*	*Cumulative % of words*
1–5	1658	1658	2728	85.91	25.47
6–10	137	1795	3736	93.01	34.88
11–15	35	1830	4181	94.82	39.03
16–20	26	1856	4649	96.17	43.40
21–100	60	1916	7173	99.27	66.96
101–200	8	1924	8149	99.69	76.07
201–899	6	1930	10712	100.00	100.00

* Starting with the least frequently used words.

As most of the detail occurs in the range of x_i/W from 1/10,712 to 10/10,712, there are obvious scaling problems. Taking logarithms and plotting $\ln(n_i)$ against $\ln(x_i)$ is one solution[17] and we obtain a representation as in Figure 2.1. The length of the right-hand displacement is an indication of the author's extensive usage of a few words. In the next chapter, concerning 17th century literature, it was an examination of representation like this which produced the explanation of our failure to utilise the writers' habits with 'be'. In 19th century writing, it is noticeable that 'be' is represented in the far right tail of the distribution, yet in 17th century writing there is far less reliance on a few words, and 'be' is not used sufficiently frequently to be the basis of statistical analysis. In terms

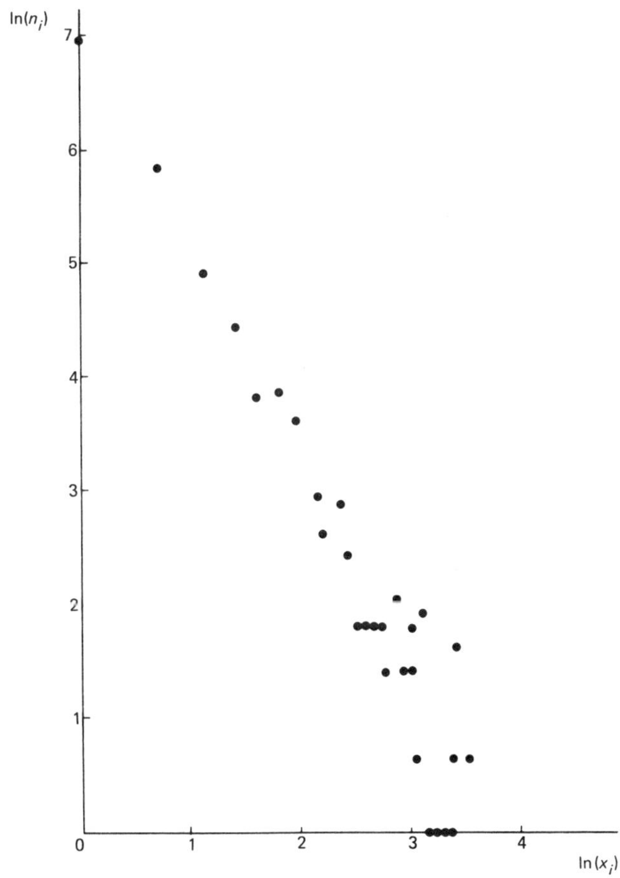

FIGURE 2.1 The logarithmic frequency distribution of Huskisson vocabulary

of Figure 2.1, the corresponding 17th century distributions have, relatively speaking, markedly shorter right-hand displacements; i.e. while it is still true that the early literature exhibits a reliance on a set of a few words, that reliance is less strong than we have observed in 19th century material.

A more familiar way of representing the data is to draw a Lorenz Curve, as in Figure 2.2. The intense usage of only a small fraction of the vocabulary set is highlighted by the diagram, and for purposes of comparison we have drawn the Huskisson Resumption speech distribution and that corresponding to Child's *New Discourse of Trade.*[18] While there is obviously great concentration exhibited by the two authors (both of whom are, incidently, quite typical of their respective periods), it is evident that the degree of concentration is greater in the later period.

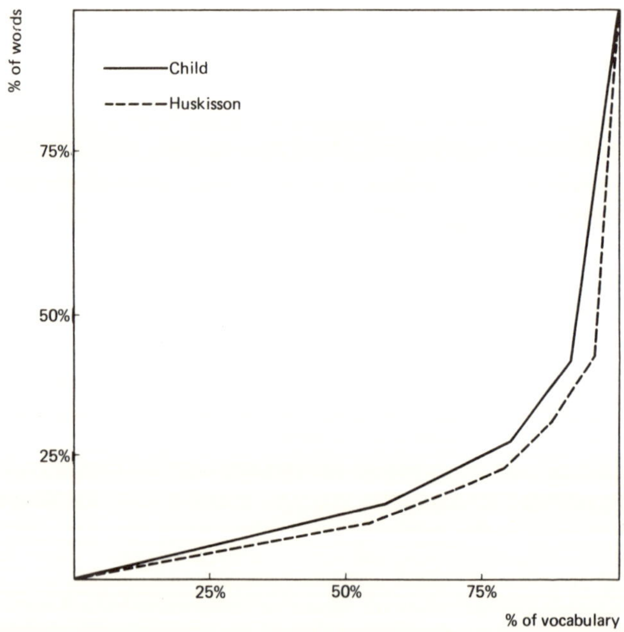

FIGURE 2.2 Lorenz Curve of Huskisson and Child vocabularies

Having described the nature of the distribution, and having noted the particular words which appear in the class of most frequently used words, we will now turn to the question of which literary habits may be employed to generate statistical data. We suggested above that the positions of particular words relative to other particular words might be a useful avenue to explore – such couplings, as noted in Chapter 1, had already been explored by Morton and his associates – and indeed we have had success in this respect. The most frequently used of all words, 'the', is itself most frequently preceeded by words such as 'of', 'to', 'and', 'in', 'that', 'which', 'for', 'as', 'from', 'with' and 'by'. Expressions such as 'to the' are called 'collocations of "the"'. We may use the relative frequency of occurrence of such collocations as a test of authorship, for, as will be explained below and illustrated in the ensuing chapters, their use by an author typically exhibits a pattern unique to his work and thus they may be used to discriminate successfully between authors. Similarly, we may use collocations with 'be', such as 'will be' or 'can be', in exactly the same way.[19] We have also examined other collocations with other 'key' words (in the above, 'the' and 'be' are key words), but we have had no success. This is, however, not at all surprising since, by the use of 'the' and 'be', we have virtually exhausted all useful information on collocations. The other frequently used collocations are either not distinguished from the collocations we are already using or simply not of sufficient frequency in the samples we have used to be amenable to statistical analysis. For example, if we examine usage of 'and', there is no concentration at all in words *preceeding* 'and' and the concentration in words *following* 'and' is wholly dominated by 'the', which is the habit we have already identified above as a collocation of 'the'. In terms of collocations, therefore, there is no useable information ignored by our study of the collocations with 'the' and 'be'. We now turn to an examination of the way in which we may operationalise the concepts of 'consistent usage' and 'distinguishing usage'.

(b) The statistical analysis of the chosen habits

Suppose we have two samples of work and we pose the question of whether we accept the hypothesis that they are by the same hand. The first stage in answering the question is to list the number of times a given habit occurs in each piece. To be specific, suppose we note the number of times within each sample that a sentence begins with a particular word. For each sample we may therefore categorise all sentences as either beginning or not beginning with the particular word. We may then represent this information as follows.

These data are classified according to two criteria; one is the source of the observation (author A or author B) and the other is its type (the sentence begins, or does not begin, with the particular word). Two

	Work of author A	Work of author B
No. of sentences beginning with word	a_1	b_1
No. of sentences not beginning with word	a_2	b_2
Total no. of sentences	T_a	T_b

criteria of classification are said to be independent if the distribution of the one depends in no way upon the distribution of the other. The representation above is known as a contingency table, and under the hypothesis of independence we may calculate expected values for each cell entry. Clearly, if the hypothesis is true we should expect to observe close correspondence between the observed and expected values, and an application of some simple probability enables us to quantify the concept of 'close correspondence'. However, before we embark upon a discussion of the manner in which we test the hypothesis of independence, we should examine its relationship to the hypothesis of authorship.

The hypothesis we are interested in (which we label as H'_0) is that authors A and B are indistinguishable in their use of this habit, and the alternative hypothesis (which we label H'_1) is that they are distinguishable. Let us suppose that H'_0 is true. In that case, we are assuming the truth of the statement that the parent distribution of observations according to the classification of 'first word' and 'not first word' is the same for each source, i.e. is independent of the source. Equally, we are assuming that the distribution across sources is independent of the usage classification. Thus a test of H'_0 against H'_1 is equivalent to a test of H_0 against H_1 as defined below:

H_0: the source of the test and the first word classification are independent.

H_1: the source of the text and the first word classification are not independent.

We may test the above in a very simple way. Suppose we wish to estimate the probability that from the population in question a sentence picked at random belongs to the classification: 'sentence begins with particular word'. From the table, our best estimator is given by $(a_1 + b_1)/(T_a + T_b)$ because in our sample this is the proportion of sentences so classified. Similarly, our best estimator of the probability that, from the population in question, a sentence picked at random has author A as source is $T_a/(T_a+T_b)$. We now wish to estimate the probability that a sentence picked at random is characterised *both* by having the particular word as its first word *and* by having author A as source. In the absence of any hypothesis regarding the two classification criteria, we estimate this by $a_1/(T_a+T_b)$; but the object of this exercise is to test H_0, and under the truth of H_0 we may utilise the rule of probability which states that if two events are independent then the probability of their joint occurrence is equal to the product of their individual probabilities. Hence under the truth of H_0, the best estimator is given by

$$\frac{(a_1+b_1)}{(T_a+T_b)}\cdot\frac{T_a}{(T_a+T_b)},$$

and in order to convert this probability to an expected value we multiply by our sample size, (T_a+T_b). Thus we obtain the expected value under H_0 as:

$$\frac{(a_1+b_1)\cdot T_a}{(T_a+T_b)}$$

which may be seen as

$$\frac{(\text{row total})\times(\text{column total})}{\text{grand total}}$$

and may be generalised to yield the rule that, denoting E_{ij} as the expected value of the cell in the ith row and jth column of the contingency table, we compute E_{ij} as:

$$E_{ij}=\frac{(\text{total of row } i)\times(\text{total of column } j)}{\text{grand total}}.$$

Denoting the observed value in the (i,j)th cell by O_{ij} we would clearly expect close correspondence between O_{ij} and E_{ij} for all i and j. How 'close' is 'close'? In order to answer this question, we compute the 'test statistic' X^2 according to:

$$X^2=\sum\frac{(O_{ij}-E_{ij})^2}{E_{ij}}.$$

The importance of X^2 is that for large samples it is distributed approximately as χ^2 and this fact enables us to formulate a decision rule.[20] By large samples is meant those sufficiently large to ensure that not more than 20 per cent of all cells have expected values less than 5.

The appropriate rule may be formulated as follows: from the relevant tabulated values of the χ^2 distribution, we note that critical value, $\chi^2_{1-\alpha}$, which will be exceeded by a χ^2 variable with probability α. Suppose that X^2 exceeds $\chi^2_{1-\alpha}$. This may be explained in one of two ways. Either H_0 is true, and our sample is one which will be observed on only α per cent of all repeated samples, or H_0 is false. By setting α sufficiently small – 0.05 is typical – we can regard the first interpretation as implausible and reject H_0. It is important to note that in hypothesis testing we can make two sorts of error, namely the rejection of a true null hypothesis or the rejection of a true alternative hypothesis (the latter is equivalent to the acceptance of a false null hypothesis). The above decision rule accords 0.05 to the probability of the former error, i.e. if $X^2 > \chi^2_{0.95}$ we reject H_0, recognising that there is a 5 per cent probability of our being mistaken. This is called a type I error. On the other hand, if $X^2 < \chi^2_{1-\alpha}$ we accept H_0 (i.e. fail to reject H_0) and we may be mistaken; however, X^2 is a statistic computed assuming H_0 to be true, and since H_1 does not define uniquely any E_{ij} (since H_1 simply states a lack of independence, between row and column values, it does *not* specify the exact nature of the dependence), we cannot formulate a test statistic under the truth of H_1. Thus we are unable to quantify the probability of a type II error, that of accepting a false null hypothesis. This is a common situation in hypothesis testing and is not to be seen as a particular weakness of our procedure.

The only two additional points to be made about the test procedure concern the 'degrees of freedom' and the 'level of significance'. In a contingency table such as that shown above, given the observed row and column totals, it is clearly possible to fill in any three of the cells if the fourth cell value is also given. Such a table is therefore said to have one degree of freedom. If we were to disaggregate the habits and use, say, r individual habits in a table which had c columns (i.e. pieces of work in our case), then there would be $(r-1)(c-1)$ degrees of freedom and this dictates the critical value of χ^2 for a given α. The significance level is the probability of the type I error and is, as has been stated, typically set at 5 per cent. However, this is quite arbitrary, and in what follows we shall, on some occasions, remark that 'independence may be rejected at a 10 per cent [or occasionally even higher] level of significance', by which is meant that the type I error is 10 per cent. In many statistical problems it is possible to quantify the costs of making a wrong decision. Thus, for example, if the costs associated with erroneous rejection of H_0 are high we set a very small α, a small type I error. In our work it would be foolish to attempt to think of such 'costs', and consequently we are not led to the rigid application of a particular type I error. When hypotheses are rejected by us, therefore, we will always indicate the maximum probability of our being wrong.

In their analysis of literary habits by the use of contingency tables and the χ^2 distribution, Michaelson *et al.*[21] follow a procedure whereby, for example, for each frequently used first word, a table of two rows like the contingency table above is constructed. Since no two such tables derived from data of one broad class of habit (e.g. first word usage) can yield statistically independent results, we prefer to disaggregate the rows into individual habits or small sets of habits and thus present a single table which represents the whole of our analysis of first word usage. This procedure, therefore, allows us to use all the available information on a particular class of habit (such as first word usage) simultaneously rather than sequentially, and does, of course, ensure that our contingency tables have more than one degree of freedom. This, in turn, ensures that we can utilise a wide set of individual habits in the one test which our analysis requires, having as it does a focal point *not* of individual habits *per se* but of a broad class of habits. Thus analysis of first words, or collocations with 'the' and with 'be' may each be carried out summarising all the relevant information in the one table, and using one test statistic. The various stages of our analysis proceed as follows:

(i) We examine extracts of the work of each author under consideration and produce a contingency table of r rows, each row corresponding to an individual first word or a set of first words. The categorisation is chosen so that for each author's work, H_0 is accepted, i.e. so that using the particular classification scheme, each author exhibits internal consistency of usage.

(ii) We apply this classification scheme to the anonymously written piece and test H_0 on the data. If H_0 is accepted (i.e. H_0 is not rejected), we carry on. If the anonymously written piece exhibits internal inconsistency we go back to stage one and look for another suitable classification scheme.

(iii) We make pairwise comparisons of the work of our selected authors, seeking a rejection of H_0 in all tests, for only a rejection of H_0 indicates that the habits considered are capable of discriminating between the authors.

(iv) Given that the classification is a good discriminator between the work of different authors, we now compare each author with the anonymous piece. We have typically found that we reject independence in the case of all potential authors bar one, i.e. we are typically in the position of concluding, for example, that the anonymous material in question is not the work of authors A or B, but is the work of author C since the habits exhibited by the anonymous writer are inconsistent with those of authors A and B while wholly consistent with those of author C.

What we seek then is that classification of first word usage (and similarly of collocations with 'the' and 'be') which is capable of establishing each author's own internal consistency, and the internal consistency of the anonymous material, whilst discriminating between the work of the known authors, and thus being capable of discriminating between an unknown hand and the known hands.

One final word is necessary before we examine this procedure at work. The classification schemes chosen are almost certain to be case and sample specific. By this we mean that classifications of habits capable of discriminating between authors A and B are *not necessarily* capable of discriminating between authors B and C. Equally, it seems not unlikely that using a particular sample of author A's work we shall obtain a set of habits used consistently by him which will *not be identical* to the set we would obtain using a different sample. This is, however, not at all a surprising statement. If we think of the way we would proceed to estimate the value of some parameter θ by the method of sampling, we know with certainty that there will be differences between estimates taken from different samples. Our case is entirely analogous, and it seems clear that the larger the sample, the closer will our chosen sample set be to the true set of discriminators.

V. CONCLUSION

We have, in this chapter, attempted to indicate the bases upon which rest the statistical procedures employed in this book. It should be clear that we are satisfied that a non-parametric approach is the most fruitful one to employ in tackling the sort of authorship problems which concern us in the study. We have applied the approach outlined in this chapter to six problems of disputed authorship in the history of the literature of economics, one stemming from the 17th century, the remainder from the 19th. It will be apparent to the reader who examines subsequent chapters, and the details of the results presented therein, that our preference for a non-parametric approach would seem to be justified, in that the results obtained are, in the main, remarkably satisfactory.

3 Sir Josiah Child's Economic Writings

I. HISTORICAL BACKGROUND

(a) Philopatris

The main problem discussed in this chapter is the supposed authorship of a work defending the East India Company, the author of which gives his name as 'Philopatris'.[1] It is called *A Treatise Wherein is Demonstrated, I. That the East-India Trade is the most national of all foreign trades; II. that the clamors . . . against the present East-India Company are sinister, selfish, or groundless . . . .*[2] A number of authorities have attributed this to Sir Josiah Child who was an important, and at times dominant, figure in the company from 1673 until his death in 1699.[3] The pamphlet was originally attributed to Child by Charles King in *The British Merchant* of 1721,[4] and this attribution was endorsed by McCulloch, who considered that the style was the same as that of a work which had appeared with Child's name on its title page, *A New Discourse of Trade.*[5] W. R. Scott also seems to have believed that the work was by Child.[6] Viner considered that it was by Child,[7] and Chaudhuri, the outstanding contemporary authority on the East India Company, also takes this view.[8]

The background to the writing of the pamphlet was set out with great clarity by an earlier historian, Sir W. W. Hunter, who, in his *History of British India*, wrote of the East India Company in the late 17th century:

> There had thus grown up within the realm a body standing apart from the nation, yet wielding in India the national powers of coining money, levying taxes, building forts, maintaining troops, and making war or peace. That such a body should continue exempt from Parliamentary control must depend either on the absence of public envy, or on the popularity of the Sovereign by whose prerogative it was maintained. Under Charles I. the profits of the India Trade had

> proved too uncertain to excite the jealousy of the Commons: under Charles II. the royal authority sufficed to protect it from their interference.[9]

For although royal protection proved adequate, and the Court, mainly through the dexterity with which Child distributed bribes,[10] continued to take the side of the Company, its monopolistic privileges were under considerable attack from the 1670s onwards. This has two aspects which are of significance for our present purpose. Firstly, the stock of the Company was held in relatively few hands, with Child in a predominant position,[11] and the value of the assets was estimated to be very considerably in excess of the nominal value of the stock, so that there was considerable pressure for an enlargement of the stock – and on the wisdom of this, members of the Company were divided. Secondly, the Company sought to defend itself through the publication of pamphlets. At least one of these was written by one Robert Ferguson, who was employed by the Company for this purpose and paid for his pains; another was ultimately the joint product of several members of the Company.[12] This last means that any attribution of authorship is treading on potentially treacherous ground.

In his book *The Origins of Scientific Economics*, Professor W. Letwin gives three reasons why it is, in his opinion, impossible that Child was the author of the Philopatris pamphlet. Firstly, he says that Child commended in another work, called *Brief Observations Concerning Trade and Interest of Money* (1668), the Dutch practice of appointing trading merchants to their Councils of State, while Philopatris apparently disapproves of this both because merchants are not the best judges of the interest of the kingdom and because the Dutch do not in fact have them on their councils.[13] This particular point of contrast is, however, less than completely persuasive. All that Child had claimed in his earlier pamphlet was that 'They [the Dutch] have in their greatest *Councils of State and War*, trading Merchants that have lived abroad in most parts of the World; who have not only the Theoretical Knowledge, but the Practical Experience of Trade, by whom Laws and Orders are contrived, and Peaces with forreign Princes projected, to the great advantage of their Trade.'[14] Now while it is true that Philopatris was not entirely happy about trading merchants, still actively engaged in business, being the best judges of the interest of the country, he was 'of a Opinion, and have found by experience, That a mixt Assembly of Noblemen, Gentlemen, and Merchants are the best Constitution that can be established for the making Rules, Orders, and By-Laws, for the carrying on any Trade for the Publick Utility of the Kingdom'.[15] It is apparently satisfactory to have members of the mercantile class in the councils of the country if they are retired merchants or the sons of merchants (the former presumably having the experience of active trading which Child required), and if they are only a part of the ruling council. There is *some* contrast between Child and 'Philopatris'; but it is not really quite strong enough to regard it as a decisive test of authorship – at least in our view.

Professor Letwin's second ground is that Child asserts that the value of land always rises or falls as trade increases or declines, while Philopatris 'seems to question this view implicitly' when he says that all trade which does not increase the value of English lands should be not only discouraged but rejected.[16] But in fact Philopatris says: 'That Domestick and Foreign trade do (as we vulgarly say of Twins, but more truly of Trade) wax and wain together; and if it were not an impropriety of Speech, Land might be coupled with them.'[17] In fact, this is rather remarkably similar to the following quotation from Child's *New Discourse*: 'in all Nations, and at all times between Land and Trade, which are Twins, and have always, and ever will wax and wain together, *It cannot be ill with Trade, but Land will fall, nor ill with Lands, but Trade will feel it*' [italics in original].[18]

Professor Letwin's third ground is, however, much more secure. It is that Philopatris was in favour of a new issue of stock in the Company, while Child was against it.[19] Now, there seems no doubt that the Court of the Company, although only 'upon a very great debate', agreed to a new stock.[20] They also agreed to make a present to the King of 10,000 guineas[21] – this on 5 October 1681, before Child had complete control of the Company. (The dating is important in assessing the reliability of Macaulay's account of the proceedings, since Macaulay indicates that the present came from Child after Papillon had been ousted from the Company,[22] which suggests that the Historian was not quite clear in his own mind about the sequence of events.) The Company received from the royal Court a message, through Sir Joseph Ashe, to the effect that it would be better to leave the question of the new stock until later and not to link this to the gift of 10,000 guineas.[23] But the Company was anxious for protection; and on 11 November 1681, the Court debated a draft supplied by Papillon asking the King for a proclamation against interlopers into the Company's monopoly of the East India Trade.[24] This draft contained a statement of the willingness of the Company to have a new stock. This is not apparent from the Court Book of the Company which merely records that a petition to the King was approved by the Court of the Company on that day. But in a book published in 1887, by a descendant of Papillon, the draft of the petition, with the passage about a new stock, was reproduced, together with some manuscript notes apparently by Papillon himself.[25] From the reproduction of this document, both Hunter and, subsequently, Letwin have deduced that the discussion of the petition was the occasion for a major confrontation between Child and Papillon, with Child victorious and the offer to issue a new stock removed from the draft.[26] We have located the original of this manuscript; and although there are a number of inaccuracies in the reproduction (apart from modernised spelling), it is substantially accurate.[27] Both the petition and the marginal notes are in Papillon's hand. This is important. For at the end of Papillon's draft there was a passage expressing the willingness of the Directors to agree to a new stock; and Papillon noted that this was left out on debate. He also noted that the Governor (Child) had said the clause had been brought in 'to do us a mischeif [sic]. Upon wch the deputy [Papillon] vindicated himself.' It thus certainly poses difficulties over the attribution of the pamphlet by Philopatris to Child. Despite confusion in some of the historical accounts – apart from that of Macaulay noted above, W. R. Scott seems to have managed to argue that both Papillon and Child were at one stage in favour of a new stock, by attributing the Philopatris pamphlet to Child and citing Somer's *Tracts* in support of his statement about Papillon when the passage in Somer's *Tracts* turns out to be Philopatris again[28] – it does seem clear that there was a major dispute (Papillon was ultimately ousted from the Company) and it seems likely that the question of a new stock became an issue in the dispute. But the Philopatris pamphlet was published *before* the debates in October and November 1681, for there is a reply to it (cited by Letwin)[29] – a reply which clearly thought that Child was the author of the Philopatris work – entitled *An Arrest on the East-India Privatier* of 16 September 1681. So it is *possible* that the issue became really contentious only in the following month.

Nevertheless, Professor Letwin seems on strong ground here. The best that one can say is that the historical evidence is inconclusive. Moreover, on his side it has to be said that the stylistic impression left by the Philopatris pamphlet can strike a reader as being different from that left by the work of Child – indeed, to have more in common with Ferguson – and that Philopatris concedes that he parts company with most of his colleagues over the need for a new stock.[30] On the other hand, as Chaudhuri has pointed out: 'There is no doubt that in spite of his cautious support to [sic] the idea of a new stock, the author preferred to carry on with the old one and he took some trouble to point out the good value of the existing East India stock.'[31] Indeed, Philopatris defends the limited number of stock holders.

> Object, 7. *They complain that the present Stock is ingrossed into a few hands: some single Adventurers have 16 or 17000l principal Stock in their own names.*
> An. If this be true, the Complaint of it would sound better out of the mouth of an old Leveller, than a Merchants living under a free and Royal Monarchy. And yet to give the maddest of men their due, neither the late *English* Levellers, nor their Elder Brethren, The Tribunes of the People of *Rome*; nor yet the more Ancient *Lacedemonians* or other *Greeks*; none of them had ever that excess of Indiscretion, as to pretend to Stint, much less to Level Personal Estates: Which if they could be made even at noon, would be unequal before night.
> 2. If there were any thing in this Objection, certainly the *Dutch*, being a Republick, Would have found a Remedy for it before this time: Whereas on the contrary they think who-ever Adventures most in their joynt stocks, doth most oblige the Commonwealth, tho he be a stranger; . . .
> 3. The more any Adventurer hath in the Stock, the more he is engaged to study and promote the good of it, by all possible means within his power. An Adventurer that hath the smallest Interest, may be as just and true to the Stock as he that hath the greatest: but I can never believe that a small interest will awaken a man so often in the night, nor keep him so long from sleeping, in the meditation of any business; as a very great and principal concern may do.
> 4. Notwithstanding the largeness of any of the Adventurers Stocks, There are yet Five Hundred fifty six Adventurers: which is a greater number than are to be found in any Trade, that hath not a Joynt Stock.[32]

The historical and internal evidence seems, then, less than completely conclusive, although there is no doubt that the balance of the case, as far as this single piece of internal evidence goes, lies with Professor Letwin's view that the Philopatris pamphlet, in advocating a new stock, was inconsistent with Child's view. But Chaudhuri has suggested that such an inconsistency may well be explained by the insertion of material by other directors.[33] This seems reasonable. It is clear from the Court Book that the publication of pamphlets was a matter in which the Court of the

Company took a keen interest. It is quite possible that the draft of the pamphlet by Philopatris was discussed by at least some of the directors and debated by them in the same way as Papillon's draft petition to the King.[34] Since any such debate must have taken place before 30 September 1681, when a majority of the Court was still in favour of a new stock,[35] it is possible that this insertion could have been made by the Court at that time in a draft which was basically the work of Child.

Of course, this possibility itself raises serious problems for the historian of ideas. For it means that the attribution to any writer of a particular intellectual position, on the basis of his published work, runs the risk that the point in question may have been inserted by other hands. But given that this did seem a real possibility, and that the historical evidence was – as usual – less than conclusive, the authorship problem outlined here seemed to be an obvious one on which to try a statistical test.

(b) Subsidiary problems

Given the necessity of using samples, not only of the writings of Sir Josiah Child, but also of Robert Ferguson, we took the opportunity to attempt to investigate the authorship of a number of other works of doubtful attribution which are also discussed in Letwin's book.

Answer of the Said East India Company[36]

This is a pamphlet of about 4,500 words. It is in the form of a reply to papers by the Turkey Company. Letwin[37] notes that Khan[38] thought that the *Answer* was the work of Child because of 'general considerations of style and context [sic]' and notes the reference in the Court Book of the East India Company to this work which indicates that a draft, proceeding from an unnamed pen, was referred by the Directors to Child, Papillon and others for amendment as they saw fit.[39] He concludes that there is nothing in the *Answer* which proves or disproves Child's authorship of the original draft.

This is undoubtedly true. At the same time, there are a number of elements in the *Answer* which are certainly suggestive of Child. In particular, there is defence of the existence of concentrated holdings of shares and the assertion that the greater is any man's interest, the greater his vigilance. There is also emphasis on the desirability of reduction of the rate of interest. It is interesting to note that there are also a number of parallels with the 'Philopatris' pamphlet, including a reference to a Jewish merchant with a large stockholding in the Dutch East India Company,[40] a denial that the East India trade has interfered with exports to Turkey,[41] and that silk imports have interfered with British manufacture.[42] Of course, these matters were probably common currency amongst the Directors of the Company; but there is enough here to indicate that an attempt to use statistical analysis might be interesting.

Humble Answer of the Governor . . . of the East India Company[43]

This is of about 3,500 words. Letwin[44] notes that this work was attributed to Child, possibly under the misapprehension that he was still Governor at the time of its publication in 1692. Letwin also reads into a section of the pamphlet dealing with individual dominance within the company an 'unflattering' reference to Child's to-be-anticipated demise.[45] This is, in itself, not very conclusive, as the reference could have been to some other wealthy Director.

The document does, however, read like the product of a Committee. The only thing one can say is that whoever wrote the 'Philopatris' pamphlet may have influenced the document – there is some material in the pamphlet which parallels an argument in Philopatris, although this may have been quite a common argument amongst the Directors.[46] But the presence of common material suggests that statistical investigation might be helpful.

The Great Honour . . . of the East-India Trade[47]

This pamphlet is about 3,500 words long and appeared in 1697. Letwin[48] notes that the work was attributed to Child by the London Bibliography (III 908); this is presumably on the basis that the author gives his initials as 'J. C.'. This was not unreasonable – Child had identified himself as the author of his 1668 pamphlet *Brief Observations*[49] by the initials 'J. C.'. Moreover, one might take the view that Child was so well known in an East India context that it was unlikely that anyone else would have used the initials. While dismissing Foxwell's suggestion that the author might be John Carey, Letwin is unable to offer an opinion upon the possibility of the pamphlet being by Child. A perusal of the content would suggest that the pamphlet *could* be by Child, written in his retirement from active direction of the Company, but still a substantial stockholder. It seemed worth investigation.

An Essay on Wool[50]

This is a pamphlet of just over 4,000 words which appeared in 1693. Letwin[51] notes that this is attributed to Child by the London Bibliography (III 1215) and Kress (1810). He feels, however, that the pamphlet is not by Child, on the grounds that the author's insistence that the government should forcibly maintain high standards in woollen manufacture is directly contrary to the view advocated by Child in *New Discourse of Trade* Chapter 8, and that the author argues, contrary to Child, that independent merchants are ruining the wool trade, which should therefore be confined to a company.

In substance,[52] this view seems persuasive. Not only does the style of the pamphlet seem different from that of Child but the emphases also appear different. While Child laid stress upon the harm of a high rate of interest and religious intolerance, which he believed to be driving out the woollen manufacturers, the burden of the pamphlet is that, under the impact of Dutch and other competition, English cloth has become debased and there is a need to raise its quality while its sales should be regulated by a Parliamentary Committee. The pamphlet engages in sweeping numerical calculations about the resources available for potential English output and exports, and suggests that private traders have glutted the market for wool which can be improved only by confining the trade to merchant companies. Nevertheless, it seemed reasonable to check our subjective impressions that the work was not by Child against the numerical analysis of the text.

Discourse of the Nature . . . of Trade[53]

This is a pamphlet of about 5,500 words which appeared in 1694. Letwin[54] notes that the pamphlet proposes Child-like policies such as a registry of lands, a reduction of interest rates, and the naturalisation of foreigners. But these were common ideas, as Letwin points out, and there is a contradiction between the defence by Child of the export of treasure by the East India Company[55] and the view of the author of this pamphlet that the export of coin should be prevented. Moreover, he thinks it unlikely that Child would have published a work with a rather similar title to his earlier one but containing some contradiction of its position.

All this is very reasonable; but the clinching factor is undoubtedly the style of the pamphlet, to which Letwin also draws attention. It is literary and quite elegant, and contrasts sharply with Child's own abrasive and telegraphic approach. However, the work has been attributed to Child and it seemed worth testing it against our sample of material by Child.

(c) Texts

Apart from the subsidiary texts discussed above, we used for statistical analysis a number of texts relating to our main problem, the authorship of the pamphlet by 'Philopatris'. We used pp. 3–16 of Child's *Brief Observations*[56] amounting to about 4,500 words and pp. i–xxxvii of his *New Discourse of Trade*[57] giving us about another 6,500 words. We also used the whole 'Philopatris' pamphlet[58] which is about 13,000 words long, and a pamphlet written by Ferguson for Papillon which is 10,000 words in length.[59] We also used an extract of rather over 10,000 words in length from a pamphlet written by the prolific Ferguson and published under his own name,[60] and, as a particularly appropriate comparison, a pamphlet of nearly 5,000 words by Culpepper[61] which Child incorporated into his *New Discourse of Trade*.

II. STATISTICAL ANALYSIS

(a) 17th-century literary peculiarities

It is somewhat ironic to have to report that the statistical analysis which we used in an attempt to throw further light on the problems discussed so far in this chapter was completed after the other studies in this book, and presented us with much greater difficulty than we had experienced with the preceding five examples of statistical analysis. This chapter is not one in which to study our statistical procedures at their most comprehensive and it is only chronological considerations which persuade us to present the results of our analysis of the 17th century literature at this point in the book. For this literature has proved to be by far the most difficult of all from which to obtain satisfactory statistical results. The results presented below are *in themselves* not in the least unsatisfactory; but they relate to a narrow range of statistical data and we should have liked to have been able to present additional statistical evidence to support the conclusions obtained. The material at our disposal only allowed us to utilise habits in the use of 'the' and we were not able to obtain satisfactory results from an analysis of habits in the choice of first word or in couplings with 'be', although these proved highly satisfactory throughout most of the rest of our study.

Our normal starting point in the statistical analysis of a given work has been typically an analysis of first word usage. Clearly, it is necessary that we are able to identify sentences in order to carry out such an analysis. But in the 17th century literature even this elementary condition is not met. The use of punctuation has changed markedly since the 17th century and the writers of that period frequently used the semi-colon where a 19th or 20th century writer would use a full stop. Thus we find, in the writings of Sir Josiah Child, entire paragraphs which may be as long as 140 words, broken only by commas and semi-colons. The same is generally true of the other 17th century writers that we have examined. It would hardly be too much to say that paragraphs and sentences are *typically* coincident. Thus, with 'sentences' in excess of 150 words, 1,000 words of 17th century literature will contain less than 10 'sentences'; a sample of 1,000 words of 19th century literature of the kind which we have examined in this book would typically give us more than 20 sentences. The texts, as published, provide us, then, with insufficient information for analysis of first word usage. It is true that we could have attempted to remedy this by imposing modern punctuation upon the 17th century texts; but such a strategy is open to many criticisms, not the least of which is that no other researcher could reproduce our results unless possessed of the same judgement of standards of correct punctuation. But this itself springs from the overriding problem that there are no clear rules by which we could select sentence endings, so that a significant degree of subjective judgement would enter into our proceedings. We preferred to resign ourselves to the fact that within our framework, because of the lack of full stops to identify sentences, we cannot follow the procedure for analysing first word usage which we have used elsewhere. The numbers of first words are simply too small to enable inference to be made from them and, because of the difficulty of identifying sentences at all, we necessarily find ourselves omitting from our frequency count many words which would count as first words, given more modern punctuation. Our sample of first words would then be not only small but extremely unrepresentative.

It is perhaps rather more surprising that we were also unsuccessful in using data from the frequency of different collocations with 'be' to obtain satisfactory statistical results. The reasons for this are rather less obvious. They seem to lie in marked differences in vocabulary usage between 17th century literature and the 19th century literature we have analysed elsewhere. It is not, as one might expect, that later writers consistently used a wider vocabulary – for even though this is typically the case, the problem does not lie here. Rather it lies in the relative frequency of different words within the vocabulary. It is noticeable that the most frequently used word, 'the', is used more frequently by the later writers. Typical figures per thousand words are 59 and 86 occurrences of 'the' in 17th century and 19th century works respectively. Indeed, contrary to what one might expect, the most frequently used five words ('the', 'of', 'and', 'in' and 'to', a set the composition of which is virtually consistent over all the writers studied in this book) occupy a much larger proportion of total words used in the later works. The relative frequency of 'be' is also markedly higher in the 19th century literature, with a typical frequency of 18 per 1,000 words compared with 11 in the 17th century literature. Thus the distribution of words in the 19th century texts we have analysed has a very thick right-hand tail, containing the relative frequency of 'be', while the earlier work is characterised by a distribution which is not only flatter but, although skewed, does not include 'be' in its far right-hand tail.[62] The immediate effect of all this is that we have a much smaller sample of occurrences of 'be' from which to obtain data on typical couplings; and this problem is intensified by the small size of some of the 17th century pieces. Thus we were not able to run tests of internal consistency on some of the anonymous texts, using data derived from collocations with 'be', with any confidence. Since the size of the texts limits the data available, the problem cannot be remedied by increasing the 'sample' size.

We are thus left only with data derived from collocations with 'the' as a basis for analysis in this chapter.

(b) Collocations with 'the'

It was some compensation for the difficulties we experienced in analysing the 17th century literature that we were able to use a markedly disaggregated set of collocations with 'the'. The contingency tables have 8 rows corresponding to the following collocations with 'the': 'and'; 'of'; 'be' or 'if'; 'which' or 'upon' or 'for'; 'in' or 'by' or 'on'; 'that' or 'from'; 'with' or 'all' or 'into' or 'as' or 'at' or 'is'; and all other collocations with 'the'. The summary results are set out in Table 3.1 and the details may be found in the contingency tables 3.2(i) to 3.2(xxxvi). The contingency tables each have seven degrees of freedom, for which the corresponding 95 per cent critical value of the χ^2 distribution is 14.07.

The first 10 rows of Table 3.1 exhibit the results obtained from

TABLE 3.1 Collocations with 'the'

Texts analysed	X^2	d.f.	$\chi^2_{0.95}$	*Decision*	*Maximum type I error (where applicable)*	*Contingency table*
Brief Observations vs *New Discourse of Trade*	8.59	7	14.07	Accept the hypothesis of the internal consistency of Child	–	3.2(i)
Tract against Usury internally	6.31	7	14.07	Accept the hypothesis of the internal consistency of Culpepper	–	3.2(ii)
Interest of Reason in Religion internally	8.43	7	14.07	Accept the hypothesis of the internal consistency of Ferguson	–	3.2(iii)
East India-Trade . . . most profitable internally	6.70	7	14.07	Accept the hypothesis of the internal consistency of 'Papillon' pamphlet	–	3.2(iv)
East India-Trade . . . the most National internally	8.46	7	14.07	Accept the hypothesis of the internal consistency of 'Philopatris'	–	3.2(v)
Answer of the Said East India Co. internally	20.48	7	14.07	Reject the hypothesis of the internal consistency of *Answer*	0.005	3.2(vi)
Humble Answer internally	4.35	7	14.07	Accept the hypothesis of the internal consistency of *Humble Answer*	–	3.2(vii)
Great Honour and Advantage internally	5.99	7	14.07	Accept the hypothesis of the internal consistency of *Great Honour*	–	3.2(viii)
Essay on Wool internally	7.48	7	14.07	Accept the hypothesis of the internal consistency of *Essay on Wool*	–	3.2(ix)

Discourse of Nature of . . . Trade 1694 internally	19.83	7	14.07	Reject the hypothesis of the internal consistency of *Discourse of . . . Trade*	0.01	3.2(x)
Child vs Culpepper	16.96	7	14.07	Reject the hypothesis of consistency between Child and Culpepper	0.02	3.2(xi)
'Papillon' vs Culpepper	27.13	7	14.07	Reject the hypothesis of consistency between 'Papillon' and Culpepper	0.005	3.2(xii)
Ferguson vs Culpepper	27.50	7	14.07	Reject the hypothesis of consistency between Ferguson and Culpepper	0.005	3.2(xiii)
Child vs Ferguson	13.55	7	13.53[1]	Reject the hypothesis of consistency between Child and Ferguson	0.06	3.2(xiv)
Child vs 'Papillon'	11.19	7	11.18[2]	Reject the hypothesis of consistency between Child and 'Papillon'	0.13	3.2(xv)
Ferguson vs 'Papillon'	3.10	7	14.07	Accept the hypothesis of consistency between Ferguson and 'Papillon'	–	3.2(xvi)
Child vs Ferguson and 'Papillon'	14.86	7	14.07	Reject the hypothesis of consistency between Child and Ferguson plus 'Papillon'	0.04	3.2(xvii)
Ferguson and 'Papillon' vs Culpepper	29.90	7	14.07	Reject the hypothesis of consistency between Ferguson plus 'Papillon' and Culpepper	0.005	3.2(xviii)
'Philopatris' vs Culpepper	15.34	7	14.07	Reject the hypothesis of consistency between 'Philopatris' and Culpepper	0.04	3.2(xix)
Answer of the Said East India Co. vs Culpepper	15.10	7	14.07	Reject the hypothesis of consistency between *Answer of the Said East India Co.* and Culpepper	0.04	3.2(xx)

TABLE 3.1 (*contd.*)

Texts analysed	X^2	d.f.	$\chi^2_{0.95}$	*Decision*	*Maximum type I error (where applicable)*	*Contingency table*
Humble Answer vs Culpepper	25.87	7	14.07	Reject the hypothesis of consistency between *Humble Answer* and Culpepper	0.005	3.2(xxi)
Great Honour and Advantage vs Culpepper	29.40	7	14.07	Reject the hypothesis of consistency between *Great Honour and Advantage* and Culpepper	0.005	3.2(xxii)
Essay on Wool vs Culpepper	13.91	7	13.53[1]	Reject the hypothesis of consistency between *Essay on Wool* and Culpepper	0.06	3.2(xxiii)
Discourse of Nature of . . . Trade 1694 vs Culpepper	19.85	7	14.07	Reject the hypothesis of consistency between *Discourse of Nature of . . . Trade* and Culpepper	0.01	3.2(xxiv)
'Philopatris' vs Child	5.52	7	14.07	Accept the hypothesis of consistency between 'Philopatris' and Child	–	3.2(xxv)
'Philopatris' vs Ferguson and 'Papillon'	12.89	7	12.68[3]	Reject the hypothesis of consistency between 'Philopatris' and Ferguson plus 'Papillon'	0.08	3.2(xxvi)

Answer of the Said East India Co. vs Child	5.17	7	14.07	Accept the hypothesis of consistency between *Answer of the Said East India Co.* and Child	–	3.2(xxvii)
Answer of the Said East India Co. vs Ferguson and 'Papillon'	9.17	7	14.07	Accept the hypothesis of consistency between *Answer of the Said East India Co.* and Ferguson plus 'Papillon'	–	3.2(xxviii)
Humble Answer vs Child	14.28	7	14.07	Reject the hypothesis of consistency between *Humble Answer* and Child	0.05	3.2(xxix)
Humble Answer vs Ferguson and 'Papillon'	8.05	7	14.07	Accept the hypothesis of consistency between *Humble Answer* and Ferguson plus 'Papillon'	–	3.2(xxx)
Great Honour and Advantage vs Child	8.39	7	14.07	Accept the hypothesis of consistency between *Great Honour and Advantage* and Child	–	3.2(xxxi)
Great Honour and Advantage vs Ferguson and 'Papillon'	12.14	7	12.02[4]	Reject the hypothesis of consistency between *Great Honour and Advantage* and Ferguson plus 'Papillon'	0.10	3.2(xxxii)
Essay on Wool vs Child	11.31	7	11.18[2]	Reject the hypothesis of consistency between *Essay on Wool* and Child[5]	0.13	3.2(xxxiii)
Essay on Wool vs Ferguson and 'Papillon'	33.21	7	14.07	Reject the hypothesis of consistency between *Essay on Wool* and Ferguson plus 'Papillon'	0.005	3.2(xxxiv)

TABLE 3.1 (*contd.*)

Texts analysed	X^2	d.f.	$\chi^2_{0.95}$	*Decision*	*Maximum type I error (where applicable)*	*Contingency table*
Discourse of Nature of . . . Trade 1694 vs Child	6.77	7	14.07	Accept the hypothesis of consistency between *Discourse of Nature of . . . Trade* and Child	–	3.2(xxxv)
Discourse of Nature of . . . . Trade 1694 vs Ferguson and 'Papillon'	7.37	7	14.07	Accept the hypothesis of consistency between *Discourse of Nature of . . . Trade* and Ferguson plus 'Papillon'	–	3.2(xxxvi)

1 13.53 is the $\chi^2_{7,\,0.94}$ value
2 11.18 is the $\chi^2_{7,\,0.87}$ value
3 12.68 is the $\chi^2_{7,\,0.92}$ value
4 12.02 is the $\chi^2_{7,\,0.90}$ value
5 But see the text.

TABLE 3.2 Contingency tables – collocations with 'the'

(i) Child

Brief Observations 1668		*New Discourse of Trade* 1693		
12	(7.83)	4	(8.17)	16
38	(34.74)	33	(36.26)	71
6	(5.38)	5	(5.62)	11
14	(14.19)	15	(14.81)	29
24	(27.40)	32	(28.60)	56
13	(12.23)	12	(12.77)	25
24	(20.06)	17	(20.94)	41
145	(154.15)	170	(160.85)	315
276		288		564

$X^2 = 8.59$, $\chi^2_{7,\,0.95} = 14.07$.

(ii) Culpepper, *Tract against Usury*

pp. 205–17		pp. 217–30		
6	(4.91)	3	(4.09)	9
7	(10.36)	12	(8.64)	19
5	(3.82)	2	(3.18)	7
9	(7.63)	5	(6.37)	14
22	(21.80)	18	(18.20)	40
1	(2.18)	3	(1.82)	4
14	(15.81)	15	(13.19)	29
81	(78.50)	63	(65.50)	144
145		121		266

$X^2 = 6.31$, $\chi^2_{7,\,0.95} = 14.07$.

(iii) Ferguson, *Interest of Reason in Religion*

pp. 200–26		pp. 226–33, 276–97		
7	(9.12)	11	(8.88)	18
44	(49.67)	54	(48.33)	98
4	(2.53)	1	(2.47)	5
20	(23.32)	26	(22.68)	46
42	(43.59)	44	(42.41)	86
24	(19.26)	14	(18.74)	38
28	(24.84)	21	(24.16)	49
163	(159.66)	152	(155.34)	315
332		323		655

$X^2 = 8.43$, $\chi^2_{7,\,0.95} = 14.07$.

TABLE 3.2 (*contd.*)

(iv) 'Papillon', *East India-Trade . . . most profitable*

pp. 1–14		pp. 14–27		
6	(7.73)	10	(8.27)	16
62	(60.36)	63	(64.64)	125
7	(5.31)	4	(5.69)	11
18	(23.18)	30	(24.82)	48
42	(45.39)	52	(48.61)	94
17	(19.80)	24	(21.20)	41
27	(28.01)	31	(29.99)	58
188	(177.22)	179	(189.78)	367
367		393		760

$X^2 = 6.70, \quad \chi^2_{7, 0.95} = 14.07.$

(v) 'Philopatris', *East India Trade . . . the most national*

pp. 1–22		pp. 22–43		
7	(10.69)	15	(11.31)	22
54	(49.55)	48	(52.45)	102
10	(10.20)	11	(10.80)	21
21	(21.37)	23	(22.63)	44
50	(43.72)	40	(46.28)	90
12	(15.06)	19	(15.94)	31
23	(28.66)	36	(30.34)	59
182	(179.74)	188	(190.26)	370
359		380		739

$X^2 = 8.46, \quad \chi^2_{7, 0.95} = 14.07.$

(vi) *Answer of the Said East India Co.* 1681

pp. 7–11		pp. 11–15		
6	(3.12)	1	(3.88)	7
29	(24.92)	27	(31.08)	56
6	(3.56)	2	(4.44)	8
13	(11.57)	13	(14.43)	26
24	(17.80)	16	(22.20)	40
6	(5.34)	6	(6.66)	12
16	(15.13)	18	(18.87)	34
70	(88.56)	129	(110.44)	199
170		212		382

$X^2 = 20.48, \quad \chi^2_{7, 0.995} = 20.28.$

TABLE 3.2 (*contd.*)

(vii) *Humble Answer* 1692

pp. 620–4		pp. 624–7		
3	(2.61)	2	(2.39)	5
18	(15.68)	12	(14.32)	30
13	(10.97)	8	(10.03)	21
11	(13.07)	14	(11.93)	25
4	(4.70)	5	(4.30)	9
7	(5.23)	3	(4.77)	10
48	(51.74)	51	(47.26)	99
104		95		199

$X^2 = 4.35, \quad \chi^2_{7,\,0.95} = 14.07.$

(viii) *Great Honour and Advantage* 1697

pp. 1–19		pp. 20–39		
4	(5.10)	6	(4.90)	10
20	(19.36)	18	(18.64)	38
3	(2.04)	1	(1.96)	4
5	(5.10)	5	(4.90)	10
6	(9.17)	12	(8.83)	18
4	(6.11)	8	(5.89)	12
5	(4.59)	4	(4.41)	9
60	(55.54)	49	(53.46)	109
107		103		210

$X^2 = 5.99, \quad \chi^2_{7,\,0.95} = 14.07.$

(ix) *Essay on Wool*

pp. 1–9		pp. 10–18		
10	(7.36)	5	(7.64)	15
11	(10.80)	11	(11.20)	22
4	(2.94)	2	(3.06)	6
9	(6.38)	4	(6.62)	13
9	(7.85)	7	(8.15)	16
3	(2.45)	2	(2.55)	5
7	(6.87)	7	(7.13)	14
54	(62.33)	73	(64.67)	127
107		111		218

$X^2 = 7.48, \quad \chi^2_{7,\,0.95} = 14.07.$

TABLE 3.2 (*contd.*)

(x) *Discourse of Nature of . . . Trade* 1694

pp. 1–15		pp. 15–31		
6	(5.38)	5	(5.62)	11
24	(24.93)	27	(26.07)	51
0	(2.44)	5	(2.56)	5
0	(4.89)	10	(5.11)	10
16	(19.55)	24	(20.45)	40
7	(7.33)	8	(7.67)	15
15	(11.24)	8	(11.76)	23
85	(77.23)	73	(80.77)	158
153		160		313

$X^2 = 19.83, \quad \chi^2_{7,\,0.99} = 18.48.$

(xi)

Child		Culpepper		
16	(16.99)	9	(8.01)	25
71	(61.16)	19	(28.84)	90
11	(12.23)	7	(5.77)	18
29	(29.22)	14	(13.78)	43
56	(65.23)	40	(30.77)	96
25	(19.71)	4	(9.29)	29
41	(47.57)	29	(22.43)	70
315	(311.90)	144	(147.10)	459
564		266		830

$X^2 = 16.96, \quad \chi^2_{7,\,0.98} = 16.62.$

(xii)

'Papillon'		Culpepper		
16	(18.52)	9	(6.48)	25
125	(106.67)	19	(37.33)	144
11	(13.33)	7	(4.67)	18
48	(45.93)	14	(16.07)	62
94	(99.26)	40	(34.74)	134
41	(33.33)	4	(11.67)	45
58	(64.44)	29	(22.56)	87
367	(378.52)	144	(132.48)	511
760		266		1026

$X^2 = 27.13, \quad \chi^2_{7,\,0.995} = 20.28.$

TABLE 3.2 (*contd.*)

(xiii)

Ferguson		Culpepper		
18	(19.20)	9	(7.80)	27
98	(83.21)	19	(33.79)	117
5	(8.53)	7	(3.47)	12
46	(42.67)	14	(17.33)	60
86	(89.61)	40	(36.39)	126
38	(29.87)	4	(12.13)	42
49	(55.47)	29	(22.53)	78
315	(326.43)	144	(132.57)	459
655		266		921

$X^2 = 27.50, \quad \chi^2_{7,\,0.995} = 20.28.$

(xiv)

Child		Ferguson		
16	(15.73)	18	(18.27)	34
71	(78.19)	98	(90.81)	169
11	(7.40)	5	(8.60)	16
29	(34.70)	46	(40.30)	75
56	(65.70)	86	(76.30)	142
25	(29.15)	38	(33.85)	63
41	(41.64)	49	(48.36)	90
315	(291.48)	315	(338.52)	630
564		655		1219

$X^2 = 13.55, \quad \chi^2_{7,\,0.94} = 13.53.$

(xv)

Child		'Papillon'		
16	(13.63)	16	(18.37)	32
71	(83.49)	125	(112.51)	196
11	(9.37)	11	(12.63)	22
29	(32.80)	48	(44.20)	77
56	(63.90)	94	(86.10)	150
25	(28.11)	41	(37.89)	66
41	(42.17)	58	(56.83)	99
315	(290.52)	367	(391.48)	682
564		760		1324

$X^2 = 11.19, \quad \chi^2_{7,\,0.87} = 11.18.$

TABLE 3.2 (*contd.*)

(xvi)

Ferguson		'Papillon'		
18	(15.74)	16	(18.26)	34
98	(103.23)	125	(119.77)	223
5	(7.41)	11	(8.59)	16
46	(43.51)	48	(50.49)	94
86	(83.32)	94	(96.68)	180
38	(36.57)	41	(42.43)	79
49	(49.53)	58	(57.47)	107
315	(315.70)	367	(366.30)	682
655		760		1415

$X^2 = 3.10$, $\chi^2_{7,\,0.95} = 14.07$.

(xvii)

Child		Ferguson and 'Papillon'		
16	(14.25)	34	(35.75)	50
71	(83.79)	223	(210.21)	294
11	(7.69)	16	(19.31)	27
29	(35.05)	94	(87.95)	123
56	(67.26)	180	(168.74)	236
25	(29.64)	79	(74.36)	104
41	(42.18)	107	(105.82)	148
315	(284.14)	682	(712.86)	997
564		1415		1979

$X^2 = 14.86$, $\chi^2_{7,\,0.96} = 14.69$.

(xviii)

Ferguson and 'Papillon'		Culpepper		
34	(36.20)	9	(6.80)	43
223	(203.71)	19	(38.29)	242
16	(19.36)	7	(3.64)	23
94	(90.91)	14	(17.09)	108
180	(185.19)	40	(34.81)	220
79	(69.87)	4	(13.13)	83
107	(114.48)	29	(21.52)	136
682	(695.29)	144	(130.71)	826
1415		266		1681

$X^2 = 29.90$, $\chi^2_{7,\,0.995} = 20.28$.

TABLE 3.2 (*contd.*)

(xix)

'Philopatris'		Culpepper		
22	(22.80)	9	(8.20)	31
102	(88.97)	19	(32.03)	121
21	(20.59)	7	(7.41)	28
44	(42.65)	14	(15.35)	58
90	(95.59)	40	(34.41)	130
31	(25.74)	4	(9.26)	35
59	(64.71)	29	(23.29)	88
370	(377.96)	144	(136.04)	514
739		266		1005

$X^2 = 15.34, \quad \chi^2_{7,\,0.96} = 14.69.$

(xx)

Answer of the Said East India Co. 1681		Culpepper		
7	(9.43)	9	(6.57)	16
56	(44.21)	19	(30.79)	75
8	(8.84)	7	(6.16)	15
26	(23.58)	14	(16.42)	40
40	(47.16)	40	(32.84)	80
12	(9.43)	4	(6.57)	16
34	(37.14)	29	(25.86)	63
199	(202.20)	144	(140.80)	343
382		266		648

$X^2 = 15.10, \quad \chi^2_{7,\,0.96} = 14.69.$

(xxi)

Humble Answer 1692		Culpepper		
5	(5.99)	9	(8.01)	14
30	(20.97)	19	(28.03)	49
0	(3.00)	7	(4.00)	7
21	(14.98)	14	(20.02)	35
25	(27.82)	40	(37.18)	65
9	(5.56)	4	(7.44)	13
10	(16.69)	29	(22.31)	39
99	(103.99)	144	(139.01)	243
199		266		465

$X^2 = 25.87, \quad \chi^2_{7,\,0.995} = 20.28.$

TABLE 3.2 (*contd.*)

(xxii) *Great Honour and Advantage*		Culpepper		
10	(8.38)	9	(10.62)	19
38	(25.15)	19	(31.85)	57
4	(4.85)	7	(6.15)	11
10	(10.59)	14	(13.41)	24
18	(25.59)	40	(32.41)	58
12	(7.06)	4	(8.94)	16
9	(16.76)	29	(21.24)	38
109	(111.62)	144	(141.38)	253
210		266		476

$X^2 = 27.40, \quad \chi^2_{7,\,0.995} = 20.28.$

(xxiii) *Essay on Wool*		Culpepper		
15	(10.81)	9	(13.19)	24
22	(18.47)	19	(22.53)	41
6	(5.86)	7	(7.14)	13
13	(12.16)	14	(14.84)	27
16	(25.22)	40	(30.78)	56
5	(4.05)	4	(4.95)	9
14	(19.37)	29	(23.63)	43
127	(122.06)	144	(148.94)	271
218		266		484

$X^2 = 13.91, \quad \chi^2_{7,\,0.94} = 13.53.$

(xxiv) *Discourse of Nature of . . . Trade* 1694		Culpepper		
11	(10.81)	9	(9.19)	20
51	(37.84)	19	(32.16)	70
5	(6.49)	7	(5.51)	12
10	(12.97)	14	(11.03)	24
40	(43.25)	40	(36.75)	80
15	(10.27)	4	(8.73)	19
23	(28.11)	29	(23.89)	52
158	(163.26)	144	(138.74)	302
313		266		579

$X^2 = 19.85, \quad \chi^2_{7,\,0.99} = 18.48.$

TABLE 3.2 (*contd.*)

(xxv)

'Philopatris'		Child		
22	(21.55)	16	(16.45)	38
102	(98.12)	71	(74.88)	173
21	(18.15)	11	(13.85)	32
44	(41.40)	29	(31.60)	73
90	(82.80)	56	(63.20)	146
31	(31.76)	25	(24.24)	56
59	(56.72)	41	(43.28)	100
370	(388.50)	315	(296.50)	685
739		564		1303

$X^2 = 5.52, \quad \chi^2_{7,\,0.95} = 14.07.$

(xxvi)

'Philopatris'		Ferguson and 'Papillon'		
22	(19.21)	34	(36.79)	56
102	(111.50)	223	(213.50)	325
21	(12.69)	16	(24.31)	37
44	(47.35)	94	(90.65)	138
90	(92.63)	180	(177.37)	270
31	(37.74)	79	(72.26)	110
59	(56.95)	107	(109.05)	166
370	(360.92)	682	(691.08)	1052
739		1415		2154

$X^2 = 12.89, \quad \chi^2_{7,\,0.92} = 12.68.$

(xxvii)

Answer of the Said East India Co. 1681		Child		
7	(9.29)	16	(13.71)	23
56	(51.28)	71	(75.72)	127
8	(7.67)	11	(11.33)	19
26	(22.21)	29	(32.79)	55
40	(38.77)	56	(57.23)	96
12	(14.94)	25	(22.06)	37
34	(30.29)	41	(44.71)	75
199	(207.56)	315	(306.44)	514
382		564		946

$X^2 = 5.17, \quad \chi^2_{7,\,0.95} = 14.07.$

TABLE 3.2 (*contd.*)

(xxviii)

Answer of the Said East India Co. 1681		Ferguson and 'Papillon'		
7	(8.72)	34	(32.28)	41
56	(59.31)	223	(219.69)	279
8	(5.10)	16	(18.90)	24
26	(25.51)	94	(94.49)	120
40	(46.77)	180	(173.23)	220
12	(19.34)	79	(71.66)	91
34	(29.97)	107	(111.03)	141
199	(187.28)	682	(693.72)	881
382		1415		1797

$X^2 = 9.17, \quad \chi^2_{7, 0.95} = 14.07.$

(xxix)

Humble Answer 1692		Child		
5	(5.48)	16	(15.52)	21
30	(26.34)	71	(74.66)	101
0	(2.87)	11	(8.13)	11
21	(13.04)	29	(36.96)	50
25	(21.13)	56	(59.87)	81
9	(8.87)	25	(25.13)	34
10	(13.30)	41	(37.70)	51
99	(107.98)	315	(306.02)	414
199		564		763

$X^2 = 14.28, \quad \chi^2_{7, 0.95} = 14.07.$

(xxx)

Humble Answer 1692		Ferguson and 'Papillon'		
5	(4.81)	34	(34.19)	39
30	(31.19)	223	(221.81)	253
0	(1.97)	16	(14.03)	16
21	(14.18)	94	(100.82)	115
25	(25.28)	180	(179.72)	205
9	(10.85)	79	(77.15)	88
10	(14.43)	107	(102.57)	117
99	(96.29)	682	(684.71)	781
199		1415		1614

$X^2 = 8.05, \quad \chi^2_{7, 0.95} = 14.07.$

TABLE 3.2 (*contd.*)

(xxxi)

Great Honour and Advantage		Child		
10	(7.05)	16	(18.95)	26
38	(29.57)	71	(79.43)	109
4	(4.07)	11	(10.93)	15
10	(10.58)	29	(28.42)	39
18	(20.08)	56	(53.92)	74
12	(10.04)	25	(26.96)	37
9	(13.57)	41	(36.43)	50
109	(115.04)	315	(308.96)	424
210		564		774

$X^2 = 8.39$, $\chi^2_{7,\,0.95} = 14.07$.

(xxxii)

Great Honour and Advantage		Ferguson and 'Papillon'		
10	(5.69)	34	(38.31)	44
38	(33.73)	223	(227.27)	261
4	(2.58)	16	(17.42)	20
10	(13.44)	94	(90.56)	104
18	(25.59)	180	(172.41)	198
12	(11.76)	79	(79.24)	91
9	(14.99)	107	(101.01)	116
109	(102.22)	682	(688.78)	791
210		1415		1625

$X^2 = 12.14$, $\chi^2_{7,\,0.90} = 12.02$.

(xxxiii)

Essay on Wool		Child		
15	(8.64)	16	(22.36)	31
22	(25.93)	71	(67.07)	93
6	(4.74)	11	(12.26)	17
13	(11.71)	29	(30.29)	42
16	(20.07)	56	(51.93)	72
5	(8.36)	25	(21.64)	30
14	(15.33)	41	(39.67)	55
127	(123.22)	315	(318.78)	442
218		564		782

$X^2 = 11.31$, $\chi^2_{7,\,0.87} = 11.18$.

TABLE 3.2 (*contd.*)

(xxxiv)

Essay on Wool		Ferguson and 'Papillon'		
15	(6.54)	34	(42.46)	49
22	(32.71)	223	(212.29)	245
6	(2.94)	16	(19.06)	22
13	(14.28)	94	(92.72)	107
16	(26.17)	180	(169.83)	196
5	(11.21)	79	(72.79)	84
14	(16.15)	107	(104.85)	121
127	(108.00)	682	(701.00)	809
218		1415		1633

$X^2 = 33.21, \quad \chi^2_{7,\,0.995} = 20.28.$

(xxxv)

Discourse of Nature of . . . Trade 1694		Child		
11	(9.64)	16	(17.36)	27
51	(43.54)	71	(78.46)	122
5	(5.71)	11	(10.29)	16
10	(13.92)	29	(25.08)	39
40	(34.26)	56	(61.74)	96
15	(14.28)	25	(25.72)	40
23	(22.84)	41	(41.16)	64
158	(168.81)	315	(304.19)	473
313		564		877

$X^2 = 6.77, \quad \chi^2_{7,0.95} = 14.07.$

(xxxvi)

Discourse of Nature of . . . Trade 1694		Ferguson and 'Papillon'		
11	(8.15)	34	(36.85)	45
51	(49.63)	223	(224.37)	274
5	(3.80)	16	(17.20)	21
10	(18.84)	94	(85.16)	104
40	(39.85)	180	(180.15)	220
15	(17.03)	79	(76.97)	94
23	(23.55)	107	(106.45)	130
158	(152.15)	682	(687.85)	840
313		1415		1728

$X^2 = 7.37, \quad \chi^2_{7,\,0.95} = 14.07.$

examining the work of Child, Culpepper, Ferguson and Papillon, as well as each of the six anonymous pieces, for internal consistency. It is immediately apparent that each of the four named writers shows internal consistency in the choice of couplings with 'the' but that only four of the anonymous pieces are internally consistent in this respect, suggesting that both *Answer of the Said . . . Company* and *Discourse* (1694) may be the product of more than one hand.

The next eight entries in Table 3.1 report the results of comparing the habits in the use of 'the' exhibited by the known authors. It is clear from this that Culpepper's work is significantly different from that of Child, Papillon and Ferguson, with computed χ^2 values of 16.96, 27.13, and 27.50 respectively. This result was to be expected if our procedure is appropriate and it was, indeed, for this reason that Culpepper was included as a test since he was writing earlier in the 17th century than the others and yet his pamphlet was reprinted within a work by Child. Thus this result provides some confirmation of the appropriateness and efficiency of the one test remaining to us. A test on this basis, as the next row indicates, shows significant differences between the work of Child and that of Ferguson, with a computed χ^2 value of 13.55. There are also differences between the work of Child and that appearing under the name of Papillon, although there is an uncomfortably large type I error of 13 per cent attached to this rejection of consistency. However, it is gratifying to find that Ferguson did indeed write the work which appeared under the name of Papillon, as the East India Company records would indicate, for comparison of habits in the use of 'the' produces a computed χ^2 of only 3.10. This is particularly interesting for it shows that Professor Letwin's conjecture, that the Ferguson who wrote the pamphlet 'at the instance of Thomas Papillon' was in fact the religious controversialist whose work we have used as a basis for comparison, is correct.

In the light of this conclusion, we have felt able to amalgamate the acknowledged work by Ferguson and the piece appearing under the name of Papillon in the subsequent tests in order to provide a larger sample. A test of consistency between this enlarged sample and the work of Child yields a computed χ^2 value of 14.86, indicating discrimination, while comparison with that of Culpepper yields a computed χ^2 of 29.90.

The next six rows of Table 3.1 again exhibit the results of using Culpepper as a test piece, given that he cannot possibly have written any of the disputed texts. It is gratifying to be able to report that we achieve clear discrimination between his work and all six of the anonymous pieces and that the largest type I error in reaching this conclusion is only

6 per cent – for the *Essay on Wool.* The remaining results are extremely strong with two type I errors of 4 per cent, one of 1 per cent, and two of not more than 0.5 per cent.

Given the strength of the results so far, it is possible to turn to the key question of the authorship of the anonymously written pieces. The first, and most important, conclusion is that it does indeed appear to be correct after all that Child was the author of the pamphlet by 'Philopatris'. It is also significant that it is clear that Ferguson did not write that pamphlet. The computed χ^2 values are 5.52 (for Child) and 12.89. In rejecting Ferguson as the author, the probability of error is only 8 per cent at most.

The *Answer of the Said . . . Company* is, as already indicated in the first part of this chapter, a pamphlet in which more than one hand was involved, and thus it is not surprising that we have been able to report internal inconsistency. It is now interesting to see that it turns out to be statistically insignificantly different, on the basis of the present tests, from the work of both Child *and* Ferguson. We are not able to assign authorship of the original draft on the basis of our test; but it does seem plausible to take the view that the original draft was supplied to the Company by Ferguson, at their request, and that Child had a major hand in the alterations to it which have already been mentioned. This is consistent with our conclusion that Ferguson supplied another such document to the Company – the *Humble Answer.* For this does not seem to be the work of Child, but is indistinguishable from that of Ferguson – the computed χ^2 values are 14.28 and 8.05 respectively. The presence of the material which suggested an association with 'Philopatris' turns out, as anticipated, to be insignificant.

However, it does appear that the circumstantial evidence suggesting that Child was the author of the *Great Honour* pamphlet is consistent with the statistical results ; the computed χ^2 resulting from comparing the work of Child with this pamphlet is only 8.39, and a similar comparison using the work of Ferguson yields 12.14, which would lead us to reject Ferguson as the author, although with a type I error of 10 per cent.

Perhaps not surprisingly, we obtain very much less clear cut results from analysing the habits in the use of 'the' exhibited by the author of the *Essay on Wool.* It does seem fairly clear that Ferguson was not the author – a computed χ^2 value of 33.21 does not leave much room for doubt. It is, however, *possible* that Child may have had a hand in the pamphlet although, as indicated in part I of this chapter, it seems unlikely that the pamphlet was wholly his because of its differences in approach. The χ^2 value obtained by comparing the pamphlet with the work of Child is 11.31; and rejection of consistency of the *Essay* with Child's work would imply a type I error of 13 per cent. Moreover, it is apparent from an examination of Tables 3.2(xxxiii) and 3.2(i) that the major contributor to the figure of 11.31 in Table 3.2(xxxiii) is row 1 ('and the'); and this same row is the major contributor to the figure of 8.59 in Table 3.2(i). Thus the inconsistency of habit between Child and the author of the pamphlet is the same as an inconsistency of habit exhibited by Child himself. In view of the internal evidence provided by an examination of the content of the pamphlet, which was discussed above, it would seem unwise to be any more definite than this.

The 1694 *Discourse of Trade* has already been shown to be internally inconsistent, suggesting that more than one hand was involved. Intriguingly, it proves impossible to reject either Child or Ferguson as the author. Given the literary flourish of this pamphlet, it is tempting to speculate that Ferguson again supplied a draft and that Child altered this. But this can be no more than speculation and, given that it would not be too difficult to construct an *a priori* case suggesting that this was unlikely, it seems safer not to press this point further.

III. CONCLUSION

Our study of the 17th century economic writing considered in this chapter has found that only one form of literary habit, the choice of collocations with 'the', has proved successful in producing statistical results which were of use in dealing with the problem. First word usage and collocations with 'be' proved, in contrast to the experience in other chapters, unsatisfactory. Nevertheless, the results obtained from the tests on collocations with 'the' seem fairly strong and we have been able, through the use of the Culpepper material, to provide a test of the ability of our procedure to discriminate even in the difficult area of 17th century literature. It seems clear, perhaps most importantly, that Child did write the 'Philopatris' pamphlet, the material on a new stock not withstanding. Moreover, it is clear that Professor Letwin's conjecture about the identity of Robert Ferguson has also been borne out by our analysis. Some of the texts analysed have proved to offer insuperable difficulties. Yet this itself is reassuring. For it does mean that where a text is the work of several hands, and cannot safely be attributed to any one writer, the method will indicate that there is internal inconsistency in the text under consideration and that subsequent attempts to identify it with the work of any one author are likely, happily, to be unsuccessful.

Our remaining chapters take us out of the minefield of 17th century pamphlets and it is to a much disputed 19th century problem that we now turn.

4 Torrens, McCulloch, and the *Edinburgh Review*, 1819

I. HISTORICAL BACKGROUND

The problem discussed in this chapter, like those in our remaining chapters, deals with a matter of authorship identification in which the text is written in 19th century English prose.

In October 1819, an article appeared in the *Edinburgh Review* entitled 'Mr Owen's Plans for Relieving the National Distress'.[1] The authorship of this article has been a matter of dispute for some time and it was, indeed, this problem which first drew us into the study of the statistical analysis of authors' habits.

The two authors whose names have been linked with the article are Robert Torrens and J. R. McCulloch. The link with Torrens is strong. The article draws heavily upon a speech by Torrens – as reported in the *Scotsman*, of which, it is true, McCulloch was editor.[2] The first ten pages of the article draw upon the speech and paraphrase it in places,[3] and the next five pages reproduce material directly from the speech, as does the last page of the article. However, in between the two sections which relate directly to the speech, there is a critical section dealing with Sismondi;[4] and it is this section which has been the basis for doubt about the attribution of the article to Torrens.

Most authorities have, nevertheless, assumed that the entire article was the work of Torrens. Those who have taken this view include such illustrious names in economic scholarship as Lord Robbins, Mr P. Sraffa and Professor F. W. Fetter.[5] Recent authors who have supported the view include Professors J. S. Chipman[6] and T. Sowell.[7] Torrens' contemporary Ricardo[8] was also convinced that the article was by Torrens and the background to this belief turns out to be fairly strong supporting evidence for its correctness. There is also material in the text of the article itself which would suggest Torrens as the author.

The case for attributing the article to Torrens rests upon a number of factors. They include the reproduction of material from his speech; the reply by Torrens in his *Essay on the Production of Wealth* to an attack by Malthus on this very article;[9] Ricardo's belief in the authorship, at a time when he was intimate with Torrens; the acceptance by Malthus, who, as noted above, had attacked the article, that the author was Torrens;[10] the use of numerical examples, to which Torrens was particularly addicted; and the reproduction of arguments which occur in the article, in Torrens' *Essay* of two years later.

The scholarly concensus on this matter has, however, been challenged on at least two occasions. The late Jacob Viner, undoubtedly one of the leading historians of economic thought in this century, attributed the authorship to J. R. McCulloch, in his *Studies in the Theory of International Trade* published in 1937;[11] and 37 years later Professor W. O. Thweatt expressed support for this view.[12] Viner gave no reasons for his attribution in his book, although those familiar with his methods realised that this was no snap judgement on his part. However, through the courtesy of Professor Donald Winch, we have learnt that, in correspondence with Sraffa, Viner relied on five main grounds.[13] These were: (i) a reference in the article to a previous *Edinburgh Review* article which is known to be by McCulloch;[14] (ii) McCulloch's claim to a monopoly of economic articles in the *Edinburgh Review* for the period 1819–29; (iii) Sismondi's belief that McCulloch was the author of the article; (iv) praise of Mrs Marcet in the article – Viner attributed this praise to a request from Leonard Horner to McCulloch to praise Mrs Marcet; and (v) laudatory references to the Say–Mill Law of Markets, and citations from French economists.

There are a number of fairly important objections to these grounds, as Sraffa made clear to Viner in their correspondence. However, we should also note the grounds upon which Professor Thweatt's conclusion is based before going on to consider the difficulties with the attribution of the article to McCulloch.

Professor Thweatt has argued that the material in the *Essay on the Production of Wealth* which replies to Malthus is in fact based upon arguments found in Ricardo's *Notes on Malthus*; and Torrens received these by means of their incorporation by McCulloch in a subsequent article in the *Edinburgh Review*[15] – thus McCulloch replied to Malthus *before* Torrens. McCulloch, it is argued, was unwilling to claim authorship of the article when Ricardo attributed it to Torrens, because of the amount of Torrens' own material which had been incorporated into it.[16] Thirdly, Professor Thweatt has pointed out that material in Torrens' speech about colonisation as a remedy for economic distress was not incorporated in the article; and he believes this to be significant on the grounds that Torrens was an enthusiast for colonisation and McCulloch, in his view, was not. Fourthly, he points to opposition elsewhere in Torren's work to the Say–Mill Law of Markets;[17] the position in the article which is in accord with the same Law of Markets he believes to conflict with Torrens' position in other places. Fifthly, he believes that Torrens never mentioned Sismondi elsewhere in his work;[18] and, finally, he points to the reference to the earlier *Edinburgh Review* article which Viner had also regarded as significant.

It is in the nature of disputes about authorship that circumstantial evidence of this sort is never completely convincing. In particular, there seem to be a number of *a priori* objections to the arguments summarised above dealing with this particular problem. The argument that Torrens was relying upon McCulloch's version of the *Notes on Malthus* seems unconvincing in the light of Torrens' mental vitality and flair for controversy. It would be hard to accept such a view unless the internal evidence were overwhelming, which it does not seem to be. But perhaps more importantly, whatever the *origin* of the ideas, and however far Torrens was borrowing from Ricardo, whether via McCulloch or not, it was Torrens himself who publicly undertook the refutation of Malthus' attack; and it is *this*, the very act of replying to an attack upon the article, which is held to be acknowledgement of authorship of the original article. The view that McCulloch was unwilling to claim authorship of the article in correspondence with Ricardo seems less than persuasive when one examines the correspondence in question. For Ricardo, in a letter of 28 February 1820, says quite plainly that Torrens is the author of the article; and McCulloch, in a letter of 19 March which is a direct reply to that of 28 February, lays no claim to the authorship of the article, but instead refers to a different *Edinburgh Review* article, one which is undoubtedly his, for Ricardo's approbation.[19] The omission of the material about colonisation is also less than completely convincing as an argument for Torrens' authorship. McCulloch was, in fact, an advocate of colonisation and emigration from his earliest days and an enthusiastic supporter of the colonisation schemes of Wilmot-Horton. It was retaining control of colonies, as an empire ruled from home, to which he objected, not the establishment of colonies as an outlet for surplus population. It seems reasonable, then, to take the view that the omission of the colonisation material has no real significance in relation to differences of opinion between McCulloch and Torrens and, more particularly in the present context, in relation to the attribution of the disputed article to one or other of them.[20] Again, although it is true that Torrens was, in general, an opponent of the Say–Mill Law of Markets, his position was not entirely consistent on this, as can be seen from the *Essay*. In a reading of pages 370–430 of that work we find that Torrens spends no less than 14 pages showing that production of commodities constitutes demand for commodities, and that increased productive power does not upset this – the basic Say–Mill proposition. He then dismisses Malthus' vision of excessively rapid accummulation of capital leading to effective demand failure as 'vague, fallacious, and inconsistent throughout'.[21] Too rapid accummulation will check itself through bidding up of wages and lowering of profits – a standard Ricardian position.[22] Finally, Torrens establishes that gluts can only occur either from 'erroneous calculations of producers' or from 'irregularity of the seasons'.[23] All this is hardly the work of a man who consistently and immovably opposed Say's Law. In any case, Torrens was not a man who could be accused of rigid consistency in thought. Indeed, given the vicissitudes of his thought on other matters, especially monetary theory,[24] it would have been rather remarkable if he had been totally consistent in his attitude towards Say's Law. The fact that Torrens did not mention Sismondi elsewhere does not seem particularly important, given that he was mainly concerned with the writings of Malthus on the question of effective demand failure; and the form of the reference to a previous *Edinburgh Review* article, in a journal in which everything was published anonymously, can surely be represented quite reasonably as a straightforward exercise of the editor's hand.

In addition to doubts about the *a priori* case for McCulloch having been the author of the article, there are other factors which seem to suggest Torrens' authorship. Firstly, McCulloch was not a plagiarist (as distinct from a *self*-plagiarist).[25] In any case, Torrens, who was a very touchy character, would not have allowed plagiarism of his speech on this scale. Secondly, there seems to us to be close correspondence between the six pages of the article which lie at the root of the dispute, and the corresponding section of Torrens' *Essay*.[26] *Per contra*, there is *not* any very obvious correspondence between the *Edinburgh Review* article and three other pieces by McCulloch referring to Sismondi where, given his penchant for self-plagiarism, one might well have expected to find such correspondence.[27] Another factor which would suggest that McCulloch was not the author is that the article was not included in the list of McCulloch's *Edinburgh* contributions compiled by his confidential clerk and son-in-law H. G. Reid, who had access to McCulloch's own list. Nor is it in McCulloch's own bound volumes of his *Edinburgh* articles at Reading or the corresponding set in the Goldsmith Library.[28] The very style of the article, which is distinctly florid, seems redolent of

Torrens' work, rather than that of McCulloch which is of a rather more rough-hewn nature. Moreover, there is a reference to an article by McCulloch in the disputed article itself; and it is not a straightforward footnote reference but what was known in the 19th century as a 'puff', praising the excellence of that article. This would have amounted to self-advertisement of a kind which the editor, Jeffrey, would have been unlikely to allow, given that he did his best to keep McCulloch under control.[29] The monopoly which McCulloch is supposed to have had of the *Edinburgh*'s economic articles was never really complete, even at its height, so that not much weight can be laid upon this in attributing the article to McCulloch;[30] and finally, on the positive side, the *Wellesley Index* cites the Copinger list, as well as the letter by Ricardo, as authority for the attribution to Torrens – and this list is believed to have been based upon a record of the *Edinburgh*'s publishers, Longmans.[31]

On balance, both positive and negative factors would seem to support the majority opinion that Torrens is the author of the article in question. But the opposing case is by no means negligible and the problem of attribution in this case is clearly one to which a statistical approach can make some contribution.

The texts used for analysis were as follows. We used pp. 51–84 of McCulloch's *Treatise on Taxation*[32] which amounts, after removal of quotations, footnotes and other extraneous material, to about 13,000 words. We used pp. 142–64 of the 5th edition of the same author's *Principles of Political Economy*,[33] which is just slightly under 9,000 words. We also include McCulloch's article 'Machinery and Accumulation'[34] which amounts to about 8,500 words.

The length of the disputed article in the *Edinburgh Review* itself[35] is about 10,500 words.

The main Torrens text which we used for analysis was a section of his *Essay on the External Corn Trade*,[36] Part II, pp. 174–266, amounting to about 16,000 words. His Speech[37] discussed in the text was also included for comparative purposes and amounts to slightly under 5,000 words in length. We also used a short section of his *Essay on the Production of Wealth*,[38] pp. 371–83, which is slightly over 2,000 words in length.

II. STATISTICAL ANALYSIS

Our first task in conducting statistical analysis of authorship is to identify those habits of style which are used consistently by both authors and which can also be used to distinguish successfully between their work. We also have to test the article in dispute for internal consistency of style and then to compare the whole of it with the habits of both possible authors. We are able to test the internal consistency of the 1819 article by splitting the work into its three component parts. These are the section which has been a particular matter of dispute, dealing with Sismondi, the direct quotation from Torrens' speech, and the section of paraphrase of material from that speech.

(a) First word usage

We used the following classification of first word usage: 'it'; 'but'; 'the' or 'we'; 'in'; 'suppose' or 'this'; and 'all other first words'. We found this to be the most successful classification in terms of establishing consistency within the work of each of our authors and discrimination between their work. Each contingency table has six rows, corresponding to our six classifications of first word. The summary results are presented in Table 4.1 and the details upon which this is based are to be found in the contingency Tables 4.2(i) to 4.2(viii).

We found Torrens to be consistent in his choice of first word; using data obtained from the frequency of choice in his speech, in his *Essay on the Production of Wealth*, and in his *External Corn Trade*, we obtained a calculated χ^2 of 10.02, well below the 95 per cent critical value, from the distribution with 10 degrees of freedom, of 18.31. In the case of the samples of McCulloch's work which we used, we were able to obtain a calculated χ^2 value of 6.68 from data drawn from the sections of his *Principles* and *Treatise on Taxation* which we used and from his *Edinburgh Review* article 'Effects of Machinery and Accumulation'.

Applying the same classification of first word usage to the article in dispute, we found that it is internally consistent, with a computed χ^2 value of 12.61, still well below the critical value of 18.31. However, the contingency Table 4.2(iii) suffers from having 6 of its 18 cells with expected values below 5. This could cast doubt upon our result and so it is desirable to amalgamate rows in order to check the outcome. Amalgamation of rows 1 and 5 indicated no change in our conclusion. We present a summary of the results obtained from contingency tables with amalgamated rows in Table 4.1, but have not included the extra contingency tables since our conclusions remain unaffected.

The original classification produces satisfactory discrimination between Torrens and McCulloch, yielding a computed χ^2 value of 25.34 where the 95 per cent critical value, with 5 degrees of freedom, is 11.07. Since this classification discriminates well between our two possible

TABLE 4.1 First word usage

Texts analysed	X^2	d.f.	$\chi^2_{0.95}$	*Decision*	*Maximum type I error (where applicable)*	*Contingency table*	*After row amalgamations* X^2	d.f.	$\chi^2_{0.95}$	*Maximum type I error (where applicable)*
Speech vs *Wealth* vs *Corn Trade*	10.02	10	18.31	Accept the hypothesis of Torrens' internal consistency	–	4.2(i)	9.50	8	15.51	–
Principles vs 'Machinery' vs*Taxation*	6.68	10	18.31	Accept the hypothesis of McCulloch's internal consistency	–	4.2(ii)	6.65	8	15.51	–
'Digression' vs Speech vs Paraphrase	12.61	10	18.31	Accept the hypothesis of the internal consistency of disputed article 1819	–	4.2(iii)	12.55	8	15.51	–
Torrens vs McCulloch	25.34	5	11.07	Reject the hypothesis of consistency between Torrens and McCulloch	0.005	4.2(iv)	17.67	4	9.49	0.005
McCulloch vs *whole* of disputed article 1819	17.46	5	11.07	Reject the hypothesis of consistency between McCulloch and disputed article 1819	0.005	4.2(v)	13.34	4	9.49	0.01
Torrens vs *whole* of disputed article 1819	3.83	5	11.07	Accept the hypothesis of consistency between Torrens and disputed article 1819	–	4.2(vi)	3.62	4	9.49	–
McCulloch vs 'Digression'	9.67	5	9.52*	Reject the hypothesis of consistency between McCulloch and the 'Digression'	0.09	4.2(vii)	9.14	4	9.04*	0.06
Torrens vs 'Digression'	7.61	5	11.07	Accept the hypothesis of consistency between Torrens and the 'Digression'	–	4.2(viii)	7.61	4	9.49	–

* 9.52 is the $\chi^2_{5,\,0.91}$ value.

* 9.04 is the value $\chi^2_{4,\,0.94}$.

TABLE 4.2 Contingency tables – first word usage

(i) Torrens

Speech		*Wealth*		*Corn Trade*		
8	(5.90)	2	(2.45)	17	(18.64)	27
15	(11.58)	6	(4.82)	32	(36.60)	53
9	(15.52)	9	(6.45)	53	(49.03)	71
7	(7.21)	5	(3.00)	21	(22.79)	33
6	(5.68)	3	(2.36)	17	(17.95)	26
68	(67.10)	22	(27.91)	217	(211.99)	307
113		47		357		517

$X^2 = 10.02, \quad \chi^2_{10,\,0.95} = 18.31.$

(ii) McCulloch

Principles		'Machinery'		*Taxation*		
23	(25.23)	32	(30.75)	43	(42.02)	98
30	(27.29)	35	(33.26)	41	(45.45)	106
40	(35.79)	49	(43.61)	50	(59.60)	139
15	(12.62)	12	(15.37)	22	(21.01)	49
8	(9.01)	12	(10.98)	15	(15.01)	35
99	(105.05)	122	(128.02)	187	(174.93)	408
215		262		358		835

$X^2 = 6.68, \quad \chi^2_{10,\,0.95} = 18.31.$

(iii) *Edinburgh* 1819

'Digression'		Speech		Paraphrase		
2	(2.07)	4	(2.22)	2	(3.71)	8
3	(5.96)	7	(6.38)	13	(10.66)	23
14	(9.07)	7	(9.70)	14	(16.23)	35
6	(5.44)	3	(5.82)	12	(9.74)	21
2	(2.59)	5	(2.77)	3	(4.64)	10
30	(31.87)	35	(34.10)	58	(57.03)	123
57		61		102		220

$X^2 = 12.61, \quad \chi^2_{10,\,0.95} = 18.31.$

TABLE 4.2 *(contd.)*

(iv)

Torrens		McCulloch		
27	(47.80)	98	(77.20)	125
53	(60.80)	106	(98.20)	159
71	(80.30)	139	(129.70)	210
33	(31.36)	49	(50.64)	82
26	(23.33)	35	(37.67)	61
307	(273.41)	408	(441.59)	715
517		835		1352

$X^2 = 25.34$, $\chi^2_{5,\,0.995} = 16.75$.

(v)

Edinburgh 1819		McCulloch		
8	(22.10)	98	(83.90)	106
23	(26.90)	106	(102.10)	129
35	(36.28)	139	(137.72)	174
21	(14.60)	49	(55.40)	70
10	(9.38)	35	(35.62)	45
123	(110.73)	408	(420.27)	531
220		835		1055

$X^2 = 17.46$, $\chi^2_{5,\,0.995} = 16.75$.

(vi)

Edinburgh 1819		Torrens		
8	(10.45)	27	(24.55)	35
23	(22.69)	53	(53.31)	76
35	(31.64)	71	(74.36)	106
21	(16.12)	33	(37.88)	54
10	(10.75)	26	(25.25)	36
123	(128.36)	307	(301.64)	430
220		517		737

$X^2 = 3.83$, $\chi^2_{5,\,0.95} = 11.07$.

TABLE 4.2 (*contd.*)

(vii) 'Digression'		McCulloch		
2	(6.39)	98	(93.61)	100
3	(6.97)	106	(102.03)	109
14	(9.78)	139	(143.22)	153
6	(3.51)	49	(51.49)	55
2	(2.36)	35	(34.64)	37
30	(27.99)	408	(410.01)	438
57		835		892

$X^2 = 9.67, \quad \chi^2_{5,\,0.91} = 9.52.$

(viii) 'Digression'		Torrens		
2	(2.88)	27	(26.12)	29
3	(5.56)	53	(50.44)	56
14	(8.44)	71	(76.56)	85
6	(3.87)	33	(35.13)	39
2	(2.78)	26	(25.22)	28
30	(33.47)	307	(303.53)	337
57		517		574

$X^2 = 7.61, \quad \chi^2_{5,\,0.95} = 11.07.$

authors, it seems sensible to use it to test for consistency between the work of one or other of them and the anonymous text. This leads us to reject, fairly conclusively, the hypothesis that McCulloch was the author of the article on Owen. While his work is distinguished from the text of the disputed article, with a computed χ^2 of 17.46, Torrens' work is indistinguishable from it on the present test, with a computed χ^2 of only 3.83.

This result might be attributable to the inclusion in the article of material reproduced directly from Torrens' speech, even though there is also a good deal of paraphrase. However, if we examine the relatively small section dealing with Sismondi, we obtain identical conclusions with respect to authorship, even though the type I error associated with the rejection of the hypothesis that McCulloch could have been the author is slightly higher. This increase in type I error is, almost certainly, wholly attributable to the reduction in sample size when we take only a section of the article instead of the entire article. The section is only equivalent to about one quarter of the article. This means that there is less information available and the reduction in information is reflected in the increased type I error. Nevertheless, the differences between the 'Digression on Sismondi', as it has been called, and McCulloch's work, are sufficiently large to be statistically significant, and in rejecting the hypothesis that McCulloch was the author of this section, the probability of error is certainly not larger than 9 per cent. Comparing this small sample of the disputed article with Torrens' work we find that, in respect of first word usage, the habits of the anonymous author differ only slightly from those exhibited by Torrens himself; the differences are so small as to be statistically insignificant.

Analysis of data from first word usage thus leads us to conclude that Torrens, not McCulloch, was the author, not only of the article as a whole but also of the particular section of it, the 'Digression on Sismondi', which seems to lie at the basis of the dispute about authorship. This last is an extremely important conclusion. It might be possible to argue – though only by disregarding our tests of homogeneity – that the inclusion of material from Torrens' speech gives the article as a whole its distinctive literary characteristics. But, as we have indicated, the particular section which has been the basis for attribution of the article to McCulloch, despite the inclusion of other material by Torrens, turns out to be written in a style which is consistent with that of the work of Torrens but not that of McCulloch.

(b) Collocations with 'the'

In selecting collocations with 'the' which produce consistent results within the texts of one author, while discriminating between authors, we found it best to use a fairly highly aggregated approach, and one which did not exhaust all possible collocations with 'the'. The collocations we found to be most successful were: 'in' or 'on' or 'upon' or 'and' or 'that' or 'by'; 'of' or 'at'; 'from' or 'than' or 'to' or 'into'. Each collocation table thus has only three rows. Quite a high degree of amalgamation proved necessary in order to obtain sufficient consistency within the work of Torrens; McCulloch is a highly consistent writer but Torrens rather less so. Because the set of collocations used here is not exhaustive, those in the use of which Torrens was most inconsistent having been disregarded, the column totals in the tables discussed below do not indicate the total occurrences of 'the' in each piece. We also disregarded some collocations because, although both writers were consistent in their use, the habit failed to discriminate between the authors.

However, the remaining collocations proved perfectly adequate for the purposes in hand – obtaining consistency within the work of one author and discriminating between authors – and the results of analysis of data obtained from the frequency of collocations with 'the' accord with the conclusions drawn as a result of the analysis of first word usage. The results are summarised in Table 4.3, and the details are to be found in the contingency tables 4.4(i) to 4.4(viii).

As the first three rows of Table 4.3 indicate, Torrens, McCulloch, and the author of the anonymous article are each consistent in their use of the selected collocations, with computed χ^2 values of 4.13, 7.06 and 5.24 respectively, each of which is well within the relevant 95 per cent critical value of 9.49. The fourth row of Table 4.3 indicates that the selected collocations discriminate extremely well between Torrens and McCulloch, with a computed χ^2 value of 15.00. The relevant critical value, with 2 degrees of freedom, is 5.99, and hence we may safely conclude that discrimination is achieved.

Comparison of McCulloch's habitual use of the selected collocations with those of the anonymous author indicates the presence of large differences, and these differences are statistically significant – the computed χ^2 is 7.06 while the critical value is 5.99. In contrast, a comparison of Torrens' habits with those of the anonymous author yields a computed χ^2 as low as 0.74. We thus conclude from analysis of collocations with 'the' that Torrens, not McCulloch, was the author of the disputed 1819 article; and, perhaps most significantly, for the reasons indicated above, we obtain the same conclusion in respect of the so-called 'Digression' taken on its own. This last is particularly important, given the very small sample with which we have to work; the computed χ^2 value when comparing McCulloch's habits in the use of 'the' with those of the 'Digression' is 6.18, outside the critical value of 5.99, while for Torrens the computed χ^2 is only 3.13.

(c) Collocations with 'be'

The results of our tests using data obtained from the frequency of collocations with 'be' are presented in Table 4.5, which summarises the detailed contingency tables 4.6(i) to 4.6(vi). Each contingency table has four rows, which correspond to the following groupings of collocations: 'could' or 'shall'; 'would' or 'may'; 'should' or 'must'; 'can' or 'might'. Thus this list does not exhaust all the occurrences of 'be'. This is because the Torrens material exhibits inconsistencies in the use of particular collocations such as 'will be' and 'to be' and these had to be eliminated from the analysis in order to produce consistency within Torrens' work. Unfortunately, the removal of data relating to collocations which are

TABLE 4.3 Collocations with 'the'

Texts analysed	X^2	d.f.	$\chi^2_{0.95}$	*Decision*	*Maximum type I error (where applicable)*	*Contingency table*
Speech vs *Wealth* vs *Corn Trade*	4.13	4	9.49	Accept the hypothesis of Torrens' internal consistency	–	4.4(i)
Principles vs 'Machinery' vs *Taxation*	7.06	4	9.49	Accept the hypothesis of McCulloch's internal consistency	–	4.4(ii)
'Digression' vs Speech vs Paraphrase	5.24	4	9.49	Accept the hypothesis of the internal consistency of disputed article 1819	–	4.4(iii)
Torrens vs McCulloch	15.00	2	5.99	Reject the hypothesis of consistency between Torrens and McCulloch	0.005	4.4(iv)
McCulloch vs *whole* of disputed article 1819	7.06	2	5.99	Reject the hypothesis of consistency between McCulloch and disputed article 1819	0.03	4.4(v)
Torrens vs *whole* of disputed article 1819	0.74	2	5.99	Accept the hypothesis of consistency between Torrens and disputed article 1819	–	4.4(vi)
McCulloch vs 'Digression'	6.18	2	5.99	Reject the hypothesis of consistency between McCulloch and the 'Digression'	0.05	4.4(vii)
Torrens vs 'Digression'	3.13	2	5.99	Accept the hypothesis of consistency between Torrens and the 'Digression'	–	4.4(viii)

TABLE 4.4 Contingency tables – collocations with 'the'

(i) Torrens

Speech		*Wealth*		*Corn Trade*		
82	(80.48)	32	(37.29)	361	(357.23)	475
51	(47.44)	28	(21.98)	201	(210.58)	280
31	(36.09)	16	(16.72)	166	(160.19)	213
164		76		728		968

$X^2 = 4.13, \quad \chi^2_{4,\,0.95} = 9.49.$

(ii) McCulloch

Principles		'Machinery'		*Taxation*		
142	(126.84)	161	(157.19)	227	(245.97)	530
96	(102.43)	126	(126.94)	206	(198.64)	428
42	(50.74)	60	(62.88)	110	(98.39)	212
280		347		543		1170

$X^2 = 7.06, \quad \chi^2_{4,\,0.95} = 9.49.$

(iii) *Edinburgh* 1819

'Digression'		Speech		Paraphrase		
51	(44.48)	42	(48.06)	89	(89.47)	182
22	(25.17)	34	(27.20)	47	(50.63)	103
14	(17.35)	18	(18.75)	39	(34.90)	71
87		94		175		356

$X^2 = 5.24, \quad \chi^2_{4,\,0.95} = 9.49.$

(iv)

Torrens		McCulloch		
475	(455.02)	530	(549.98)	1005
280	(320.55)	428	(387.45)	708
213	(192.42)	212	(232.58)	425
968		1170		2138

$X^2 = 15.00, \quad \chi^2_{2,\,0.995} = 10.60.$

TABLE 4.4 (*contd.*)

(v)

Edinburgh 1819		McCulloch		
182	(166.10)	530	(545.90)	712
103	(123.88)	428	(407.12)	531
71	(66.02)	212	(216.98)	283
356		1170		1526

$X^2 = 7.06, \quad \chi^2_{2,\,0.97} = 7.01.$

(vi)

Edinburgh 1819		Torrens		
182	(176.66)	475	(480.34)	657
103	(102.98)	280	(280.02)	383
71	(76.36)	213	(207.64)	284
356		968		1324

$X^2 = 0.74, \quad \chi^2_{2,\,0.95} = 5.99.$

(vii)

'Digression'		McCulloch		
51	(40.21)	530	(540.79)	581
22	(31.15)	428	(418.85)	450
14	(15.64)	212	(210.36)	226
87		1170		1257

$X^2 = 6.18, \quad \chi^2_{2,\,0.95} = 5.99.$

(viii)

'Digression'		Torrens		
51	(43.38)	475	(482.62)	526
22	(24.90)	280	(277.10)	302
14	(18.72)	213	(208.28)	227
87		968		1055

$X^2 = 3.13, \quad \chi^2_{2,\,0.95} = 5.99.$

TABLE 4.5 Collocations with 'be'

Texts analysed	X^2	d.f.	$\chi^2_{0.95}$	Decision	Maximum type I error (where applicable)	Contingency table	After row amalgamations X^2	d.f.	$\chi^2_{0.95}$	Maximum type error (where applicable)
Speech vs *Wealth* vs *Corn Trade*	3.20	6	12.59	Accept the hypothesis of Torrens' internal consistency	–	4.6(i)	1.33	2	5.99	–
Principles vs 'Machinery' vs *Taxation*	9.74	6	12.59	Accept the hypothesis of McCulloch's internal consistency	–	4.6(ii)	3.13	2	5.99	–
'Digression' vs Speech vs Paraphrase	5.62	6	12.59	Accept the hypothesis of the internal consistency of disputed article article 1819	–	4.6(iii)	0.76	2	5.99	–
Torrens vs McCulloch	25.33	3	7.81	Reject the hypothesis of consistency between Torrens and McCulloch	0.005	4.6(iv)	19.78	1	3.84	0.005
McCulloch vs *whole* of disputed article 1819	15.30	3	7.81	Reject the hypothesis of consistency between McCulloch and disputed article 1819	0.005	4.6(v)	3.25	1	3.07*	0.08
Torrens vs *whole* of disputed article 1819	3.49	3	7.81	Accept the hypothesis of consistency between Torrens and disputed article 1819	–	4.6(vi)	0.26	1	3.84	–
McCulloch vs 'Digression'	Not applicable due to very low						Not applicable due to very low			
Torrens vs 'Digression'	expected values in contingency tables						expected values in contingency tables			

* 3.07 is the $\chi^2_{1,\,0.92}$ value.

TABLE 4.6 Contingency tables – collocations with 'be'

(i) Torrens

Speech		*Wealth*		*Corn Trade*		
5	(3.37)	0	(1.21)	23	(23.42)	28
10	(11.54)	6	(4.15)	80	(80.31)	96
4	(3.97)	1	(1.43)	28	(27.61)	33
6	(6.13)	2	(2.21)	43	(42.66)	51
25		9		174		208

$X^2 = 3.20$, $\chi^2_{6,\,0.95} = 12.59$.

(ii) McCulloch

Principles		'Machinery'		*Taxation*		
2	(4.48)	10	(6.54)	5	(5.98)	17
74	(63.84)	91	(93.03)	77	(85.13)	242
15	(18.99)	25	(27.68)	32	(25.33)	72
14	(17.68)	27	(25.76)	26	(23.57)	67
105		153		140		398

$X^2 = 9.74$, $\chi^2_{6,\,0.95} = 12.59$.

(iii) *Edinburgh* 1819

'Digression'		Speech		Paraphrase		
0	(1.56)	2	(1.56)	8	(6.88)	10
5	(4.53)	6	(4.53)	18	(19.94)	29
2	(2.34)	2	(2.34)	11	(10.31)	15
3	(1.56)	0	(1.56)	7	(6.88)	10
10		10		44		64

$X^2 = 5.62$, $\chi^2_{6,\,0.95} = 12.59$.

(iv)

Torrens		McCulloch		
28	(15.45)	17	(29.55)	45
96	(116.01)	242	(221.99)	338
33	(36.04)	72	(68.96)	105
51	(40.50)	67	(77.50)	118
208		398		606

$X^2 = 25.33$, $\chi^2_{3,\,0.95} = 7.81$.

TABLE 4.6 (*contd.*)

(v)

Edinburgh 1819		McCulloch		
10	(3.74)	17	(23.26)	27
29	(37.54)	242	(233.46)	271
15	(12.05)	72	(74.95)	87
10	(10.67)	67	(66.33)	77
64		398		462

$X^2 = 15.30, \quad \chi^2_{3,\,0.95} = 7.81.$

(vi)

Edinburgh 1819		Torrens		
10	(8.94)	28	(29.06)	38
29	(29.41)	96	(95.59)	125
15	(11.29)	33	(36.71)	48
10	(14.35)	51	(46.65)	61
64		208		272

$X^2 = 3.49, \quad \chi^2_{3,\,0.95} = 7.81.$

used inconsistently has the effect of reducing the effective size of our samples, especially those deriving from the three subsections of the disputed 1819 *Edinburgh* article. We are left with only 10 relevant observations in that part of the article which reproduces Torrens' speech directly, and the same is true of the 'Digression'. In the speech itself, when used as a basis for comparison, we are left with only nine observations. The major consequence of this is that we are unable to use collocations with 'be' to test the authorship of the 'Digression' against the work of Torrens and McCulloch. For were we to attempt to do so we would have half our cells with expected frequencies of less than 5, which would invalidate the use of the χ^2 statistic. A secondary consequence of the inconsistency exhibited by Torrens, and the resultant pruning of usable collocations with 'be' is that, in our analysis of the internal consistency of the disputed article and of Torrens' own work, we have two-thirds and one-half, respectively, of the cells with expected values of less than 5. Nevertheless, we have decided to report the results using the data classified into four categories because although it is necessary to treat the first and third tests of consistency with caution, the direct tests of discrimination and of authorship of the whole of the disputed article are both valid and conclusive.

Before going on to summarise the results of these tests, it is perhaps worth saying that in earlier work, reported elsewhere, we did not encounter the same difficulties in securing consistency within the work of Torrens and we were thus more confident of our results from analysis of data arising from collocations with 'be'.[39] The difficulties have arisen on this occasion simply because we decided to use much enlarged samples of the work of McCulloch and Torrens; and, at least with Torrens, it turns out that the collocations which are successful in indicating uniformity within the known work of one author are sample-specific.

The results obtained from using collocations with 'be' in the present enlarged sample are presented in Table 4.5. From this it is clear that Torrens, McCulloch and the anonymous article are each internally consistent, as indicated by computed χ^2 values of 3.20, 9.74 and 5.62 respectively, each of which is well below the 95 per cent critical point of 12.59. The fourth entry in the table indicates that the data provide strong discrimination between Torrens and McCulloch; the computed χ^2 is 25.33 while the critical value is 7.81. Comparison between McCulloch's habits and those exhibited within the *Edinburgh* article indicates the presence of statistically significant differences, enabling us to reject the hypothesis that McCulloch wrote the article, with a type I error of less than 0.005, given a computed χ^2 value of 15.30. By contrast, the differences between Torrens' habits in the use of collocations with 'be' and those of the anonymous author are quite insignificant; the computed χ^2 is 3.49, well below the critical value of 7.81. These results reinforce the conclusion, obtained from the two previous sets of tests, that McCulloch was not the author of the *Edinburgh* article on Owen, while it seems entirely plausible that Torrens wrote the piece.

However, as indicated above, we were less happy about tests on collocations with 'be' than about those on first word usage or on collocations with 'the'. In order to approach this problem in another way, we amalgamated rows 1 and 4 and rows 2 and 3 to yield contingency tables with only two rows. This procedure still does not permit us to test the 'Digression' on its own; but it greatly reduces the importance of the incidence of low expected values. With only two rows in the contingency tables the only point at which we encounter the problem of low expected values is in the test for internal consistency in the disputed article itself, where one third of the cells have expected values of less than 5.

The results of the tests with contingency tables of only two rows are summarised in Table 4.5. From this it is clear that our conclusions are unaffected. The loss of information resulting from amalgamating rows is reflected in the increased possibility of type I error in rejecting McCulloch as the author; but the conclusion is still clear enough.

III. CONCLUSION

Taken together, our tests produce results which point in only one direction. The conclusion that Torrens was the author of the 1819 *Edinburgh Review* article on Robert Owen seems inevitable; and it seems equally clear that he wrote the entire article rather than contributing material which was then processed by another hand. In our judgement, our statistical results accord entirely with the balance of the historical evidence which was summarised in the first part of this chapter. But, as indicated there, historical evidence is frequently inconclusive; and we feel that it is of considerable value to add to it the results of statistical tests, as we have done in this case.

5 Samuel Bailey and Two Anonymous Pamphlets of 1821

I. HISTORICAL BACKGROUND

In 1821 there appeared two pamphlets which have been a matter of intermittent speculation ever since. They were *Observations on Certain Verbal Disputes in Political Economy, particularly relating to Value, and to Demand and Supply* (London: R. Hunter, 1821) and *An Inquiry into Those Principles Respecting the Nature of Demand and the Necessity of Consumption, lately advocated by Mr. Malthus, from which it is concluded that Taxation and the Maintenance of Unproductive Consumers can be Conducive to the Progress of Wealth* (London: R. Hunter, 1821). The two pamphlets came quickly to the notice of Ricardo, whose attention was drawn to them by Tooke; and Ricardo attempted some reply to the first pamphlet in a letter to Trower written a month after receiving them.[1]

A number of writers familiar with the Classical literature have noticed similarities between the contents of one or both of the pamphlets and the work of Samuel Bailey, and indeed both of them have been included in a modern reprint of Bailey's work.[2] Marx noted similarities between Bailey's *Critical Dissertation*[3] and the *Observations*; and although he did not like the latter pamphlet he conceded that it was 'not without a certain acuteness'.[4] However, Marx does not seem to have believed that Bailey was the author of the *Observations*; rather, he noted the similarity[5] and ultimately accused Bailey of plagiarism.[6] The *Inquiry* he described as 'A Ricardian work. Good against Malthus. Demonstrates the infinite narrow-mindedness to which the perspicacity of these fellows is reduced as they examine not landed property but capital. Nevertheless, it is one of the best polemical works of the decade.[7] Schumpeter mentioned the *Observations* in connection with Bailey,[8] his attention having perhaps been drawn to the work by Seligman;[9] but neither Schumpeter nor Seligman offered any guess as to the authorship.

Rauner, in his standard study of Bailey,[10] reported that Viner had privately advanced the hypothesis that Bailey was the author of the *Observations*; but Rauner rejected this on stylistic grounds – very reasonably in our view.

One established historian of economic thought, Professor T. Sowell, has thrown academic caution to the winds and advanced the view that both pamphlets were by Bailey.[11] In his article, Sowell found a remarkable range of similarities between the two pamphlets and other works known to be by Bailey. He presented a persuasive *a priori* case based upon similarities in discussion of (i) the role of words, (ii) value theory, (iii) methodology, (iv) the treatment of other economists and of non-economists, and (v) style. Moreover, he concluded that Bailey *must* have known of the *Observations* when he wrote his *Critical Dissertation* because the former pamphlet is cited by De Quincey in a work to which Bailey replied in his *Dissertation*. From this, Sowell concluded that Bailey was either plagiarising – which he considered unlikely – or rewriting his earlier pamphlet.

Unfortunately, the clinching evidence – the citation by De Quincey – turns out to be faulty. For De Quincey did not actually cite the *Observations*. Sowell appears to have been relying upon a reference in Rauner,[12] in which Rauner said that De Quincey had 'expressly referred' to the *Observations* in his *Dialogues of Three Templars*. But in fact all that De Quincey said was:

> Thus, for example, Mr. Ricardo sternly insists on the *true* sense of the word value, and (what is still more unusual to most men) insists on using it but in *one* sense: and hence arise consequences which naturally appear at once obscure and paradoxical to M. Say, to Mr. Malthus, to the author of an Essay on Value, and to all other lax thinkers, who easily bend their understandings to the infirmity of the popular usage.

So imprecise was De Quincey's recollection of the 'Essay on Value' that the only further illumination available is provided by a footnote in which he says: 'I forget the exact title; but it was printed for Hunter, St. Paul's Churchyard'.[13] Since Hunter printed a great many pamphlets – a point to which we shall return below – this was hardly helpful. So the crucial evidence dissolves upon inspection. Sowell was, however, satisfied of Bailey's authorship – indeed it should, in all fairness, be said that he had presented an excellent *a priori* case – and in his subsequent book, *Say's Law*,[14] he based some of the material on the assumption that both pamphlets were by Bailey.[15]

The circumstantial (as distinct from internal) evidence for Bailey's authorship was neither strongly positive nor strongly negative. Both pamphlets were published anonymously by the same bookseller, Hunter; and K. Dennis has pointed out to us, in correspondence, that Hunter was the publisher for all of Bailey's anonymous pamphlets up to 1835. But Hunter had a very long list, and it seems perfectly possible that other economic authors amongst those that he published could have been responsible.

The authoritative list of Bailey's publications, given by his friend Alexander Ireland,[16] does not contain either pamphlet; and this is also true of the *Dictionary of National Biography*, which appears to have had access to unpublished information. Halkett and Laing[17] make no mention of either pamphlet, although their work contains more than a dozen Bailey entries.

The Kress Library has copies of both pamphlets. The copy of the *Observations* is marked 'From the Author' and that of the *Inquiry* is marked 'The Editor of Blackwoods Mag. From the Author'. But the handwritings on the two pamphlets do not appear to be the same and *neither* of the handwritings tallies with Bailey's handwriting, of which there are extensive examples available in his papers. The same is true of the handwriting in copies of the pamphlets which are in the London Library, although this does tally with the handwritings in the Kress copies.[18] However, this is not conclusive negative evidence for the handwriting may well be that of a clerk – McCulloch, for instance, habitually had his works inscribed by his confidential clerk and son-in-law H. G. Reid. There are faint pencil marks on the Kress copy of the *Inquiry*; and we are indebted to Dr K. Carpenter and Ms Laura Goldberg of the Kress Library for their attempts to decipher these. The pencil marks, which are not at all clear on a Xerox copy, *may* say 'By Bailey of Sheffield'.

We have not traced a copy in any other library containing any more information which would point in the direction of an author, although extensive enquiries have been made both in the United Kingdom and in North America.[19] Bailey himself owned copies of both pamphlets, and these are still extant, but there is no indication of authorship in them.[20]

The matter of the circumstantial evidence was exhaustively investigated by Kenneth Dennis. Indeed, he pursued the historical evidence to the point where statistical analysis remains virtually the only unexplored avenue. Like Sowell, he had been impressed by similarities of phrase between the two pamphlets and Bailey's *Dissertation*. However, Mr Dennis also found a critical denial of authorship of the *Observations* on the part of Bailey. This part of his investigation has been published;[21] but, since the relevant material relates closely to Marx's accusation of plagiarism, we shall defer consideration of it for the moment. It was, indeed, this author who drew the attention of other historians of economic thought to the presence of Bailey's manuscript notebooks in Edinburgh, where they had rested, apparently unnoticed by economists, since the 1870s, despite efforts to trace Bailey's papers.[22]

(a) Content of the *Observations*

The style of this pamphlet is different from, and far less polished than, that of Samuel Bailey. Bailey had a beautiful and brillant style, an excellent mind, and a wide philosophical education. This is very much apparent from his papers in Edinburgh. But the English of the *Observations* is much poorer than that of Bailey, and at times is really clumsy. Its author's understanding of a number of issues is not as clear as that of Bailey. In particular, he does not appear to appreciate the import of Ricardo's chapter on Value and Riches – which Bailey clearly did understand. Much of the pamphlet is directed against Say rather than Ricardo, although the latter was Bailey's principal target, and the author is very much less fair to Say than Bailey was to Ricardo. Indeed, much of the criticism is arguably inaccurate, and shows a level of understanding of the literature much lower than that of Bailey.

The pamphlet also contains material about mathematics which was not really a preoccupation of Bailey. The author seems to have considerable faith in the power of mathematics: 'In order to make any science approach to the accuracy of mathematical conclusion, one would think that it might be desirable to imitate, as far as it *is* possible, the process adopted in mathematical reasoning.'[23] However, he later expresses the view that; 'The French philosophers (if I may venture to say so of our superiors in mathematical science) seem to make their mathematics impede rather than assist them in the prosecution of those speculations which are not mathematical. I cannot consider this a *necessary* consequence of mathematical habits, though we have the opinion of Gibbon that it is.'[24]

The starting point of the pamphlet is that difficulties of 'moral sciences' are often connected with words, and that this weakens the influence of economics by rendering it uncertain. However, in the view of the author, much of the subject matter turns out to be nothing more than a dispute about words, rather than a subject of importance. The confusion over words is, in his view, compounded by the propensity of economic writers to coin new terms and new definitions.

He rejects the concept of absolute value, and that of an invariable measure is seen as an impossibility because if one commodity has risen in terms of another then the latter cannot bc invariable but must *ipso facto* have fallen. It is this argument, in particular, which has led to parallels with Bailey.

It is clear, however, that Bailey did not write the pamphlet. His denial, in his notebooks, is completely explicit. In the first of six notebooks of references, Bailey has notes on the *Observations*;[25] and beside these notes, in different ink, using a different pen, and in a much later hand, there is the following note: 'NB This Book exhibits some striking coincidences with my Treatise on Value – so striking that I might possibly incur the charge of plagiarism if any one compare the two works. The truth is however that I did not see this pamphlet till my own book was published. S. B.'

It seems clear that Bailey did not write the *Observations*. Indeed, in a number of comments in his papers[26] Bailey shows that he set great store by orderly composition and logical development and style; and his own 1825 *Critical Dissertation* is outstanding in this respect. Rauner was thus correct to dismiss the *Observations* as Bailey's. The only real question is whether Bailey had seen the pamphlet and forgotten it.

It seems clear that the denial of previous knowledge was written at a different time from the notes on the pamphlet. Closer examination of other items noted in the same notebook, both before and after the entry relating to the *Observations*, suggests, at first sight, some suspicion. The notes immediately following those on the *Observations* are on an article in the *Edinburgh Review* of October 1823.[27] Moreover, as Kenneth Dennis has pointed out, there are notes on Torrens' *Essay on the Production of Wealth* a little later in the same notebook,[28] which deal with the subject of value. Yet we know that the Torrens work was published in 1821. All this does suggest, at first sight, that Bailey read the *Observations* about 1823 *before* writing his *Critical Dissertation*.

However, a closer look at the dates involved exonerates Bailey. For earlier in the same notebook we find notes on the second edition of Sydney Smith's *A Letter to the Electors on the Catholic Question*;[29] and this appears to have been published in York in 1826. Thus, the only way in which Bailey could be implicated would be if he had made a habit of leaving blank pages in the notebook and filling them in at a later date so that the Sydney Smith work could have been noted at a later date than the *Observations*. But there is no real evidence of such a practice in the notebook.[30] Moreover, it does seem to have been the case that Bailey did not make notes on periodical literature immediately that it appeared; and thus the position of the notes on an 1823 periodical is not significant. For although there are notes on *Blackwoods Magazine* for 1824 and on the *Quarterly Review* for the same year, later in the notebook, there are notes on a book by Chalmers at an earlier point in the notebook[31] – and the third volume of this book, *The Christian and Civic Economy of Large Towns*, did not appear until 1826. Yet Bailey's notes show that he had read volume three. There does not then really seem to be any basis for Marx's accusation of plagiarism.

It seems quite clear that Bailey was not only not the author of the *Observations*, but also that he did not read the work for some time after it was published. A return to the internal evidence of the pamphlet to search for other clues as to a possible author suggests itself. The author displayed a number of characteristics which, though not unique, were unusual in combination. For one thing, his apparent familiarity with mathematical literature is fairly unusual in the economic literature of the period. For another, the pamphlet, although written with great fluency, displays some superficiality. More seriously, it shows marked unfairness at times, particularly to J. B. Say. The author was obviously a highly educated man with a knowledge of mathematics, philosophy and Greek, but he was also a man who had little patience with those he considered foolish. All this was highly general. However, at one point in the article, there is a parenthetical – almost throw-away – reference to an article in the *Edinburgh Review* of 1804.[32] This article, 'Lord Lauderdale on Public Wealth',[33] is known to be the work of Henry Brougham.[34] At first sight, this was not a very helpful discovery. Brougham is famous as a distinguished lawyer and politician. However, further investigation revealed that Brougham was in fact trained in mathematics and philosophy. According to *DNB* 'He delighted in the study of mathematics and physics, and at the age of eighteen sent a paper to the Royal Society on . . . Light, which was read and printed in the Society's "Transactions" '. He also, at Edinburgh, followed a four year course 'of humanity and philosophy' and it was not until after that that he began to read law. The comments in *DNB* on his reviewing are particularly interesting: 'His reviews were slashing, but his work was often superficial and his criticisms were sometimes scandalously unjust.' But of his ability there is no doubt. As *DNB* puts it: 'His versatility and his power of despatch were extraordinary.'[35]

Not only do Brougham's educational background and his propensities as a critic qualify him to be the author of the *Observations*, but episodes in his public life at the time the pamphlet was published might well have suggested to him that it would be wise to make the pamphlet anonymous – his involvement in the Queen Caroline divorce case had made him a number of powerful enemies.

Unfortunately, the mass of the Brougham papers at University College London has not yet been catalogued; it is possible that conclusive historical evidence lies therein. We have, however, compared the handwriting on the Kress Library copies with a sample of Brougham's handwriting;[36] and it is clear that the hands are different. But, as indicated above, this is not a serious negative point because of the role of clerks in the dispatch of complimentary copies. It certainly seemed worthwhile testing the style of the 1804 *Edinburgh* article against that of the *Observations* to see if there were similarities. The results of our investigations are reported in part II of this chapter.

(b) The *Inquiry*

The *Inquiry* is far better written than the *Observations*, although it does not seem to be quite as good as other work of Bailey, either with respect to analysis or style. There are also some fragments of internal evidence which would suggest another of our authors – William Huskisson.[37] But the extent of the author's acquaintance with the work of Ricardo would appear to rule out Huskisson, as should be clear from the discussion in Chapter 8. There is also some internal evidence, first noted by Kenneth Dennis, which would point in the direction of Bailey. There is a reference to the cutlery trade[38] and another[39] to the value of rents in the United States, in a manner which suggests first-hand knowledge. According to *DNB*, Bailey was sent to the United States 'in order to establish business connections with that country'.[40] It is also possible to make out a convincing *a priori* case that Henry Brougham may have been responsible for this pamphlet.[41]

The main concern of the pamphlet is with the possibility of effective demand failure which had been raised by Malthus, and with the latter author's emphasis upon the need for unproductive consumption. While the author of the *Inquiry* accepts the basic circularity of the economic system, and also accepts the Ricardian view that Smith was in error in believing that profits were lowered by the competition of accumulated capital, he does not accept that output can always be marketed profitably. Nevertheless, he believes that demanding labour by laying out capital means proportionately more demand for 'necessaries', and proportionately less demand for 'superfluities'. Producers may well be happy to save, even with the prospect of earning a lower rate of profit than before; if they find *ex post* that profits are even lower than expected, this may still not be a sufficient inducement to them to withdraw capital. If, however, they are not satisfied with their rate of profit they will not invest anyway. Thus, if people continue to accumulate they must find the level of profits a sufficient incentive, even if that level is low. If the rich agree to postpone consumption by saving, they are permitting the poor to consume more. So long as the rich do not then produce more of those items, the consumption of which they are reducing, there will be no demand problem; and if they do produce more of these goods, this will be sectional, and not general, over-production. Malthus, in the view of the author of the *Inquiry*, has been misled by the current slump. Transitional distress is indeed important; and uncertainty and panic interfere with the free flow of capital. The ending of the Napoleonic Wars had produced, in the author's view, sudden changes in the channels of trade with ill-advised speculation added to this. These factors meant that, in the view of the writer of the *Inquiry*, there was no need for Malthus' theory to explain the prevailing economic distress. Although the barter statement of Say's Law was invalid in a monetary economy, the basic circularity of the economic system meant that it had a long-run tendency towards equilibrium. Views such as these constitute an interesting part of the literature in the debate concerning underconsumption. It is certainly of interest to attempt to establish the identity of the author of the *Inquiry*. There is little direct evidence, either positive or negative, as already indicated, concerning Bailey and this pamphlet; there is certainly no explicit denial of authorship as there was of the authorship of the *Observations*. In the circumstances, and given the widespread belief that Bailey was the author of this work, it seemed reasonable to test the literary habits of its author against those of Bailey. The results of our tests are given in part II of the chapter.

For our tests we used pp. 2–32 of the *Observations*, amounting to rather over 9,000 words, and pp. 1–37 of the *Inquiry*, which is of very much the same length. For comparison we used pp. 1–70 of Bailey's *Critical Dissertation* of 1825, amounting to about 13,500 words, and pp. 1–61 of his *Letter to a Political Economist* of 1826,[42] amounting to about 10,500 words. We also used a well-known critical work on value theory from the same period, *An Examination of the Doctrines of Value* by C. F. Cotterill dating from 1831,[43] as this seemed a good comparative text. The extract we used was pp. 1–54, amounting to about 12,000 words. Finally, to test the possibility that the author of the *Observations* was Henry Brougham, we used the *Edinburgh Review* article of 1804 already referred to. This is about 15,000 words in length.

II. STATISTICAL ANALYSIS

We have, for the purposes of our tests, data derived from three named authors, Bailey, Cotterill, and Brougham, as well as two pamphlets which may well be by different hands. Clearly, we must attempt to discover those habits which are observed consistently within the work of one author and which are sufficiently distinctive to enable his work to be distinguished from that of another author; and we have then to discover whether the same habits indicate any distinction between the literary habits of the authors of the two pamphlets in question. We have extracts from two separate works by Bailey but, in the case of Cotterill and Brougham, we have divided the large sample into two parts since each comes from only one work. Since our data is derived from collocations and first word usage, our division of the samples into two parts must be such as to preserve the literary form; we could not, for example, randomly sample from the individual words, and it would be unwise, as already noted, randomly to sample individual sentences. However, the procedure of splitting up each of the two texts into roughly equal halves seems perfectly satisfactory and it has proved to be most effective, as the results below indicate.

(a) First word usage

It is interesting to report that our analysis of habits of first word usage, which has proved successful in discriminating between authors elsewhere, did not prove successful in dealing with the problem under review here. It was easy enough to obtain internal consistency within the work of each author; but we were not able to obtain discrimination between Bailey and Cotterill, between Bailey and Brougham, or between Cotterill and Brougham, with respect to their habits in the choice of first word. In turn, it proved impossible to distinguish the texts produced by each of our three authors from the two anonymous pamphlets. The only possible conclusion at this stage of the analysis was that first word usage did not indicate that it was impossible for any of our three authors to have produced either of the pamphlets.

(b) Collocations with 'the'

It is gratifying to be able to report that an examination of habits in the use of 'the' proved very much more satisfactory. The results are summarised in Table 5.1, and the details are presented in Tables 5.2(i) to 5.2(xv).

TABLE 5.1 Collocations with 'the'

Texts analysed	X^2	d.f.	$\chi^2_{0.95}$	*Decision*	*Maximum type I error (where applicable)*	*Contingency table*
Critical Dissertation vs *Letter to a Political Economist*	2.77	5	11.07	Accept the internal consistency of Bailey	–	5.2(i)
Doctrines of value internally	6.71	5	11.07	Accept the internal consistency of Cotterill	–	5.2(ii)
Edinburgh 1804 internally	8.43	5	11.07	Accept the internal consistency of Brougham	–	5.2(iii)
Observations internally	2.65	5	11.07	Accept the internal consistency of *Observations*	–	5.2(iv)
Inquiry internally	1.76	5	11.07	Accept the internal consistency of *Inquiry*	–	5.2(v)
Bailey vs Cotterill	33.46	5	11.07	Reject the hypothesis of consistency between Bailey and Cotterill	0.005	5.2(vi)
Bailey vs Brougham	7.73	5	7.29*	Reject the hypothesis of consistency between Bailey and Brougham	0.20	5.2(vii)
Cotterill vs Brougham	31.60	5	11.07	Reject the hypothesis of consistency between Cotterill and Brougham	0.005	5.2(viii)
Inquiry vs *Observations*	8.54	5	8.10**	Reject the hypothesis of consistency between *Observations* and *Inquiry*	0.15	5.2(ix)
Cotterill vs *Observations*	11.35	5	11.07	Reject the hypothesis of consistency between Cotterill and *Observations*	0.05	5.2(x)

Brougham vs *Observations*	4.81	5	11.07	Accept the hypothesis of consistency between Brougham and *Observations*	–	5.2(xi)
Bailey vs *Observations*	11.98	5	11.07	Reject the hypothesis of consistency between Bailey and *Observations*	0.05	5.2(xii)
Cotterill vs *Inquiry*	16.49	5	11.07	Reject the hypothesis of consistency between Cotterill and *Inquiry*	0.01	5.2(xiii)
Brougham vs *Inquiry*	8.21	5	8.10**	Reject the hypothesis of consistency between Brougham and *Inquiry*	0.15	5.2(xiv)
Bailey vs *Inquiry*	4.24	5	11.07	Accept the hypothesis of consistency between Bailey and *Inquiry*	–	5.2(xv)

* 7.29 is the $\chi^2_{5,0.80}$ value.

** 8.10 is the $\chi^2_{5,0.85}$ value.

TABLE 5.2 Contingency tables – collocations with 'the'

(i) Bailey

Critical Dissertation		*Letter*		
42	(36.37)	27	(32.62)	69
137	(142.86)	134	(128.14)	271
34	(33.21)	29	(29.79)	63
57	(55.88)	49	(50.12)	106
52	(49.55)	42	(44.45)	94
454	(458.11)	415	(410.89)	869
776		696		1472

$X^2 = 2.77$, $\chi^2_{5,\,0.95} = 11.07$.

(ii) Cotterill, *Doctrines of Value*

pp. 1–27		pp. 27–54		
17	(16.22)	17	(17.78)	34
81	(70.62)	67	(77.38)	148
35	(37.70)	44	(41.30)	79
19	(22.43)	28	(24.57)	47
13	(17.66)	24	(19.34)	37
201	(201.37)	221	(220.63)	422
366		401		767

$X^2 = 6.71$, $\chi^2_{5,\,0.95} = 11.07$.

(iii) Brougham 1804

pp. 343–60		pp. 360–77		
29	(23.44)	18	(23.56)	47
91	(89.77)	89	(90.23)	180
26	(29.42)	33	(29.58)	59
42	(38.40)	35	(38.60)	77
36	(45.88)	56	(46.12)	92
358	(355.08)	354	(356.92)	712
582		585		1167

$X^2 = 8.43$, $\chi^2_{5,\,0.95} = 11.07$.

TABLE 5.2 (*contd.*)

(iv) *Observations*

pp. 2–16		pp. 16–32		
6	(8.22)	9	(6.78)	15
40	(37.81)	29	(31.19)	69
18	(19.18)	17	(15.82)	35
17	(18.63)	17	(15.37)	34
16	(17.54)	16	(14.46)	32
160	(155.62)	124	(128.38)	284
257		212		469

$X^2 = 2.65, \quad \chi^2_{5,\,0.95} = 11.07.$

(v) *Inquiry*

pp. 1–18		pp. 18–37		
16	(15.33)	13	(13.67)	29
59	(57.10)	49	(50.90)	108
16	(16.39)	15	(14.61)	31
23	(25.91)	26	(23.09)	49
20	(22.73)	23	(20.27)	43
170	(166.54)	145	(148.46)	315
304		271		575

$X^2 = 1.76, \quad \chi^2_{5,\,0.95} = 11.07.$

(vi)

Bailey		Cotterill		
69	(67.72)	34	(35.28)	103
271	(275.47)	148	(143.53)	419
63	(93.36)	79	(48.64)	142
106	(100.59)	47	(52.41)	153
94	(86.12)	37	(44.88)	131
869	(848.75)	422	(442.25)	1291
1472		767		2239

$X^2 = 33.46, \quad \chi^2_{5,\,0.995} = 16.75.$

TABLE 5.2 (*contd.*)

(vii)

Bailey		Brougham		
69	(64.70)	47	(51.30)	116
271	(251.56)	180	(199.44)	451
63	(68.05)	59	(53.95)	122
106	(102.08)	77	(80.92)	183
94	(103.75)	92	(82.25)	186
869	(881.86)	712	(699.14)	1581
1472		1167		2639

$X^2 = 7.73, \quad \chi^2_{5, 0.80} = 7.29.$

(viii)

Cotterill		Brougham		
34	(32.12)	47	(48.88)	81
148	(130.08)	180	(197.92)	328
79	(54.73)	59	(83.27)	138
47	(49.18)	77	(74.82)	124
37	(51.16)	92	(77.84)	129
422	(449.73)	712	(684.27)	1134
767		1167		1934

$X^2 = 31.60, \quad \chi^2_{5, 0.995} = 16.75.$

(ix)

Observations		*Inquiry*		
15	(19.77)	29	(24.23)	44
69	(79.51)	108	(97.49)	177
35	(29.65)	31	(36.35)	66
34	(37.29)	49	(45.71)	83
32	(33.69)	43	(41.31)	75
284	(269.09)	315	(329.91)	599
469		575		1044

$X^2 = 8.54, \quad \chi^2_{5, 0.85} = 8.10.$

TABLE 5.2 (*contd.*)

(x)

Observations		Cotterill		
15	(18.59)	34	(30.41)	49
69	(82.34)	148	(134.66)	217
35	(43.26)	79	(70.74)	114
34	(30.74)	47	(50.26)	81
32	(26.18)	37	(42.82)	69
284	(267.89)	422	(438.11)	706
469		767		1236

$X^2 = 11.35, \quad \chi^2_{5,\,0.95} = 11.07.$

(xi)

Observations		Brougham		
15	(17.77)	47	(44.23)	62
69	(71.38)	180	(177.62)	249
35	(26.95)	59	(67.05)	94
34	(31.82)	77	(79.18)	111
32	(35.55)	92	(88.45)	124
284	(285.53)	712	(710.47)	996
469		1167		1636

$X^2 = 4.81, \quad \chi^2_{5,\,0.95} = 11.07.$

(xii)

Observations		Bailey		
15	(20.30)	69	(63.70)	84
69	(82.15)	271	(257.85)	340
35	(23.68)	63	(74.32)	98
34	(33.83)	106	(106.17)	140
32	(30.45)	94	(95.55)	126
284	(278.60)	869	(874.40)	1153
469		1472		1941

$X^2 = 11.98, \quad \chi^2_{5,\,0.95} = 11.07.$

TABLE 5.2 (*contd.*)

(xiii)

Inquiry		Cotterill		
29	(26.99)	34	(36.01)	63
108	(109.69)	148	(146.31)	256
31	(47.13)	79	(62.87)	110
49	(41.13)	47	(54.87)	96
43	(34.28)	37	(45.72)	80
315	(315.78)	422	(421.22)	737
575		767		1342

$X^2 = 16.49, \quad \chi^2_{5,\,0.995} = 15.09.$

(xiv)

Inquiry		Brougham		
29	(25.09)	47	(50.91)	76
108	(95.06)	180	(192.94)	288
31	(29.71)	59	(60.29)	90
49	(41.59)	77	(84.41)	126
43	(44.56)	92	(90.44)	135
315	(338.99)	712	(688.01)	1027
575		1167		1742

$X^2 = 8.21, \quad \chi^2_{5,\,0.85} = 8.10.$

(xv)

Inquiry		Bailey		
29	(27.53)	69	(70.47)	98
108	(106.46)	271	(272.54)	379
31	(26.40)	63	(67.60)	94
49	(43.54)	106	(111.46)	155
43	(38.48)	94	(98.52)	137
315	(332.58)	869	(851.42)	1184
575		1472		2047

$X^2 = 4.24, \quad \chi^2_{5,\,0.95} = 11.07.$

We used the following collocations with 'the': 'at' or 'by'; 'in' or 'to' or 'as'; 'and' or 'be' or 'into' or 'is'; 'if' or 'that' or 'from'; 'which' or 'on' or 'but' or 'with'; and all other collocations with 'the'. We thus have six rows in our contingency tables. Using these six rows we are able to show that Bailey, Cotterill and Brougham, are all consistent in their use of collocations with 'the' and the same is true of each of the anonymous pamphlets taken separately. Because each contingency table has six rows, we are working with 5 degrees of freedom. The 95 per cent point from the χ^2_5 distribution is 11.07, and our computed χ^2 values in the consistency tests range from 1.76 (for the *Inquiry*) to 8.43 (for Brougham's *Edinburgh Review* article). In each of the five cases, then, the authors used collocations with 'the' consistently.

When we turn to the question of discrimination between authors we find that it proves possible to separate the work of Cotterill from that of both Bailey and Brougham very easily, although the differences in literary habits between Bailey and Brougham are less marked. In the first two cases, we have computed χ^2 values in excess of 30, but in the third case it is only 7.73. This can, however, be compared with the 80 per cent point of 7.29 under the null hypothesis that Bailey and Brougham are indistinguishable in respect to their habits in the employment of 'the'; this observed value falls in a range in which one would only expect the computed value to lie with a probability of less than 0.2. The value could be interpreted either as an atypical result or by rejection of the null hypothesis on the grounds that interpretation of the result as atypical is implausible. We chose the latter course and conclude that there is some discrimination, while recognising that the probability of our being wrong is rather higher than elsewhere. On the same reasoning we reject the hypothesis that the *Observations* and the *Inquiry* proceed from the same hand, and this time our maximum probability of error, at 0.15, is rather smaller. This result is, however, consistent with the view that it is possible that Bailey wrote the *Inquiry*; while the evidence in part II of this chapter shows that he quite clearly denied having written the *Observations*.

It is certainly quite clear from our tests on data derived from uses of 'the' that Cotterill was not the author of the *Observations*; the computed χ^2 is 11.35, so that there is only a 5 per cent chance of our being in error here. But, very interestingly, the rejection of the possibility that Bailey wrote the *Observations* is even stronger; the computed χ^2 figure is 11.98. It is, therefore, rather exciting to find that while our tests on 'the' indicate clearly that neither Bailey nor Cotterill was involved in production of the *Observations*, Brougham's literary habits in the use of 'the' are insignificantly different, from a statistical point of view, from those exhibited by the author of the *Observations*. The computed χ^2 is only 4.81. Consequently, it seems entirely reasonable to argue that the hypothesis that Brougham was the author of this pamphlet seems distinctly persuasive.

It is abundantly clear that Cotterill was not the author of the other pamphlet either. The computed χ^2 value in comparing his work with that of the *Inquiry* is 16.49. It is also reasonable to conclude that Brougham, whose work was indistinguishable from the first pamphlet, was not the author of the second one. The probability of our being in error in the rejection of Cotterill's authorship is no larger than 0.01; the discrimination between the text of the *Inquiry* and the work of Brougham is rather less strong and we have a type I error of 0.15. However, this is an acceptable type I error, particularly as we find that in comparing Bailey's literary habits with the author of the *Inquiry*, insofar as the use of 'the' is concerned, we obtain a computed χ^2 of only 4.24. It does rather look as if Bailey may well have written the *Inquiry*.

In summary, then, our tests on collocations with 'the' indicate that Brougham may well have been the author of the *Observations*, particularly when this statistical result is taken in conjunction with the evidence presented in the first part of this chapter; and the statistical evidence would also suggest that the suspicions of Sowell, and others, that Bailey was the author of the *Inquiry*, are eminently reasonable on stylistic grounds.

(c) Collocations with 'be'

The conclusions we have obtained from our analysis of data derived from collocations with 'the' are strengthened when we examine data derived from habits in the use of 'be'. We used the following amalgamations: 'will' or 'can' or 'must' or 'shall'; 'would' or 'could' or 'may' or 'might' or 'should'; 'to'; 'noun'. From these amalgamations we obtained the results presented in summary form in Table 5.3 which derives from the contingency tables, with their four rows, 5.4(i) to 5.4(xv).

We found that each of our three known authors, and the two anonymous pamphlets, exhibited consistency in the use of 'be'. Each contingency table has 3 degrees of freedom, and the 95 per cent critical value with 3 degrees of freedom is 7.81. In testing the work of our authors for internal consistency we obtained computed χ^2 figures of 2.26 for Bailey, 3.72 for Cotterill, 4.60 for Brougham, 5.58 for the author of the

TABLE 5.3 Collocations with 'be'

Texts analysed	X^2	d.f.	$\chi^2_{0.95}$	*Decision*	*Maximum type I error (where applicable)*	*Contingency table*
Critical Dissertation vs *Letter to a Political Economist*	2.26	3	7.81	Accept the internal consistency of Bailey	–	5.4(i)
Doctrines of value internally	3.72	3	7.81	Accept the internal consistency of Cotterill	–	5.4(ii)
Edinburgh 1804 internally	4.60	3	7.81	Accept the internal consistency of Brougham	–	5.4(iii)
Observations internally	5.58	3	7.81	Accept the internal consistency of *Observations*	–	5.4(iv)
Inquiry internally	3.58	3	7.81	Accept the internal consistency of *Inquiry*	–	5.4(v)
Bailey vs Cotterill	13.65	3	7.81	Reject the hypothesis of consistency between Bailey and Cotterill	0.005	5.4(vi)
Bailey vs Brougham	9.77	3	7.81	Reject the hypothesis of consistency between Bailey and Brougham	0.025	5.4(vii)
Cotterill vs Brougham	10.47	3	7.81	Reject the hypothesis of consistency between Cotterill and Brougham	0.025	5.4(viii)
Inquiry vs *Observations*	13.43	3	7.81	Reject the hypothesis of consistency between *Inquiry* and *Observations*	0.005	5.4(ix)

TABLE 5.3 (*contd.*)

Texts analysed	X^2	d.f.	$\chi^2_{0.95}$	*Decision*	*Maximum type I error (where applicable)*	*Contingency table*
Cotterill vs *Observations*	15.71	3	7.81	Reject the hypothesis of consistency between Cotterill and *Observations*	0.005	5.4(x)
Brougham vs *Observations*	6.94	3	7.81	Accept the hypothesis of consistency between Brougham and *Observations*	–	5.4(xi)
Bailey vs *Observations*	16.30	3	7.81	Reject the hypothesis of consistency between Bailey and *Observations*	0.005	5.4(xii)
Cotterill vs *Inquiry*	9.11	3	7.81	Reject the hypothesis of consistency between Cotterill and *Inquiry*	0.03	5.4(xiii)
Brougham vs *Inquiry*	13.37	3	7.81	Reject the hypothesis of consistency between Brougham and *Inquiry*	0.005	5.4(xiv)
Bailey vs *Inquiry*	2.12	3	7.81	Accept the hypothesis of consistency between Bailey and *Inquiry*	–	5.4(xv)

TABLE 5.4 Contingency tables – collocations with 'be'

(i) Bailey

Critical Dissertation		*Letter*		
50	(48.78)	29	(30.22)	79
66	(67.31)	43	(41.69)	109
28	(30.26)	21	(18.74)	49
11	(8.65)	3	(5.35)	14
155		96		251

$X^2 = 2.26, \quad \chi^2_{3,\,0.95} = 7.81.$

(ii) Cotterill, *Doctrines of Value*

pp. 1–27		pp. 27–54		
20	(19.09)	22	(22.91)	42
27	(24.55)	27	(29.45)	54
16	(15.00)	17	(18.00)	33
7	(11.36)	18	(13.64)	25
70		84		154

$X^2 = 3.72, \quad \chi^2_{3,\,0.95} = 7.81.$

(iii) Brougham 1804

pp. 343–60		pp. 360–77		
22	(26.55)	26	(21.45)	48
22	(22.68)	19	(18.32)	41
27	(23.79)	16	(19.21)	43
7	(4.98)	2	(4.02)	9
78		63		141

$X^2 = 4.60, \quad \chi^2_{3,\,0.95} = 7.81.$

(iv) *Observations*

pp. 2–16		pp. 16–32		
8	(10.49)	16	(13.51)	24
15	(18.79)	28	(24.21)	43
26	(20.10)	20	(25.90)	46
3	(2.62)	3	(3.38)	6
52		67		119

$X^2 = 5.58, \quad \chi^2_{3,\,0.95} = 7.81.$

TABLE 5.4 (*contd.*)

(v) *Inquiry*

pp. 1–18		pp. 18–37		
12	(16.12)	21	(16.88)	33
32	(31.26)	32	(32.74)	64
14	(11.23)	9	(11.77)	23
5	(4.40)	4	(4.60)	9
63		66		129

$X^2 = 3.58, \quad \chi^2_{3, 0.95} = 7.81.$

(vi)

Bailey		Cotterill		
79	(74.99)	42	(46.01)	121
109	(101.02)	54	(61.98)	163
49	(50.82)	33	(31.18)	82
14	(24.17)	25	(14.83)	39
251		154		405

$X^2 = 13.65, \quad \chi^2_{3, 0.995} = 12.84.$

(vii)

Bailey		Brougham		
79	(81.32)	48	(45.68)	127
109	(96.05)	41	(53.95)	150
49	(58.91)	43	(33.09)	92
14	(14.73)	9	(8.27)	23
251		141		392

$X^2 = 9.77, \quad \chi^2_{3, 0.975} = 9.35.$

(viii)

Cotterill		Brougham		
42	(46.98)	48	(43.02)	90
54	(49.59)	41	(45.41)	95
33	(39.67)	43	(36.33)	76
25	(17.75)	9	(16.25)	34
154		141		295

$X^2 = 10.47, \quad \chi^2_{3, 0.975} = 9.35.$

TABLE 5.4 (*contd.*)

(ix)

Observations		*Inquiry*		
24	(27.35)	33	(29.65)	57
43	(51.34)	64	(55.66)	107
46	(33.11)	23	(35.89)	69
6	(7.20)	9	(7.80)	15
119		129		248

$X^2 = 13.43, \quad \chi^2_{3,\,0.995} = 12.84.$

(x)

Observations		Cotterill		
24	(28.77)	42	(37.23)	66
43	(42.28)	54	(54.72)	97
46	(34.44)	33	(44.56)	79
6	(13.51)	25	(17.49)	31
119		154		273

$X^2 = 15.71, \quad \chi^2_{3,0.995} = 12.84.$

(xi)

Observations		Brougham		
24	(32.95)	48	(39.05)	72
43	(38.45)	41	(45.55)	84
46	(40.73)	43	(48.27)	89
6	(6.87)	9	(8.13)	15
119		141		260

$X^2 = 6.94, \quad \chi^2_{3,0.95} = 7.81.$

(xii)

Observations		Bailey		
24	(33.13)	79	(69.87)	103
43	(48.89)	109	(103.11)	152
46	(30.55)	49	(64.45)	95
6	(6.43)	14	(13.57)	20
119		251		370

$X^2 = 16.30, \quad \chi^2_{3,\,0.995} = 12.84.$

TABLE 5.4 (*contd.*)

(xiii)

Inquiry		Cotterill		
33	(34.19)	42	(40.81)	75
64	(53.79)	54	(64.21)	118
23	(25.53)	33	(30.47)	56
9	(15.50)	25	(18.50)	34
129		154		283

$X^2 = 9.11, \quad \chi^2_{3,0.97} = 8.94.$

(xiv)

Inquiry		Brougham		
33	(38.70)	48	(42.30)	81
64	(50.17)	41	(54.83)	105
23	(31.53)	43	(34.47)	66
9	(8.60)	9	(9.40)	18
129		141		270

$X^2 = 13.37, \quad \chi^2_{3,\,0.995} = 12.84.$

(xv)

Inquiry		Bailey		
33	(38.02)	79	(73.98)	112
64	(58.73)	109	(114.27)	173
23	(24.44)	49	(47.56)	72
9	(7.81)	14	(15.19)	23
129		251		380

$X^2 = 2.12, \quad \chi^2_{3,\,0.95} = 7.81.$

Observations, and 3.58 for the author of the *Inquiry*. Thus, in each case we can accept the null hypothesis of consistency.

This set of tests also produced admirable discrimination between authors. The lowest χ^2 obtained in these tests is 9.77, and this is quite sufficient to distinguish between the work of Bailey and of Brougham. Bailey's work is distinguished from that of Cotterill as before, whose work, in turn, is clearly distinct from that of Brougham. Similarly, our two anonymous pamphlets seem to come from different pens.

The critical question, however, given that we have managed to find consistency within authors and discrimination between them, is whether the two anonymous pamphlets exhibit any similarities to the work of our authors. It is clear that the author of the *Observations* exhibits habits in the use of 'be' which are dissimilar, and statistically significantly different from, those exhibited by both Cotterill and Bailey. The computed χ^2 values are 15.71 and 16.30 respectively, so that it is possible to reject both Cotterill and Bailey as possible authors of this pamphlet with a type I error of only 0.005 in each case. Brougham's habits are, however, consistent with those of the author of the *Observations*; the computed χ^2 value is only 6.94.

It does not, however, seem that Brougham was the author of the *Inquiry*. The computed χ^2 is 13.37. Neither was Cotterill the author, it would seem, since the computed χ^2 is 9.11. However, it does seem that Bailey's habits are compatible with those of the author of the *Inquiry* and the computed χ^2, at 2.12, is extremely low. The chances of our making an error in rejecting either Cotterill or Brougham as authors are only 0.03 and 0.005, while Bailey's work appears to be extremely similar to that of the anonymous author.

It therefore seems reasonable to conclude from the analysis of habits in the use of 'be' that Brougham, not Cotterill or Bailey, was the author of the *Observations*, while Bailey, not Brougham or Cotterill, was responsible for the *Inquiry*. The evidence is very strong and it is fully in accord with the background evidence presented in the first part of this chapter and from the results obtained in analysing habits in the use of 'the'.

III. CONCLUSION

The statistical results obtained in dealing with the problems discussed in this chapter are highly satisfactory, and accord with the balance of the historical evidence, which is itself, however, inconclusive, discussed in the first part of the chapter. Even though we found that, in dealing with this particular problem, we were unable to achieve any discrimination using data derived from first word habits, the evidence from the collocations points unambiguously in one direction. Habits in the use of 'be' provide the most clear cut conclusions; but those with 'the' yield identical results even though they are, on their own, not quite so strong. In summary, then, it seems reasonable to conclude that Brougham was the author of the *Observations* and Bailey of the *Inquiry*.

6 The Authorship of the *Westminster Review* Attack on Samuel Bailey and the Authorship of James Mill's *Elements*

I. HISTORICAL BACKGROUND

In 1825, Bailey published his famous *Critical Dissertation on the Nature, Measure and Causes of Value.*[1] In January 1826 the *Westminster Review* published an extremely sharp and critical review of Bailey's book.[2] McCulloch, who, if he knew the author of this attack, did not care to reveal it, referred to the *Westminster Review* piece as 'a very captious article'[3] and it seems fair to say that this was not an untypical reaction. The authorship of the review was not, however, made public and has remained a matter of speculation ever since. Both James and John Stuart Mill were known to be connected with the *Westminster*, which had been founded in 1824 as a review presenting the views of the utilitarians and radicals; and Fetter has written: 'It was understood that James Mill, whose position at the India House made it inadvisable for him to appear as editor, would contribute on economics.'[4] James Mill has undoubtedly been the prime suspect, and was believed to be the author by Henry Higgs, Viner, and Hayek, while both Edgeworth and Schumpeter believed that John Stuart Mill was the author of the attack. Rauner, who reviewed the matter extensively, concluded that James Mill was certainly the author.[5]

Rauner, in fact, prepared an excellent *a priori* case for believing that James Mill must be held responsible. In particular, he lighted on the following points.

1. The reviewer was particularly concerned to defend James Mill and Ricardo.

2. The books listed in J. S. Mill's *Autobiography* as having been read at Grote's were those cited by the reviewer. Viner pointed out to Rauner that Hobbes followed Whately on the reading list, but Whately was not published till 1828. It follows from this that the reviewer did not learn about Hobbes from the discussions at Grote's. But in 1825 James Mill was writing his *Analysis of the Human Mind*[6] and reading Hobbes. Hobbes is referred to with considerable emphasis in the review and drawn upon as a source of authority.

3. In both the *Analysis of the Human Mind* and the *Westminster Review* article, great stress is laid on precision in expression. There is a long section on 'Naming' in the former work.[7]

4. The article makes a contrast between chemistry, where innovations in language are permissible, and economics, which does not require them. James Mill was a close friend of Thomas Thomson, Professor of Chemistry at the University of Glasgow.[8]

5. The reviewer conceded that Ricardo had been too ambitious in his attempt to use the word 'value' in two senses, which accords with James Mill's decision to deal only with 'exchangeable' or 'relative' value in the first edition of his *Elements*.[9]

6. The reviewer, like James Mill, failed to understand the importance of time in value, although the problems involved were appreciated by Ricardo.[10]

7. Bailey had objected to the inverse relationship of wages and profits in Ricardo, and the reviewer interpreted the relationship in a similar manner to that in James Mill's *Elements*.[11]

8. The treatment of demand and value is similar to that in the *Elements*.[12]

9. The reviewer concludes with a hint that he is expecting to review favourably another Bailey work; and in the July 1826 issue Mill reviewed Bailey's *Formation and Publication of Opinions*.[13]

10. Rauner draws attention to the strong tone of the review and draws a parallel with Mill's attack on Sir James Mackintosh.[14]

11. The charge of excessive length which the reviewer levels against Bailey would accord with the austerity of Mill's own presentation.

12. The article is written in the staccato style which is typical of Mill in polemic.

13. There is excessive use of the semi-colon, which is typical of Mill under such circumstances.

14. There are old fashioned negatives of a kind to which Mill was unusual in adhering.

Most of these points stand up to examination. Mill's vanity was well-known,[15] and his role in placing before the world Ricardo's economic theories is also widely appreciated;[16] and both of these are consistent with the concentration of the defence on the intellectual reputations of James Mill and Ricardo.

The point about Hobbes is also important. It is quite clear that not only did James Mill greatly (indeed uncritically) admire Hobbes, but Chapter 4 of his *Analysis of the Phenomena of the Human Mind* shows very clear Hobbesian influences. Indeed Halevy goes so far as to say: 'James Mill, who admired him [Hobbes] profoundly, reproduced almost word for word his reflections on language, which have become classical.'[17] There is a passionate defence of Hobbes in Mill's *Fragment on Mackintosh*.[18] J. S. Mill does say quite explicitly[19] that Hobbes was read by the circle at Grote's *after* Whately. Although Locke is cited frequently, the influence of Hobbes on Mill's *Analysis of the Phenomena of the Human Mind* is clear enough, even though he is not cited frequently by name.[20] One can certainly envisage the author of the *Westminster Review* material on the meaning of 'value' being the same as the author of the section on naming in the *Analysis*. There is no doubt of James Mill's friendship with Thomson, the Professor of Chemistry at Glasgow, which is confirmed by Bain.[21] Mill's use of strong language was sufficiently marked to be felt by Bain to require defence: 'The use of strong language must be judged by the provocation. Mill, all his life, waged a war against those that he considered enemies of human welfare. He often gave vent to strong language but never to coarse invective. The cause that he fought under was public and not personal.'[22] Indeed, the preface to the *Fragment on Mackintosh*, a work which is really rather shrill, implies that the book had been moderated in tone before publication because Mackintosh was no longer alive to defend himself. If that is the case, one cannot help wondering what it was like before.

Yet there are some grounds for doubt. For one thing, it is by no means as clear as Rauner asserts that Mill was busy composing his *Analysis* (and thus particularly familiar with Hobbes) at the date in question. Rauner says that 'in 1825 James Mill was in the midst of writing his *Analysis of the Human Mind*'[23] and cites Bain and J. S. Mill's *Autobiography*. In fact, however, Bain states that the composition went on in the summers of 1824–29[24] and this statement seems in turn to be based upon J. S. Mill's *Autobiography*. But J. S. Mill's *Autobiography* is even less explicit; the younger Mill gives the summers of 1822–9.[25]

Again, although it is true that the circle at Grote's read Hobbes after Whately, and thus after the publication of the *Westminster Review* article, J. S. Mill himself read Hobbes in childhood.[26] It appears he read it before he was 14,[27] which would have been in 1820. It is true of course, that the references to Hobbes in J. S. Mill's *Logic*[28] are uniformly hostile. Although Hobbes is cited quite frequently (a matter which is made clear by the admirable bibliographic index in the new Toronto edition), it is perfectly obvious that the younger Mill was not an admirer of Hobbes. He thought him over-rated compared to Locke,[29] he referred to his 'ultra-nominalism',[30] accused him of reasoning in a circle,[31] referred to the 'double sophism of an original contract'[32] and at numerous points in the book was at pains to draw attention to the fallacies and deficiencies in Hobbes' work. But this is hardly conclusive, because there is no evidence that Mill had such an uncompromisingly critical attitude towards Hobbes (or indeed a critical attitude at all) at the time of the *Westminster Review* article. His mental crisis, which is well known, is dated in his *Autobiography* as occurring from the *autumn* of 1826[33] and it would be perfectly possible to argue (indeed it seems highly likely) that his view of Hobbes, assimilated under the influence of his father, at a time when he was hardly mature enough for this, could well have been one of the intellectual beliefs affected by the crisis. Again, on the question of precision, there is no shortage of material about this in the *Logic* (e.g. Book 1, Chapter 1 'Of the Necessity of Commencing with an Analysis of Language').

The material concerning chemistry is also inconclusive. Mill, in his *Autobiography,* recounts how he 'devoured treatises on Chemistry' at a very early age indeed – up to the age of 12 – and that he was particularly influenced himself by the work of Thomson.[34] Moreover, the *Logic* contains a section[35] on 'Chemical Method in Social Science', although Mill says that this method is, in fact, unsuitable for economics.

Thus, not all of Rauner's grounds are equally persuasive. On the other hand, there are other grounds which Rauner does not mention but which certainly suggest that James Mill was, indeed, the author of the review. For instance, Bailey, in his reply to the *Review, A Letter to a Political Economist,*[36] points to a passage in the second edition of Mill's *Elements*[37] which referred to labour as a *cause* of value, whereas the *Westminster* reviewer had said that cost of production was not a cause of value but a cause of 'non-value'. Mill had, however, removed the offending passage in the third edition of the *Elements*, published in 1826–before Bailey's *Letter* but after the review, so that the third edition was in line with the review. There is also the fact that the reviewer[38] was clearly aware that Ricardo had used 'value' in two senses – we now know that Mill had been sent the paper on Absolute and Exchangeable

Value.[39] The reviewer also seemed to understand clearly (perhaps because of having seen the posthumous paper) the object of Ricardo's invariable measure – an understanding which would rule out most candidates for authorship. The 'elite cult' defence of political economy would again be more typical of James Mill than anyone else.[40] Moreover, there is one literary clue which Rauner missed. On page 162 of the review the word 'contemn' occurs. This is a very unusual word and, interestingly enough, the *Oxford English Dictionary*[41] cites James Mill's *History of British India* as one of the few works using this unusual form.

It is also not without significance that Bailey himself clearly believed James Mill to be the author of the review. A number of passages in his *Letter*[42] seem to be particularly directed at James Mill, and McCulloch's candour is favourably contrasted with Mill's behaviour.[43] Bailey makes a point of quoting Mill's *Elements* against the reviewer (the matter about the cause of value noted above[44]) and he notes that the reviewer seemed particularly sensitive about James Mill, although Mill himself had not received much attention in the *Critical Dissertation* compared with the other authors discussed.[45]

In addition, John Stuart Mill's attack on Malthus,[46] dating from the same period, is rather different in its method of assault. J. S. Mill would have been 18 at the time, so that its tone, which is at times that of a smart undergraduate, is perhaps understandable. J. S. Mill's method is to pretend to be defending Malthus against somebody posing as Malthus in the *Quarterly Review*, but who cannot possibly be Malthus because he has written such rubbish. (J. S. Mill, of course, knew perfectly well that the author was Malthus.)

But style is a dangerous matter without quantification. Analytical content provides other clues; and it is true that parts of J. S. Mill's *Principles* (especially Book 3 Chapter 1) contain material rather similar to the *Westminster Review* attack on Bailey.[47] On the other hand, the analysis in the *Principles* is far more sophisticated than that in James Mill's *Elements*, which itself could be regarded as being analytically on a par with the *Westminster* article, and some of it, which presents a literary description of mathematical forms, with demand clearly understood as a function of price, elasticity of demand introduced, and an equation between demand and supply being described as 'the proper mathematical analogy' of their relationship, goes far beyond anything James Mill had to offer in the *Elements*.[48] Moreover, we find therein the introduction of elasticity of supply.[49] However, all this dates from 20 years after the events under consideration, so that it is, again, inconclusive.

New light has, however, been thrown on the matter by a discovery of Professor J. M. Robson. He found, in Somerville College, Oxford, a set of some volumes of the *Westminster Review* with marks by the article titles in the tables of contents.[50] A cross (+) indicates J. S. Mill, and a dash (−) James Mill. The disputed *Westminster* article is thus marked. The identification of the meaning of these symbols rests upon their being attached to some articles the authorship of which is already known from other sources. This is very reasonable; and a check of the list which Professor Robson gives agrees with what is known from sources like the MacMinn bibliography. But it is a slender thread, nonetheless; and Professor Robson very sensibly refers to 'the imperfect cannons of proof in such matters'[51] – though, in the case of one article identified with a cross, he has found supporting manuscript evidence in the Mill–Taylor collection at LSE.

We thus return to the familiar point that literary and historical evidence in such circumstances is likely to be inconclusive and that an attempt to use our statistical analysis as a supplement seemed justified. We therefore began with the disputed *Westminster Review* article, which is about 6,500 words in length after the removal of extraneous matter such as quotations. Initially, we used for comparison a substantial extract from Mill's *Elements*, dealing with value and exchange, amounting to about 21,000 words,[52] and nearly 12,000 words of J. S. Mill's *Principles* dealing with value.[53] However, partly because we wanted to use the material for another purpose discussed below, we added to this the article in the *Westminster Review* by J. S. Mill attacking Malthus (about 10,000 words),[54] and Section Two of James Mill's *Fragment on Mackintosh*[55] (about 11,000 words) – the latter both because of the emphasis on Hobbes and also because Rauner singled this out as a particularly apposite example of James Mill at his most pungent.[56] To complete the sample of J. Mill's writings, we used an extract from his *Analysis of the Phenomena of the Human Mind*,[57] amounting to about 18,000 words.

The other problem for which we wanted to use this material was to test the theory that J. S. Mill wrote James Mill's *Elements*. This is a theory which has been in circulation for some time.

It does seem highly unlikely, after reading both the *Elements* and the *Principles*, that the same hand was responsible for them both. The basis for the theory is apparently the account which J. S. Mill gives in his *Autobiography*[58] of his method of learning economics from his father and having to write (and re-write) an account of what he had learnt afterwards. J. S. Mill claims only that the results were used by his father 'as notes from which to write his Elements of Political Economy'. Now, the view which attempts to take this as a basis for attributing authorship of the *Elements* to J. S. Mill rather overlooks the fact that, according to J. S. Mill's own account *elsewhere* in the *Autobiography*,[59] he was actually in France at the time that the *Elements* was written. Moreover, there is a clear reference in the Ricardo – Mill correspondence to James Mill 'making good progress with . . . [his] School Book of Political Economy'.[60] But we thought it worthwhile to investigate the matter numerically.

II. STATISTICAL ANALYSIS

The main question which concerns us in this chapter is that of which of the two Mills, father or son, wrote the attack on Samuel Bailey which appeared in the *Westminster Review* in 1826. However, we take notice of our subsidiary question, concerning authorship of the *Elements*, as a first step.

(a) First word usage

We begin our statistical analysis by comparing characteristic choices of first word in a sentence. We used the samples from James Mill's *Fragment on Mackintosh* and from his *Analysis of the Phenomena of the Human Mind*; and from the work of J. S. Mill we used the section of his *Principles* together with the *Westminster Review* article on Malthus referred to above, which is of very much the same date as the attack on Bailey. Before comparing either the *Elements* or the *Westminster Review* article on Bailey with the work of our two possible authors, we split each of the two disputed texts into two parts in order to test for internal consistency.

The results of our analysis of first word usage are presented in summary from in Table 6.1. This summarises the contingency tables 6.2(i) to 6.2(ix). The rows of each contingency table correspond to the usage of the following words; 'but'; 'where'; 'this' or 'it' or 'thus' or 'and'; 'a' or 'by'; and all other first words. Each table thus has five rows. From examination of Table 6.1 we conclude that both Mills are internally consistent in their first word usage and also that the *Elements* is internally consistent. With 4 degrees of freedom, the 95 per cent critical value of χ^2 is 9.49 and we observe computed values of 2.42 (J. Mill), 5.87 (J. S. Mill) and 2.85 (*Elements*). Thus the two samples from the two authors, and the

TABLE 6.1 First word usage

Texts analysed	X^2	d.f.	$\chi^2_{0.95}$	*Decision*	*Maximum type I error (where applicable)*	*Contingency table*
Fragment vs *Mind* (J. Mill)	2.42	4	9.49	Accept the hypothesis of J. Mill's internal consistency	–	6.2(i)
Principles vs 'Periodical Literature' (J. S. Mill)	5.87	4	9.49	Accept the hypothesis of J. S. Mill's internal consistency	–	6.2(ii)
Elements internally	2.85	4	9.49	Accept the hypothesis of the internal consistency of the *Elements*	–	6.2(iii)
J. Mill vs J. S. Mill	21.34	4	9.49	Reject the hypothesis of consistency between J. and J. S. Mill	0.005	6.2(iv)
J. S. Mill vs *Elements*	12.48	4	9.49	Reject the hypothesis of consistency between J. S. Mill and the *Elements*	0.02	6.2(v)
J. Mill vs *Elements*	4.76	4	9.49	Accept the hypothesis of consistency between J. Mill and the *Elements*	–	6.2(vi)
W. R. 1826 internally	4.43	4	9.49	Accept the hypothesis of consistency within *Westminster* article	–	6.2(vii)
J. S. Mill vs *W. R.* 1826	8.58	4	8.33*	Reject the hypothesis of consistency between J. S. Mill and *Westminster* article	0.08	6.2(viii)
J. Mill vs *W. R.* 1826	5.63	4	9.49	Accept the hypothesis of consistency between J. Mill and *Westminster* article	–	6.2(ix)

* $\chi^2_{4,0.92} = 8.33$.

TABLE 6.2 Contingency tables – first word usage

(i) J. Mill

Fragment		*Mind*		
16	(11.90)	23	(27.10)	39
7	(7.93)	19	(18.07)	26
103	(103.43)	236	(235.57)	339
11	(10.07)	22	(22.93)	33
191	(194.66)	447	(443.34)	638
328		747		1075

$X^2 = 2.42, \quad \chi^2_{4,\,0.95} = 9.49.$

(ii) J. S. Mill

Principles		'Periodical Literature'		
29	(25.02)	9	(12.98)	38
13	(10.54)	3	(5.46)	16
69	(73.76)	43	(38.24)	112
9	(7.24)	2	(3.76)	11
177	(180.44)	97	(93.56)	274
297		154		451

$X^2 = 5.87, \quad \chi^2_{4,\,0.95} = 9.49.$

(iii) *Elements*

pp. 254–75		pp. 276–303		
12	(11.33)	15	(15.67)	27
5	(5.04)	7	(6.96)	12
78	(73.88)	98	(102.12)	176
5	(8.40)	15	(11.60)	20
172	(173.36)	241	(239.64)	413
272		376		648

$X^2 = 2.85, \quad \chi^2_{4,\,0.95} = 9.49.$

TABLE 6.2 (*contd.*)

(iv)

J. Mill		J. S. Mill		
39	(54.24)	38	(22.76)	77
26	(29.59)	16	(12.41)	42
339	(317.71)	112	(133.29)	451
33	(31.00)	11	(13.00)	44
638	(642.46)	274	(269.54)	912
1075		451		1526

$X^2 = 21.34, \quad \chi^2_{4,\,0.995} = 14.86.$

(v)

Elements		J. S. Mill		
27	(38.33)	38	(26.67)	65
12	(16.51)	16	(11.49)	28
176	(169.81)	112	(118.19)	288
20	(18.28)	11	(12.72)	31
413	(405.07)	274	(281.93)	687
648		451		1099

$X^2 = 12.48, \quad \chi^2_{4,\,0.98} = 11.67.$

(vi)

Elements		J. Mill		
27	(24.82)	39	(41.18)	66
12	(14.29)	26	(23.71)	38
176	(193.69)	339	(321.31)	515
20	(19.93)	33	(33.07)	53
413	(395.27)	638	(655.73)	1051
648		1075		1723

$X^2 = 4.76, \quad \chi^2_{4,\,0.95} = 9.49$

(vii) *Westminster* 1826

pp. 157–64		pp. 164–72		
4	(3.69)	3	(3.31)	7
3	(2.11)	1	(1.89)	4
34	(28.49)	20	(25.51)	54
2	(2.64)	3	(2.36)	5
72	(78.07)	76	(69.93)	148
115		103		218

$X^2 = 4.43, \quad \chi^2_{4,\,0.95} = 9.49.$

TABLE 6.2 (*contd.*)

(viii)

Westminster 1826		J. S. Mill		
7	(14.66)	38	(30.34)	45
4	(6.52)	16	(13.48)	20
54	(54.09)	112	(111.91)	166
5	(5.21)	11	(10.79)	16
148	(137.51)	274	(284.49)	422
218		451		669

$X^2 = 8.58, \quad \chi^2_{4,\,0.92} = 8.33.$

(ix)

Westminster 1826		J. Mill		
7	(7.76)	39	(38.24)	46
4	(5.06)	26	(24.94)	30
54	(66.26)	339	(326.74)	393
5	(6.41)	33	(31.59)	38
148	(132.52)	638	(653.48)	786
218		1075		1293

$X^2 = 5.63, \quad \chi^2_{4,\,0.95} = 9.49.$

Elements taken separately, all exhibit the required internal consistency in choice of first word. Using the same procedure to compare the work of the two Mills we find marked differences, yielding a computed χ^2 value of 21.34. This makes it possible to compare the *Elements* with each of the two Mills separately. We are able to conclude that, on the evidence of first word usage, it would appear that J. S. Mill was not the author and that his father wrote the book. The computed χ^2 figures are 12.48 and 4.76 respectively. The probability of error in rejection of J. S. Mill, at 0.02, is extremely low.

The result of a test upon the two parts of the anonymous attack upon Samuel Bailey is reported in Table 6.2(vii). The test is, unfortunately, weakened by the relatively short length of the article. Nevertheless, our test yields a computed χ^2 figure of 4.43, which leads us to accept the hypothesis of internal consistency, although confidence in this conclusion is qualified by the fact that the relevant contingency table has 6 of its 10 cells with low expected values. Consistency could be demonstrated without such qualifications by suitable aggregation of rows (by amalgamating rows 1 and 4, for example), but, for the purpose of determining its authorship, we shall retain the current five rows, since in the two most important tables for comparative purposes (6.2(viii) and 6.2(ix)) there is no difficulty at all. These two tables lead us to conclude that J. S. Mill did not write the *Westminster Review* attack on Samuel Bailey, and that his father was responsible. The computed χ^2 values are 8.58 and 5.63 respectively, and hence the probability of error in rejecting J. S. Mill as author is no greater than 0.08.

We are able, then, to conclude from our first set of tests, involving the analysis of first word usage, that it seems likely that both the *Elements* and the *Westminster* article of 1826 were written by James Mill, not by his son.

(b) Collocations with 'the'

The results of our analysis of frequencies of different couplings with 'the' are summarised in Table 6.3, which is derived from the detailed contingency tables 6.4(i) to 6.4(ix). We have used the collocations with 'the' of the following words: 'with' or 'all'; 'to' or 'by'; 'into' or 'at'; 'be' or 'for' or 'which' or 'but'; 'from' or 'or' or 'is' or 'that'. Each contingency table thus has five rows. In this case, our classification is not exhaustive of all the collocations with 'the' – we have no 'other' row.

It would seem from Table 6.3 that we may accept the hypothesis of internal consistency within the work of both James Mill and J. S. Mill with respect to their use of 'the'. The same is true of the *Elements*. The computed χ^2 figures are 1.21, 6.03, and 1.46 respectively, while the 95 per cent point of the χ^2_4 distribution is 9.49. Each contingency table (6.4(i), (ii) and (iii)) has sufficiently large numbers of cells with expected values greater than 5 to make acceptance of this result unproblematical. Table 6.4(iv) indicates that collocations with 'the' discriminate clearly between the work of the two Mills, the computed χ^2 being 17.66.

Comparing the work of father and son with the *Elements* leads us to reject the hypothesis that J. S. Mill was the author; the computed χ^2 is 8.33, and the possibility of our making an error is as low as 0.08. James Mill's habits in using 'the' are totally compatible with those found in the *Elements*; the computed χ^2, at 6.77, is well within the 95 per cent critical value of 9.49. Again we conclude, as with the tests on first word usage, that the author of the *Elements* is James Mill, and reject the possibility that it was the work of his son.

Using collocations with 'the' to examine the internal consistency of the disputed *Westminster Review* article, we find, as Table 6.4(vii) shows, that the article is internally consistent. It is true that the number of cells with low expected frequences amounts to two-fifths of the table; but this is a

TABLE 6.3 Collocations with 'the'

Texts analysed	X^2	d.f.	$\chi^2_{0.95}$	*Decision*	*Maximum type I error (where applicable)*	*Contingency table*
Fragment vs *Mind* (J. Mill)	1.21	4	9.49	Accept the hypothesis of J. Mill's internal consistency	–	6.4(i)
Principles vs 'Periodical Literature' (J. S. Mill)	6.03	4	9.49	Accept the hypothesis of J. S. Mill's internal consistency	–	6.4(ii)
Elements internally	1.46	4	9.49	Accept the hypothesis of the internal consistency of the *Elements*	–	6.4(iii)
J. Mill vs J. S. Mill	17.66	4	9.49	Reject the hypothesis of consistency between J. and J. S. Mill	0.005	6.4(iv)
J. S. Mill vs *Elements*	8.33	4	8.33*	Reject the hypothesis of consistency between J. S. Mill and the *Elements*	0.08	6.4(v)
J. Mill vs *Elements*	6.77	4	9.49	Accept the hypothesis of consistency between J. Mill and the *Elements*	–	6.4(vi)
W. R. 1826 internally	2.57	4	9.49	Accept the hypothesis of consistency within *Westminster* article	–	6.4(vii)
J. S. Mill vs *W. R.* 1826	8.35	4	8.33*	Reject the hypothesis of consistency between J. S. Mill and *Westminster* article	0.08	6.4(viii)
J. Mill vs *W. R.* 1826	0.93	4	9.49	Accept the hypothesis of consistency between J. Mill and *Westminster* article	–	6.4(ix)

* $\chi^2_{0.92} = 8.33$

TABLE 6.4 Contingency tables – collocations with 'the'

(i) J. Mill

Fragment		*Mind*		
12	(12.39)	30	(29.61)	42
50	(49.85)	119	(119.15)	169
8	(5.90)	12	(14.10)	20
33	(34.81)	85	(83.19)	118
56	(56.05)	134	(133.95)	190
159		380		539

$X^2 = 1.21, \quad \chi^2_{4,\,0.95} = 9.49.$

(ii) J. S. Mill

Principles		'Periodical Literature'		
19	(21.47)	19	(16.53)	38
35	(42.37)	40	(32.63)	75
14	(12.99)	9	(10.01)	23
42	(38.98)	27	(30.02)	69
51	(45.19)	29	(34.81)	80
161		124		285

$X^2 = 6.03, \quad \chi^2_{4,\,0.95} = 9.49.$

(iii) *Elements*

pp. 254–75		pp. 276–303		
17	(19.98)	25	(22.02)	42
73	(70.87)	76	(78.13)	149
9	(10.46)	13	(11.54)	22
47	(46.14)	50	(50.86)	97
59	(57.55)	62	(63.45)	121
205		226		431

$X^2 = 1.46, \quad \chi^2_{4,\,0.95} = 9.49.$

TABLE 6.4 (*contd.*)

(iv)

J. Mill		J. S. Mill		
42	(52.33)	38	(27.67)	80
169	(159.61)	75	(84.39)	244
20	(28.13)	23	(14.87)	43
118	(122.32)	69	(64.68)	187
190	(176.61)	80	(93.39)	270
539		285		824

$X^2 = 17.66, \quad \chi^2_{4,\,0.995} = 14.86.$

(v)

Elements		J. S. Mill		
42	(48.16)	38	(31.84)	80
149	(134.84)	75	(89.16)	224
22	(27.09)	23	(17.91)	45
97	(99.92)	69	(66.08)	166
121	(120.99)	80	(80.01)	201
431		285		716

$X^2 = 8.33, \quad \chi^2_{4,\,0.92} = 8.33.$

(vi)

Elements		J. Mill		
42	(37.32)	42	(46.68)	84
149	(141.30)	169	(176.70)	318
22	(18.66)	20	(23.34)	42
97	(95.53)	118	(119.47)	215
121	(138.19)	190	(172.81)	311
431		539		970

$X^2 = 6.77, \quad \chi^2_{4,\,0.95} = 9.49.$

(vii) *Westminster* 1826

pp. 157–64		pp. 164–72		
5	(3.05)	2	(3.95)	7
12	(12.62)	17	(16.38)	29
1	(0.87)	1	(1.13)	2
6	(6.96)	10	(9.04)	16
13	(13.49)	18	(17.51)	31
37		48		85

$X^2 = 2.57, \quad \chi^2_{4,\,0.95} = 9.49.$

TABLE 6.4 (*contd.*)

(viii)

Westminster 1826		J. S. Mill		
7	(10.34)	38	(34.66)	45
29	(23.89)	75	(80.11)	104
2	(5.74)	23	(19.26)	25
16	(19.53)	69	(65.47)	85
31	(25.50)	80	(85.50)	111
85		285		370

$X^2 = 8.35, \quad \chi^2_{4,\,0.92} = 8.33.$

(ix)

Westminster 1826		J. Mill		
7	(6.67)	42	(42.33)	49
29	(26.97)	169	(171.03)	198
2	(3.00)	20	(19.00)	22
16	(18.25)	118	(115.75)	134
31	(30.10)	190	(190.90)	221
85		539		624

$X^2 = 0.93, \quad \chi^2_{4,\,0.95} = 9.49.$

feature which can easily be remedied. If we amalgamate rows 1 and 3, we obtain a computed χ^2 of 2.28, which is well below the $\chi^2_{3,\,0.95}$ value of 7.81. We thus obtain the same result as before. We return, however, to the less aggregated data for our subsequent analysis. It is then clear from Table 6.4(viii), which uses the original rows, that J. S. Mill and the author of the *Westminster* article on Bailey have very different habits; indeed, the differences are statistically significant, enabling us to reject, with a type I error of no greater than 0.08, the hypothesis of his authorship. The habits of James Mill in the use of 'the' are, however, wholly compatible with those of the anonymous article, yielding a χ^2 value of 0.93. It is, therefore, reasonable to conclude from the second set of tests that James Mill wrote the attack on Bailey.

(c) Collocations with 'be'

Our final statistical analysis was performed upon data derived from the usage of the word 'be'. We grouped together the following collocations: 'can'; 'would' or 'to'; 'noun' or 'might' or 'could' or 'will'; 'must' or 'should' or 'may' or 'shall' or 'need'. Consequently, each contingency table has four rows. Our results are summarised in Table 6.5 and the

TABLE 6.5 Collocations with 'be'

Texts analysed	X^2	d.f.	$\chi^2_{0.95}$	*Decision*	*Maximum type I error (where applicable)*	*Contingency table*
Fragment vs *Mind* (J. Mill)	2.40	3	7.81	Accept the hypothesis of J. Mill's internal consistency	–	6.6(i)
Principles vs 'Periodical Literature' (J. S. Mill)	4.88	3	7.81	Accept the hypothesis of J. S. Mill's internal consistency	–	6.6(ii)
Elements internally	4.29	3	7.81	Accept the hypothesis of the internal consistency of the *Elements*	–	6.6(iii)
J. Mill vs J. S. Mill	14.04	3	7.81	Reject the hypothesis of consistency between J. and J. S. Mill	0.005	6.6(iv)
J. S. Mill vs *Elements*	17.09	3	7.81	Reject the hypothesis of consistency between J. S. Mill and the *Elements*	0.005	6.6(v)
J. Mill vs *Elements*	1.89	3	7.81	Accept the hypothesis of consistency between J. Mill and the *Elements*	–	6.6(vi)
W. R. 1826 internally	4.27	3	7.81	Accept the hypothesis of consistency within *Westminster* article	–	6.6(vii)
J. S. Mill vs *W.R.* 1826	8.89	3	7.81	Reject the hypothesis of consistency between J. S. Mill and *Westminster* article	0.04	6.6(viii)
J. Mill vs *W. R.* 1826	1.74	3	7.81	Accept the hypothesis of consistency between J. Mill and *Westminster* article	–	6.6(ix)

details may be found in Tables 6.6(i) to 6.6(ix). The first three rows of Table 6.5 indicate that we are able to accept that both James and John Stuart Mill were consistent in their use of 'be' and that the author of the *Elements* was also consistent. The computed χ^2 values, at 2.40, 4.88, and 4.29 respectively, are well below the critical value of 7.81. The fourth row of Table 6.5 indicates that the differences between the Mills produce a statistically significant result, with a computed χ^2 of 14.04.

Table 6.6(v) compares the *Elements*, with respect to 'be', with our sample of the work of J. S. Mill. We find an extremely strong result to support rejection of J. S. Mill as author of this work; the type I error is only 0.005, or half of one per cent. Moreover, we are left in no doubt about the compatibility of James Mill's habits with those of the author of the *Elements* when we examine Table 6.6(vi). His style is wholly similar to that found in the *Elements*, and the slight differences which inevitably exist only result in a computed χ^2 of 1.89. The relevant 95 per cent critical value is 7.81. Thus, we conclude, as with the first set of tests, that J. S. Mill did not write the *Elements*, and that his father did so.

Table 6.6(vii) relates to the internal consistency of the disputed *Westminster* article. From it we may conclude that there is consistency, for the differences between the two parts are not statistically significant. It is true that 3 of the 8 cells have low expected values; but this problem may be overcome by reducing the table by one row through amalgamating rows one and three. Of the six cells remaining, only one would then have a low expected value, a figure which should remove any doubt about the result of the test. The computed χ^2 is then 2.73, which compares with a 95 per cent critical value for the χ^2 distribution with two degrees of freedom of 5.99. Our original conclusion is thus unaltered.

The last two tables compare characteristic uses of 'be' by the author of the disputed *Westminster* article with those of James and J. S. Mill. From Table 6.6(viii), it seems clear that J. S. Mill did not write the attack on Bailey (the computed χ^2 is 8.89), while the χ^2 value of 1.74 in Table 6.6(ix) would lead one to conclude that James Mill's literary habits in this, as in other respects, show complete compatibility with those of the author of the disputed text. The probability of our having made an error in rejecting J. S. Mill as the author is less than 0.04.

III CONCLUSION

The weight of our three sets of tests would lead to the conclusion, therefore, that the *Elements* was indeed written by James Mill; and our

TABLE 6.6 Contingency tables – collocations with 'be'

(i) J. Mill

Fragment		*Mind*		
3	(4.02)	10	(8.98)	13
30	(25.69)	53	(57.31)	83
10	(10.52)	24	(23.48)	34
9	(11.76)	29	(26.24)	38
52		116		168

$X^2 = 2.40, \quad \chi^2_{3,\,0.95} = 7.81.$

(ii) J. S. Mill

Principles		'Periodical Literature'		
24	(21.30)	11	(13.70)	35
35	(40.78)	32	(26.22)	67
35	(30.43)	15	(19.57)	50
32	(33.48)	23	(21.52)	55
126		81		207

$X^2 = 4.88, \quad \chi^2_{3,\,0.95} = 7.81.$

(iii) *Elements*

pp. 254–75		pp. 276–303		
11	(10.53)	15	(15.47)	26
49	(55.88)	89	(82.12)	138
28	(27.54)	40	(40.46)	68
27	(21.06)	25	(30.94)	52
115		169		284

$X^2 = 4.29, \quad \chi^2_{3,\,0.95} = 7.81.$

(iv)

J. Mill		J. S. Mill		
13	(21.50)	35	(26.50)	48
83	(67.20)	67	(82.80)	150
34	(37.63)	50	(46.37)	84
38	(41.66)	55	(51.34)	93
168		207		375

$X^2 = 14.04, \quad \chi^2_{3,\,0.995} = 12.84.$

TABLE 6.6 (*contd.*)

(v)

Elements		J. S. Mill		
26	(35.28)	35	(25.72)	61
138	(118.57)	67	(86.43)	205
68	(68.25)	50	(49.75)	118
52	(61.89)	55	(45.11)	107
284		207		491

$X^2 = 17.09, \quad \chi^2_{3,\,0.995} = 12.84.$

(vi)

Elements		J. Mill		
26	(24.50)	13	(14.50)	39
138	(138.86)	83	(82.14)	221
68	(64.09)	34	(37.91)	102
52	(56.55)	38	(33.45)	90
284		168		452

$X^2 = 1.89, \quad \chi^2_{3,\,0.95} = 7.81.$

(vii) *Westminster* 1826

pp. 157–64		pp. 164–72		
3	(3.27)	4	(3.73)	7
14	(14.93)	18	(17.07)	32
8	(5.13)	3	(5.87)	11
3	(4.67)	7	(5.33)	10
28		32		60

$X^2 = 4.27, \quad \chi^2_{3,\,0.95} = 7.81.$

(viii)

Westminster 1826		J. S. Mill		
7	(9.44)	35	(32.56)	42
32	(22.25)	67	(76.75)	99
11	(13.71)	50	(47.29)	61
10	(14.61)	55	(50.39)	65
60		207		267

$X^2 = 8.89, \quad \chi^2_{3,\,0.96} = 8.31.$

TABLE 6.6 (*contd.*)

(ix) *Westminster* 1826		J. Mill		
7	(5.26)	13	(14.74)	20
32	(30.26)	83	(84.74)	115
11	(11.84)	34	(33.16)	45
10	(12.63)	38	(35.37)	48
60		168		228

$X^2 = 1.74, \quad \chi^2_{3,\,0.95} = 7.81.$

three tests would lead us to reject the hypothesis that his son was the author, with type I errors of 0.02, 0.08, and 0.005 respectively. Similarly, the analysis of the characteristics of the disputed *Westminster Review* article indicates that it too was by James Mill. Each of our tests would lead us to reject the hypothesis that J. S. Mill was the author, and the type I errors in this case are of the order 0.08, 0.08 and 0.04.

7 McCulloch, Parnell, and the *Edinburgh Review*

I. HISTORICAL BACKGROUND

(a) Ireland

The problem dealt with in this part of the chapter concerns two articles, both entitled 'Ireland', which appeared in the *Edinburgh Review* in June 1822 and January 1825.[1] They are both substantial articles, the first being about 21,500 words, and the second about 23,500.

McCulloch claimed authorship of both these articles. They are in the three volume set of his *Edinburgh Review* articles, in his library at Reading, which is mentioned in his *Catalogue* (1862).[2] In this *Catalogue*, McCulloch referred explicitly to his authorship of the second article.[3] Both articles are also in a bound set of his *Edinburgh Review* articles in the Goldsmith Library. The markings on the Goldsmiths' set are in the handwriting of H. G. Reid, McCulloch's confidential clerk and son-in-law. There are also several lists of McCulloch's *Edinburgh Review* articles, which correspond with the two three-volume sets. One of these appeared in the 1869 edition of McCulloch's *Dictionary of Commerce*[4] (which was edited by H. G. Reid), and the second appeared in *Notes and Queries* in 1878.[5]

McCulloch does not seem to have been a plagiarist, as distinct from a self-plagiarist, the latter practice being perfectly understandable (at a time when he was living by his pen, and each appearance of a particular piece of work was confined to a relatively small circle of readers), although he certainly overdid it. If, then, he claimed work as his own there is no *prima facie* reason for disbelieving him.

Nonetheless, the articles are quite clearly and unambiguously claimed by Sir Henry Parnell, Baron Congleton. Since Parnell's name may not be known to everybody, it is perhaps worth saying a little about him. He was a member of the famous Bullion Committee of 1810 and was an economic writer with a claim to having developed the theory of international transfers in the context of Irish Absenteeism.[6] He was MP for Queen's County (now County Leix or Laoighis) for the years 1806–32. This is in the middle of Ireland, and not far from the latitude of Galway, which turns out to be relevant in relation to some internal evidence. Parnell conducted a sustained campaign on behalf of the Irish Catholics and in favour of Catholic emancipation; but he was also a writer on economic matters – his *Financial Reform* being perhaps his most famous work in this genre – and he certainly wrote about economic affairs as they affected Ireland.

In a letter of 28 February 1841, written to MacVey Napier of the *Edinburgh Review*, Parnell wrote:

> It occurs to me that I could write a useful & interesting Article on Ireland – I wrote the Articles which are in the Edinburgh Review, on this subject, in the years 1822 & 1825 (see Vol. 37. p. 61 Vol. 41. p. 356 & Vol. 43. p. 125–)
>
> I mean to employ my time in collecting materials while Parliament is sitting, and if I find they will enable me to produce a good article, I will write it early in the Autumn.[7]

The claim could hardly be clearer or more unambiguous.

Interestingly enough, the Copinger list, which is believed to be based upon Longman's records since destroyed, but which has proved inaccurate in a number of respects, gives McCulloch *and* Parnell as the joint authors of the third article on Ireland mentioned by Parnell, 'Catholic Emancipation . . . Divided Allegiance of the Catholics'.[8] This article was, however, never claimed by McCulloch. We have tested it for internal consistency and have not found any indication that it is by more than one hand.

Parnell's claim to authorship is also made, equally unambiguously, in his private papers. (We are greatful to Lord Congleton for granting us access to these, which are in private possession.) The papers contain a memorandum drawn up in 1838, apparently in connection with a Dundee election, which lists six articles published in the *Edinburgh Review* in the years 1820–6 (as well as two articles of 1841 and 1842 subsequently added to the document), and claims that Parnell was the author of them all.[9]

There is nothing else in the Parnell papers that would give a clue to authorship, even in a bundle containing a good deal about Ireland, or in another bundle concerned with the absenteeism of Irish landlords. There are letters from McCulloch in the papers; and there is one in which he writes to Parnell: 'I shall be at all times most happy to hear from you, and will be glad to render any assistance in my power to your good efforts either in favour of Ireland or of freedom in general.'[10] But there is no mention of *Edinburgh Review* articles.

The internal evidence is inconclusive, though it certainly favours McCulloch's claim. A reading of three of Parnell's relevant speeches of the period does not reveal anything directly reproduced in the two *Edinburgh Review* articles, nor any great overlap of topics.[11] Parnell concentrated on the Penal Laws and the violation of the Treaty of Limerick, which was supposed to guarantee the rights of the Catholics, on the temperate behaviour of those associated with the Catholic Association, on the corruption of the magistracy, and on the provocation given by proselytising fundamentalist Protestants.[12] He also dealt with matters of population, poverty, and the exclusion, for long practised, of Irish goods from the English market. It is noticeable that he is doubtful of the argument that subdivision was encouraged by the existence of the 40 shilling freehold which was supposed to give landlords an incentive to allow subdivision, so as to increase the number of votes which they controlled. This is in direct contrast to McCulloch, who followed an Irish writer, Wakefield, on this very closely, and regarded the matter as of considerable importance.[13] The general lack of correspondence between the speeches and the articles is all the more surprising because one of the items reviewed in the 1825 article was Parnell's speech of 24 June 1823.[14] Parnell is quoted[15] but not relied upon at all heavily.

On the other hand, there are pieces of internal evidence which certainly favour the idea that Parnell had a hand in the articles. Firstly, in the 1822 article there is a statement that: 'It is only necessary to walk through her [Dublin's] streets to be convinced of her improving condition';[16] and it is difficult to think of McCulloch writing this, since there is no evidence that he visited Ireland at that time. Again, in the same article, we find it stated that: 'Gratitude is one of the strongest marked traits in the Irish character.'[17] Similarly, in the 1825 article, we find the following passage:

> We know a Catholic parish in the south of Ireland with very nearly 10,000 inhabitants. Of these *one-sixteenth* part, or 625, only are Protestants, the remaining 9,375 being Catholics. The total amount of the dues and fees of all sorts paid to the Catholic priest, is about 240 l. a year, of which he pays 80 l. a year to an assistant. But this Catholic parish forms three Protestant parishes, and part of a fourth, the tithes of which taken together, amount to not less than 1600 l. a year; which,

> as there are very large tracts of grass land in the parish belonging to Protestants, fall almost wholly on the poor Catholic occupiers and cottiers, and occasion endless heartburnings and disputes.[18]

Again, there is no firm evidence that McCulloch was acquainted with any parishes in the south of Ireland at that date. At the same time it is true that he did visit Ireland in 1827.[19]

The article also contains lengthy quotation from the *Galway Advertiser* of 18 October 1822 about a petition against tithes.[20] This could, of course, have been supplied to McCulloch (who appears to have been soliciting material) by Parnell. McCulloch was in the habit of using his Parliamentary contacts to obtain information which he could use in his economic writings.[21] He had certainly requested Ricardo to obtain information about Ireland – indeed, some of this appears to have related to the first of the two disputed articles about Ireland.[22] On the other hand, the location of Parnell's constituency mentioned above may be relevant. Yet, even so, this might only support the view that the material originated with Parnell but was used by McCulloch.

In support of the possibility that Parnell was the author it should be noted that there is an apparent connection, pointed out to us by Professor W. E. Houghton of the *Wellesley Index*, between the second of the two disputed 'Ireland' articles and a subsequent *Edinburgh* article on Ireland which has not been claimed by anyone other than Parnell.[23] At three points[24] this article refers to the one of January 1825; but all three references are to one short section of the latter,[25] raising, at first sight, the possibiity that Parnell might be responsible for this section. However, a difficulty is immediately apparent; for as Table 7.1 shows, this section (I,2) contains material which had previously appeared in the *Scotsman*.

Indeed, the re-use of material from the *Scotsman* in the two disputed *Edinburgh Review* articles provides significant support for McCulloch's claim to authorship. For there is very substantial reproduction, in both *Edinburgh Review* articles, of material from the *Scotsman*. The details are shown in Table 7.2. In summary, the position is that 57 per cent of the first article can be traced to the *Scotsman*. 31 per cent of the second article can also be traced to the same newspaper. To put it another way, parts of the first *Edinburgh Review* article appeared in nine *Scotsman* articles; and parts of the second *Edinburgh Review* article also appeared in nine *Scotsman* articles. Since there is no evidence that Parnell ever contributed to the *Scotsman*, the link with McCulloch would seem to be clear.[26]

TABLE 7.1 Sections of *Edinburgh Review* 'Ireland' articles

*1822 Introduction, pp. 60–4**

I. Catholic Emanicipation, pp. 64–9*
II. Church Establishment and Tithes, pp. 69–79*
III. Government & Magistracy, pp. 79–87
IV. Education, pp. 87–94*
V. Revenue Laws, pp.94–103*
VI. Population, pp. 103–8*
Conclusion, p. 109.

1825 Introduction, pp. 356–60

I. [Causes of Political & Religious Discontent], pp. 360–83
  1. Catholic Disabilities, pp. 360–8
  2. Government & Magistracy, pp. 368–76*
  3. Church Establishment & Tithes, pp. 376–83*
II. [Causes of Irish Poverty], pp. 383–409
  [1.] [Population], pp. 383–8*
  [2.] [Causes of Population Increase]
    1. The Bounty Acts 1783, 1784, pp. 388–90*
    2. Gavelkind, pp. 390–9*
    3. The Forty Shilling Freehold, pp. 399–401*
    4. Education, pp. 404–5
    5. Commerce and Revenue, pp. 406–9
Conclusion, pp. 409–10*

* Indicates that the section contains material reproduced from the *Scotsman*.

The matter may be looked at in another way. The 1822 article is divided into an introduction and six sections; and material from the *Scotsman* appeared in the introduction and in five of the six sections. The 1825 article is divided and subdivided in a number of rather confusing ways; but it contains an introduction, and a conclusion, with the remainder divided into two halves with a number of subsections in each half. Of the three subsections in the first half, two contain material from the *Scotsman*. Of what are really six subsections in the second half, four contain material from the *Scotsman*, as does the conclusion. The details are shown in Table 7.1.

It should also be noted that there are clear links between the two disputed articles. Table 7.2 shows some of the overlap in the re-use of the material. Moreover, both articles end with exactly the same words. Speaking of the Irish connection with England, the articles both say that it will come to an end 'the instant it cannot be maintained *by force of arms*!'[27]

TABLE 7.2 *Scotsman* articles on Ireland

Scotsman articles on Ireland, 1820–4		*Edinburgh Review* re-use of the material*
8 April 1820	p. 113	65, 104–8
3 Feb. 1821	p. 37	–
3 Nov. 1821	p. 345	61–75, 101–2, 378
1 Dec. 1821	p. 380	–
8 Dec. 1821	pp. 388–9	61, 372–3
22 Dec. 1821	p. 401	70–7, 92–3
12 Jan. 1822	p. 9	–
19 Jan. 1822	p. 22	–
16 Feb. 1822	p. 52	–
18 May 1822	p. 153	94–5
22 June 1822	p. 196	–
27 June 1822	p. 201	70, 74–5, 376, 378, 381
7 Sept. 1822	p. 282	–
16 Nov. 1822	p. 363	–
15 Mar. 1823	p. 169	89–90, 90–1
22 Mar. 1823	p. 185	91, 91–3
17 May 1823	p. 317	–
19 July 1823	pp. 461–2	410
22 Oct. 1823	p. 673	–
3 July 1824	p. 507	104–6, 385–6, 387, 388
10 July 1824	p. 523	388–9, 390–1
31 July 1824	p. 571	399–401
4 Sept. 1824	p. 651	393–6, 397
4 Dec. 1824	p. 864	386–7

* Page numbers in the series 60–109 refer to the 1822 *E. R.* article. Page numbers in the series 356–410 refer to the 1825 *E. R.* article.

There is other internal evidence which would indicate that McCulloch was the author. Thus, at the beginning of 1822 article we find: 'It has been observed by Mr Hume, that there is, in human affairs, an extreme point of depression, from which they naturally begin to ascend in an opposite direction.' This is remarkably close to a passage from McCulloch's *Treatise on Taxation*, in which we find: 'But, as Hume has observed, there is an extreme point of depression in human affairs from which, when it has been attained, they begin to ascend.'[28] Another point of interest is that, as noted above, McCulloch had been soliciting material for the 1822 article. He approached Sir John Newport, through the good offices of Ricardo, and sought information about taxes and tax revenue in Ireland.[29] It is, then, particularly interesting that the 1822 article should contain [30] a quotation from Sir John Newport on precisely this point – the difficulty of raising taxes in Ireland because of its impoverished state. McCulloch drew on this for an earlier article on high and low taxes, and asked for more material from Newport for a forthcoming article on Ireland.[31]

The content of the 1825 article strongly suggests McCulloch's authorship. Thus it displays strenuous contempt for the leaders of the Catholic Association.[32] This contrasts remarkably with Parnell's speech of 10 February 1825,[33] which consisted of a lengthy and detailed defence of the Association. The 1825 article also contains material from Sir William Petty, which would suggest a connection with McCulloch, who was a pioneer economic bibliophile and historian of economic thought.[34] There is material in the 1825 article about primogeniture and the Scots system of indivisible leases, which is very much in accord with positions McCulloch developed elsewhere.[35] The article apparently accepts the importance of the forty shilling freehold argument, although it was noted above that Parnell did not think this an important matter while McCulloch regarded it as significant.[36] Finally, there is the style of the article, which seems clearly that of McCulloch – it is much stronger and less urbane than that of Parnell.

In this particular case, then, the historical evidence is extremely contradictory and confusing – though, despite the inconclusive nature of the evidence, it seems difficult to take Parnell's claim at its face value. In an attempt to shed further light on the matter, we have subjected to analysis the two disputed articles. For comparison, we relied upon the McCulloch material upon which we have drawn elsewhere in this study, and a number of Parnell items. We originally intended to use Parnell's three speeches referred to above: that of 24 June 1823 (about 11,500 words), that of 11 May 1824 (about 7,000 words), and that of 10 February 1825 (over 12,000 words) together with sections from Parnell's *History of the Penal Laws*[37] amounting to approximately 5,800 words; the 1820 *Edinburgh* article 'Finance', discussed below; and a section of his *Financial Reform*,[38] amounting to approximately 6,700 words. However, it proved necessary to discard the speeches, for reasons which will be discussed in part II of this chapter. As noted above, we also subjected the article in the November 1825 issue of the *Edinburgh Review*, 'Catholic Emancipation – . . . Divided Allegiance of the Catholics',[39] to analysis, both to test for internal consistency and also to try to establish whether either McCulloch or Parnell wrote it. We had about 6,300 words of this article available for analysis after deletion of extraneous matter, especially quotations.

We encountered some slight preliminary difficulties in the use of part of this material. 'By' is contextual in *Penal Laws* because sentences typically start with a phrase like 'By the Act of . . .'. For this reason, we could not use 'By' as a first word test. It would discriminate by showing Parnell's *Penal Laws* to be different from his other work, simply because of content, thus suggesting a different author where the same one was involved. Once we had found collocations which distinguished satisfactorily between acknowledged works of the two authors, while failing to produce any discrimination within the acknowledged work of one author, we could apply the resulting tests to different *sections* of the two long disputed articles, in an attempt to see whether the articles were in fact of joint authorship. It was necessary to take this preliminary step before proceeding to test whether they were in fact the work of one or other author alone.

(b) Finance

Our interest in the conflicting claims of McCulloch and Parnell to the authorship of the two *Edinburgh Review* articles on Ireland led to an investigation of the Parnell papers, as already noted. However, this investigation raised another problem. For it was discovered that, in his memorandum referred to above, Parnell also claimed authorship of the article 'Funding System – British Finances', which appeared in the *Review* for October 1823.[40] There has previously been no question that this article, which is of over 18,000 words in length, was by McCulloch. It is included in all four of the lists of his contributions referred to above. Both Fetter and the *Wellesley Index* give McCulloch as the author without any qualification. Moreover, this article also is explicitly claimed by McCulloch elsewhere.[41] Again, like the articles on Ireland, the majority of this article had previously appeared in the *Scotsman* newspaper. The details are shown in Table 7.3. In addition to this, the majority of the article, in turn, found its way into McCulloch's *Treatise on Taxation*.[42] Since McCulloch was not, so far as is known, a plagiarist, this would be important supporting evidence even if the material had not appeared in the *Scotsman*, *prior to* its appearance in the *Edinburgh Review*.

It is true that Parnell was keenly interested in finance at the time that the article appeared. Although his *On Financial Reform* did not appear until 1830, he had been concerned with the subject for more than ten years and in 1819 laid a series of 'Resolutions respecting the Retrenchment of the Publick Expenditure' (there were forty-seven in all) before the House of Commons. The last of these stated forcefully that there was

TABLE 7.3 *Scotsman* articles on finance

Scotsman	*Edinburgh Review*, October 1823 (corresponding passages in order occurring in *Scotsman*)
5 April 1823, pp. 217–8 'Finances of Great Britain–No. I. – Principles of the Funding System'	pp. 1–2, 7, 10, 6–7, 17, 3, 4, 4–5.
26 April 1823, p. 265 'Finances of Great Britain, No. II. – Progress and Present Amount of the Public Debt – Sinking Fund'	pp. 21–2, 22–3, 23, 31–2, 32, 34, 34–5.
10 May 1823, p. 297 'Finances of Great Britain, No. III. – Operation of the Sinking Fund since the Peace. – Present State of Revenue and Expenditure'	pp. 38–9, 39, 40, 41, 42.

considerable scope for reduction in public expenditure without any detriment to the public service.[43] Moreover, it does appear that Parnell contributed an earlier article on finance which both the *Wellesley Index* and Fetter failed to identify. We have tested this article – it is about 5,500 words long after deletion of tables and quotations – which appeared in 1820,[44] for consistency with Parnell's other writings and it appears to be by him.

Nevertheless, both the content and the style of the article of 1823, which is concerned with the National Debt, would seem to be so clearly from the pen of McCulloch that it is difficult to understand the basis for Parnell's claim to this article as well. However, we tested it against the writings of both Parnell and McCulloch.

II. STATISTICAL ANALYSIS

At an early stage in our attempt to throw light upon the conflicting historical evidence through statistical analysis, we encountered a difficulty. We found that, using all six of the works attributed to Parnell, it proved extremely difficult to find any consistent use of any of the literary habits which have proved so serviceable elsewhere in this study. In the light of our other successes with the technique of identifying consistently used habits within the work of one individual author, we found this outcome very surprising. We have accepted as a fundamental principle of this study that an author's work, proceeding from his own hand, exhibits characteristics of style, exemplified in choice of first words and in frequently used collocations, which are consistent. But in the case of Parnell we are confronted with an author whose work apparently falsifies this basic assumption. We may explain this outcome in several ways.

1. Parnell's writing may all be his own work, yet itself exhibit no consistently used habits. If this were true it would be a falsification of our fundamental premise.

2. Parnell's speeches, which had to be discarded almost at the outset of the statistical investigation, and which exemplify, in an extreme form, the difficulty we experienced in finding consistency within his work, may be distinct from his written work. This might be true either

(a) because he had been misreported in *Hansard*; or
(b) the spoken word is by its very nature quite different from the written word; or
(c) Parnell's speeches, in particular, were composed by another hand – 'ghosted'.

Possibility 1 can be rejected in the light of the evidence presented in the other chapters of this study. Possibility 2(a) can also be ruled out; the published – corrected – versions of Parnell's speeches, issued by Ridgway, were incorporated into *Hansard* in the case of two of the speeches used, and a published version of the 'Lord Althorp' speech was used, without reference to *Hansard*. Possibility 2(b) can also be ruled out on the grounds that we were able to use Torrens' speech in Chapter 4 and we were also able to use, with complete success, two speeches by Huskisson in Chapter 8. All this leaves us only with possibility 2(c). We have no direct evidence on this matter but, given the practice of 20th century politicians in the matter of speech writing, it is by no means inconceivable that Parnell employed a writer to whom he supplied material.

(a) First word usage

Having discarded Parnell's speeches, we conducted our analysis of first word usage on the remaining three works in our sample of his writings. We tried, as the most obvious candidate, the classification scheme utilised in our study of Torrens and McCulloch. This proved successful. The classification of first words was into the following categories: 'it';

'but'; 'the' or 'we'; 'in'; 'suppose' or 'this'; and 'all other first words'. Each contingency table thus has six rows. The summary results are presented in Table 7.4 and the details may be found in the contingency Tables 7.5(i) to 7.5(xvii).

From the first two rows of Table 7.4 it is clear that the works of both Parnell and McCulloch exhibit internal consistency in the choice of first word, yielding computed χ^2 values of 5.92 and 6.68 respectively, comfortably within the 95 per cent critical value (with 10 degrees of freedom) of 18.31. The next four rows of the table indicate that we may safely conclude that each of the disputed articles is internally consistent in its choice of first words. For each of these tests, there are five degrees of freedom, which sets the 95 per cent critical value at 11.07; but the highest computed χ^2 value is 5.96 ('Finance' 1823) and the other tests yield values of 5.43 ('Ireland' 1825), 4.69 ('Divided Allegiance'), and 2.07 ('Ireland' 1822). In the case of the two articles on Ireland we were able to test the internal consistency with particular care, as they both contained sections with material which had appeared in the *Scotsman* and other sections of which this was not true.[45] It is important to note that this classification discriminates well between the two possible authors; row 7 of Table 7.4 and Table 7.5(vii), show that the computed χ^2 of 36.58 resulting from comparing their habits in choice of first word exceeds even the critical value of 16.75 found at the 99.5 per cent point of the χ^2 distribution.

In the light of all this, it is particularly interesting to discover that habits in first word usage indicate that the four disputed articles were not from the same pen (row 8). We reject the hypothesis of consistency between them at a 1 per cent level of significance. This result becomes even more interesting when we realise that the computed χ^2 value of 30.58 is the result of the observations produced from analysis of the article 'Divided Allegiance' – see Table 7.5(viii). On omitting these observations, in order to examine the hypothesis of consistency in usage between the remaining three articles, we obtain a computed χ^2 of only 7.92, which is well below the relevant (95 per cent) critical value of 18.31. We are thus, even at this stage, presented with the interesting conclusion that the two articles on Ireland and the 1823 article on Finance proceeded from the same pen, whereas 'Divided Allegiance' was written by some other hand.

Given that three of the four articles are the work of one author, the next stage is to test for authorship by comparing first word usage with the work of Parnell and McCulloch. It is immediately apparent (Table 7.4 row 10) that Parnell did not write the 1822 paper – the possibility of

TABLE 7.4 First word usage

Texts analysed	X^2	d.f.	$\chi^2_{0.95}$	*Decision*	*Maximum type I error (where applicable)*	*Contingency table*
Penal Laws vs *Financial Reform* vs 'Finance' 1820	5.92	10	18.31	Accept the hypothesis of Parnell's internal consistency	–	7.5(i)
Principles vs 'Machinery' vs *Taxation*	6.68	10	18.31	Accept the hypothesis of McCulloch's internal consistency	–	7.5(ii)
'Ireland' 1822 internally	2.07	5	11.07	Accept the hypothesis of the internal consistency of 'Ireland' 1822	–	7.5(iii)
'Ireland' 1825 internally	5.43	5	11.07	Accept the hypothesis of the internal consistency of 'Ireland' 1825	–	7.5(iv) See also 7.5(xviii)
'Finance' 1823 internally	5.96	5	11.07	Accept the hypothesis of the internal consistency of 'Finance' 1823	–	7.5(v)
'Divided Allegiance' internally	4.69	5	11.07	Accept the hypothesis of the internal consistency of 'Divided Allegiance'	–	7.5(vi)
Parnell vs McCulloch	36.58	5	11.07	Reject the hypothesis of consistency between Parnell and McCulloch	0.005	7.5(vii)
'Ireland' 1822 vs 'Ireland' 1825 vs 'Finance' 1823 vs 'Divided Allegiance'	30.58	15	25.00	Reject the hypothesis of overall consistency between the four disputed articles	0.01	7.5(viii)

'Ireland' 1822 vs 'Ireland' 1825 vs 'Finance' 1823	7.92	10	18.31	Accept the hypothesis of consistency between the three named disputed articles	–	7.5(ix)
'Ireland' 1822 vs Parnell	17.93	5	11.07	Reject the hypothesis of consistency between Parnell and 'Ireland' 1822	0.005	7.5(x)
'Ireland' 1822 vs McCulloch	9.70	5	11.07	Accept the hypothesis of consistency between McCulloch and 'Ireland' 1822	–	7.5(xi)
'Ireland' 1825 vs Parnell	13.46	5	11.07	Reject the hypothesis of consistency between Parnell and 'Ireland' 1825	0.025	7.5(xii)
'Ireland' 1825 vs McCulloch	9.30	5	11.07	Accept the hypothesis of consistency between McCulloch and 'Ireland' 1825	–	7.5(xiii)
'Finance' 1823 vs Parnell	24.37	5	11.07	Reject the hypothesis of consistency between Parnell and 'Finance' 1823	0.005	7.5(xiv)
'Finance' 1823 vs McCulloch	1.59	5	11.07	Accept the hypothesis of consistency between McCulloch and 'Finance' 1823	–	7.5(xv)
'Divided Allegiance' vs Parnell	22.14	5	11.07	Reject the hypothesis of consistency between Parnell and 'Divided Allegiance'	0.005	7.5(xvi)
'Divided Allegiance' vs McCulloch	21.56	5	11.07	Reject the hypothesis of consistency between McCulloch and 'Divided Allegiance'	0.005	7.5(xvii)

TABLE 7.5 Contingency tables – first word usage

(i) Parnell

Penal Laws		*Financial Reform*		'Finance' 1820		
5	(6.71)	7	(7.98)	11	(8.31)	23
10	(6.41)	7	(7.63)	5	(7.95)	22
24	(23.33)	26	(27.76)	30	(28.92)	80
8	(7.00)	8	(8.33)	8	(8.67)	24
2	(3.21)	5	(3.82)	4	(3.98)	11
72	(74.35)	91	(88.48)	92	(92.17)	255
121		144		150		415

$X^2 = 5.92, \quad \chi^2_{10, 0.95} = 18.31.$

(ii) McCulloch

Principles		'Machinery'		*Taxation*		
23	(25.23)	32	(30.75)	43	(43.02)	98
30	(27.29)	35	(33.26)	41	(45.45)	106
40	(35.79)	49	(43.61)	50	(59.60)	139
15	(12.62)	12	(15.37)	22	(21.01)	49
8	(9.01)	12	(10.98)	15	(15.01)	35
99	(105.05)	122	(128.02)	187	(174.93)	408
215		262		358		835

$X^2 = 6.68, \quad \chi^2_{10, 0.95} = 18.31.$

(iii) 'Ireland' 1822

pp. 79–87		Remainder		
6	(6.03)	36	(35.97)	42
5	(7.60)	48	(45.40)	53
18	(14.49)	83	(86.51)	101
3	(2.87)	17	(17.13)	20
2	(2.01)	12	(11.99)	14
34	(35.00)	210	(209.00)	244
68		406		474

$X^2 = 2.07, \quad \chi^2_{5, 0.95} = 11.07.$

TABLE 7.5 (*contd.*)

(iv) 'Ireland' 1825 pp. 356–83		pp. 383–410		
19	(17.17)	18	(19.83)	37
22	(20.88)	23	(24.12)	45
40	(35.72)	37	(41.28)	77
6	(10.67)	17	(12.33)	23
4	(3.71)	4	(4.29)	8
102	(104.85)	124	(121.15)	226
193		223		416

$X^2 = 5.43, \quad \chi^2_{5,\,0.95} = 11.07.$

(v) 'Finance' 1823 Material used in *Scotsman*		Remainder		
14	(14.00)	16	(16.00)	30
18	(17.73)	20	(20.27)	38
17	(23.33)	33	(26.67)	50
7	(5.60)	5	(6.40)	12
8	(5.60)	4	(6.40)	12
69	(66.73)	74	(76.27)	143
133		152		285

$X^2 = 5.96, \quad \chi^2_{5,\,0.95} = 11.07.$

(vi) 'Divided Allegiance' pp. 125–45		pp. 145–63		
8	(5.90)	3	(5.10)	11
7	(8.59)	9	(7.41)	16
5	(4.29)	3	(3.71)	8
8	(6.44)	4	(5.56)	12
0	(0.54)	1	(0.46)	1
45	(47.24)	43	(40.76)	88
73		63		136

$X^2 = 4.69, \quad \chi^2_{5,\,0.95} = 11.07.$

TABLE 7.5 (*contd.*)

(vii)

Parnell		McCulloch		
23	(40.17)	98	(80.83)	121
22	(42.50)	106	(85.50)	128
80	(72.71)	139	(146.29)	219
24	(24.24)	49	(48.76)	73
11	(15.27)	35	(30.73)	46
255	(220.12)	408	(442.88)	663
415		835		1250

$X^2 = 36.58, \quad \chi^2_{5, 0.995} = 16.75.$

(viii)

'Ireland' 1822		'Ireland' 1825		'Finance' 1823		'Divided Allegiance'		
42	(43.39)	37	(38.08)	30	(26.09)	11	(12.45)	12
53	(54.96)	45	(48.23)	38	(33.04)	16	(15.77)	15
101	(85.33)	77	(74.89)	50	(51.30)	8	(24.48)	23
20	(24.22)	23	(21.26)	12	(14.57)	12	(6.95)	6
14	(12.65)	8	(11.11)	12	(7.61)	1	(3.63)	3
244	(253.45)	226	(222.44)	143	(152.39)	88	(72.72)	70
474		416		285		136		131

$X^2 = 30.58, \quad \chi^2_{15, 0.99} = 30.58.$

(ix)

'Ireland' 1822		'Ireland' 1825		'Finance' 1823		
42	(43.97)	37	(38.59)	30	(26.44)	109
53	(54.86)	45	(48.15)	38	(32.99)	136
101	(91.98)	77	(80.72)	50	(55.30)	228
20	(22.19)	23	(19.47)	12	(13.34)	55
14	(13.72)	8	(12.04)	12	(8.25)	34
244	(247.29)	226	(217.03)	143	(148.69)	613
474		416		285		1175

$X^2 = 7.92, \quad \chi^2_{10, 0.95} = 18.31.$

TABLE 7.5 (*contd.*)

(x)

'Ireland' 1822		Parnell		
42	(34.66)	23	(30.34)	65
53	(39.99)	22	(35.01)	75
101	(96.51)	80	(84.49)	181
20	(23.46)	24	(20.54)	44
14	(13.33)	11	(11.67)	25
244	(266.06)	255	(232.94)	499
474		415		889

$X^2 = 17.93, \quad \chi^2_{5,0.995} = 16.75.$

(xi)

'Ireland' 1822		McCulloch		
42	(50.70)	98	(89.30)	140
53	(57.58)	106	(101.42)	159
101	(86.91)	139	(153.09)	240
20	(24.99)	49	(44.01)	69
14	(17.74)	35	(31.26)	49
244	(236.09)	408	(415.91)	652
474		835		1309

$X^2 - 9.70, \quad \chi^2_{5,0.95} - 11.07.$

(xii)

'Ireland' 1825		Parnell		
37	(30.04)	23	(29.96)	60
45	(33.54)	22	(33.46)	67
77	(78.59)	80	(78.41)	157
23	(23.53)	24	(23.47)	47
8	(9.51)	11	(9.49)	19
226	(240.79)	255	(240.21)	481
416		415		831

$X^2 = 13.46, \quad \chi^2_{5,0.975} = 12.83.$

TABLE 7.5 (*contd.*)

(xiii) 'Ireland' 1825		McCulloch		
37	(44.89)	98	(90.11)	135
45	(50.21)	106	(100.79)	151
77	(71.83)	139	(144.17)	216
23	(23.94)	49	(48.06)	72
8	(14.30)	35	(28.70)	43
226	(210.83)	408	(423.17)	634
416		835		1251

$X^2 = 9.30, \quad \chi^2_{5,0.95} = 11.07.$

(xiv) 'Finance' 1823		Parnell		
30	(21.58)	23	(31.42)	53
38	(24.43)	22	(35.57)	60
50	(52.93)	80	(77.07)	130
12	(14.66)	24	(21.34)	36
12	(9.36)	11	(13.64)	23
143	(162.04)	255	(235.96)	398
285		415		700

$X^2 = 24.37, \quad \chi^2_{5,0.995} = 16.75.$

(xv) 'Finance' 1823		McCulloch		
30	(32.57)	98	(95.43)	128
38	(36.64)	106	(107.36)	144
50	(48.09)	139	(140.91)	189
12	(15.52)	49	(45.48)	61
12	(11.96)	35	(35.04)	47
143	(140.21)	408	(410.79)	551
285		835		1120

$X^2 = 1.59, \quad \chi^2_{5,0.95} = 11.07.$

TABLE 7.5 (*contd.*)

(xvi) 'Divided Allegiance'		Parnell		
11	(8.39)	23	(25.61)	34
16	(9.38)	22	(28.62)	38
8	(21.72)	80	(66.28)	88
12	(8.89)	24	(27.11)	36
1	(2.96)	11	(9.04)	12
88	(84.66)	255	(258.34)	343
136		415		551

$X^2 = 22.14, \quad \chi^2_{5,0.995} = 16.75.$

(xvii) 'Divided Allegiance'		McCulloch		
11	(15.27)	98	(93.73)	109
16	(17.09)	106	(104.91)	122
8	(20.59)	139	(126.41)	147
12	(8.54)	49	(52.46)	61
1	(5.04)	35	(30.96)	36
88	(69.47)	408	(426.53)	496
136		835		971

$X^2 = 21.56, \quad \chi^2_{5,0.995} = 16.75.$

(xviii) 'Ireland' 1825 pp. 360–8, 404–9		Remainder		
7	(10.23)	30	(26.77)	37
16	(12.44)	29	(32.56)	45
26	(21.29)	51	(55.71)	77
3	(6.36)	20	(16.64)	23
1	(2.21)	7	(5.79)	8
62	(62.48)	164	(163.52)	226
115		301		416

$X^2 = 7.63, \quad \chi^2_{5,0.95} = 11.07.$

Parnell being the author being rejected with a type I error of only 0.5 per cent, given that the computed χ^2 value is 17.93 compared with a 99.5 per cent critical value of 16.75. At the same time, we can accept the hypothesis of McCulloch's authorship since in his case the computed χ^2 is only 9.70. A similar result may be obtained for the 1825 article on Ireland. We can reject Parnell's claims to have written it, with a type I error of only 2.5 per cent (Table 7.4 row 12) and find no difficulty in accepting that McCulloch was the author. The conclusion regarding the 1823 Finance paper is even stronger (Table 7.4 row 14). The type I error in rejecting Parnell as the author is only 0.5 per cent, for the computed χ^2 value is 24.37, which contrasts sharply with a comparison between the article in question and McCulloch's writings which yields a computed χ^2 of only 1.59.

However, we reject *both* McCulloch and Parnell as the authors of 'Divided Allegiance'. The χ^2 values are high and rejection is at 0.5 per cent in both cases. This is a highly significant and interesting result; we did not expect to find that 'Divided Allegiance' was from the pen of McCulloch, but we did expect to find that it was by Parnell. The clear indication, on this test, that it is not his work, deepens the mystery about his writings.

In summary, then, our tests on habits of first word usage indicate that Parnell did not write any of the four anonymously written articles. The type I errors are only 0.5 per cent, 2.5 per cent, 0.5 per cent, and 0.5 per cent respectively. We accept the hypothesis that McCulloch wrote all but the article 'Divided Allegiance'. That he did not write the latter seems clear; but that he was involved in the other three disputed articles seems difficult to doubt.

(b) Collocations with 'the'

An attempt to use habits in the choice of collocations with 'the' as a means of establishing evidence on authorship proved to be extremely difficult in this case, in contrast with our experiences elsewhere. Again, the problem encountered was inconsistency on the part of Parnell. While McCulloch's works exhibit fairly consistent usage of numerous collocations, it proved very difficult to obtain sets of collocations within Parnell's works which would both show him to be consistent and yet still retain the power to discriminate between his work and that of McCulloch. The obvious starting point was to use the highly aggregated classification of Chapter 4, which analysed Torrens and McCulloch; but it failed.

In this case, the problem was that the level of aggregation was so high that it was impossible to distinguish between McCulloch and Parnell. Many other amalgamations were tried but these failed, either because they were also unsuccessful in achieving discrimination between the work of these two authors, or because Parnell's usage exhibited internal inconsistency. We were forced to discard so many possible classifications of collocations with 'the' because of inconsistency within work apparently written by Parnell, *even* after we had omitted his speeches from our sample, that we were led to speculate that Parnell's employment of literary assistance may not have been confined to the writing of his parliamentary speeches. (The matter is discussed further in the Appendix to this chapter.)

However, finding ourselves forced to discard possible collocation amalgamations because of Parnell's inconsistencies, the possibility arose that the clear evidence of Parnell's own inconsistency might itself prove useful. The usual approach taken in the investigations reported in this study has been to find those habits which are used consistently by each possible author, which discriminate between possible authors, and which are used consistently by the author of the particular anonymous text in which we are interested. We are then able to make comparisons between the characteristics displayed by an anonymous author and those displayed by known authors who might have been responsible for a disputed piece. However, an alternative approach, which builds upon *in*consistency by one author, may be formulated. Exactly what is involved will become clear as a result of an examination of Table 7.6, which is based upon the detailed contingency tables 7.7(i) to 7.7(xii).

We used collocations of 'the' with: 'with'; 'from'; 'and' or 'if'; 'of' or 'in'; 'which' or 'as'; 'on' or 'upon' or 'that' or 'by'; and 'all other collocations with the'.

This set of collocations enabled us to establish quite clearly that McCulloch's work is internally consistent in the choice of collocations with 'the'. The computed χ^2 value is 14.19, well below the critical 95 per cent value (with 12 degrees of freedom) of 21.03. However, this classification scheme serves only to illustrate Parnell's internal inconsistency. The computed χ^2 value of 20.58 is significant at 6 per cent – in rejecting the hypothesis that the author of work attributed to Parnell was consistent in the choice of collocations with 'the', the probability of our making an error is no larger than 6 per cent. Our usual approach would indicate that at this point we should stop and examine alternative collocations; instead we shall make use of this inconsistency.

Each of the four disputed texts is internally consistent using this

TABLE 7.6 Collocations with 'the' – Parnell inconsistent

Texts analysed	X^2	d.f.	$\chi^2_{0.95}$	*Decision*	*Maximum type I error (where applicable)*	*Contingency table*
Penal Laws vs *Financial Reform* vs 'Finance' 1820	20.58	12	20.37*	Reject the hypothesis of Parnell's internal consistency	0.06	7.7(i)
Principles vs 'Machinery' vs *Taxation*	14.19	12	21.03	Accept the hypothesis of McCulloch's internal consistency	–	7.7(ii)
'Ireland' 1822 internally	8.32	6	12.59	Accept the hypothesis of the internal consistency of 'Ireland' 1822	–	7.7(iii)
'Ireland' 1825 internally	10.41	6	12.59	Accept the hypothesis of the internal consistency of 'Ireland' 1825.	–	7.7(iv) See also 7.7(xiii)
'Finance' 1823 internally	3.86	6	12.59	Accept the hypothesis of the internal consistency of 'Finance' 1823	–	7.7(v)
'Divided Allegiance' internally	5.09	6	12.59	Accept the hypothesis of the internal consistency of 'Divided Allegiance'	–	7.7(vi)
Parnell vs McCulloch				N/A		
'Ireland' 1822 vs 'Ireland' 1825 vs 'Finance' 1823 vs 'Divided Allegiance'	32.61	18	28.87	Reject the hypothesis of overall consistency between the four disputed articles	0.025	7.7(vii)
'Ireland' 1822 vs 'Ireland' 1825 vs 'Finance' 1823	11.76	12	21.03	Accept the hypothesis of the consistency between the three named disputed articles	–	7.7(viii)
'Ireland' 1822 vs Parnell				N/A		
'Ireland' 1822 vs McCulloch	10.24	6	12.59	Accept the hypothesis of consistency between McCulloch and 'Ireland' 1822	–	7.7(ix)

'Ireland' 1825 vs Parnell				N/A		
'Ireland' 1825 vs McCulloch	9.84	6	12.59	Accept the hypothesis of consistency between McCulloch and 'Ireland' 1825	–	7.7(x)
'Finance' 1823 vs Parnell				N/A		
'Finance' 1823 vs McCulloch	7.36	6	12.59	Accept the hypothesis of consistency between McCulloch and 'Finance' 1823	–	7.7(xi)
'Divided Allegiance' vs Parnell				N/A		
'Divided Allegiance' vs McCulloch	13.57	6	12.59	Reject the hypothesis of consistency between McCulloch and 'Divided Allegiance'	0.04	7.7(xii)

* 20.37 is the $\chi^2_{12,0.94}$ value.

TABLE 7.7 Contingency tables – collocations with 'the' – Parnell inconsistent

(i) Parnell

Penal Laws		*Financial Reform*		'Finance' 1820		
5	(5.32)	9	(5.69)	2	(4.99)	16
12	(11.97)	7	(12.80)	17	(11.23)	36
21	(20.62)	20	(22.04)	21	(19.35)	62
126	(134.67)	157	(143.94)	122	(126.39)	405
18	(13.63)	18	(14.57)	5	(12.80)	41
71	(63.18)	62	(67.53)	57	(59.29)	190
284	(287.62)	301	(307.44)	280	(269.94)	865
537		574		504		1615

$X^2 = 20.58, \quad \chi^2_{12,\,0.94} = 20.37.$

(ii) McCulloch

Principles		'Machinery'		*Taxation*		
7	(10.38)	15	(13.39)	21	(19.23)	43
6	(10.14)	13	(13.08)	23	(18.79)	42
22	(20.03)	29	(25.84)	32	(37.12)	83
142	(143.37)	197	(184.94)	255	(265.69)	594
8	(11.34)	16	(14.63)	23	(21.02)	47
62	(63.96)	67	(82.51)	136	(118.53)	265
291	(278.78)	357	(359.61)	507	(516.62)	1155
538		694		997		2229

$X^2 = 14.19, \quad \chi^2_{12,\,0.95} = 21.03.$

(iii) 'Ireland' 1822

pp. 79–87		Remainder		
4	(4.72)	24	(23.28)	28
6	(6.40)	32	(31.60)	38
10	(12.47)	64	(61.53)	74
71	(64.55)	312	(318.45)	383
7	(5.22)	24	(25.78)	31
13	(23.60)	127	(116.40)	140
129	(123.03)	601	(606.97)	730
240		1184		1424

$X^2 = 8.32, \quad \chi^2_{6,\,0.95} = 12.59.$

TABLE 7.7 (*contd.*)

(iv) 'Ireland' 1825

pp. 356–83		pp. 383–410		
12	(8.35)	7	(10.65)	19
13	(16.69)	25	(21.31)	38
30	(31.19)	41	(39.81)	71
192	(187.56)	235	(239.44)	427
21	(15.81)	15	(20.19)	36
59	(69.40)	99	(88.60)	158
331	(329.00)	418	(420.00)	749
658		840		1498

$X^2 = 10.41, \quad \chi^2_{6,\,0.95} = 12.59.$

(v) 'Finance' 1823

Material used in *Scotsman*		Remainder		
6	(6.53)	8	(7.47)	14
13	(14.46)	18	(16.54)	31
21	(20.52)	23	(23.48)	44
155	(159.52)	187	(182.48)	342
6	(9.33)	14	(10.67)	20
70	(64.37)	68	(73.63)	138
278	(274.27)	310	(313.73)	588
549		628		1177

$X^2 = 3.86, \quad \chi^2_{6,\,0.95} = 12.59.$

(vi) 'Divided Allegiance'

pp. 125–45		pp. 145–63		
5	(5.40)	5	(4.60)	10
2	(4.32)	6	(3.68)	8
13	(11.34)	8	(9.66)	21
107	(101.00)	80	(86.00)	187
7	(8.64)	9	(7.36)	16
48	(50.77)	46	(43.23)	94
148	(148.53)	127	(126.47)	275
330		281		611

$X^2 = 5.09, \quad \chi^2_{6,\,0.95} = 12.59.$

TABLE 7.7 (*contd.*)

(vii)

'Ireland' 1822		'Ireland' 1825		'Finance' 1823		'Divided Allegiance'		
28	(21.47)	19	(22.58)	14	(17.74)	10	(9.21)	71
38	(34.77)	38	(36.58)	31	(28.74)	8	(14.92)	115
74	(63.49)	71	(66.79)	44	(52.48)	21	(27.24)	210
383	(404.83)	427	(425.86)	342	(334.61)	187	(173.70)	1339
31	(31.14)	36	(32.76)	20	(25.74)	16	(13.36)	103
140	(160.24)	158	(168.56)	138	(132.44)	94	(68.75)	530
730	(708.07)	749	(744.87)	588	(585.25)	275	(303.81)	2342
1424		1498		1177		611		4710

$X^2 = 32.61$, $\chi^2_{18,0.975} = 31.53$.

(viii)

'Ireland' 1822		'Ireland' 1825		'Finance' 1823		
28	(21.19)	19	(22.29)	14	(17.52)	61
38	(37.17)	38	(39.10)	31	(30.72)	107
74	(65.66)	71	(69.07)	44	(54.27)	189
383	(400.21)	427	(421.00)	342	(330.79)	1152
31	(30.22)	36	(31.79)	20	(24.98)	87
140	(151.47)	158	(159.34)	138	(125.19)	436
730	(718.08)	749	(755.40)	588	(593.53)	2067
1424		1498		1177		4099

$X^2 = 11.76$, $\chi^2_{12,0.95} = 21.03$.

(ix)

'Ireland' 1822		McCulloch		
28	(27.68)	43	(43.32)	71
38	(31.19)	42	(48.81)	80
74	(61.20)	83	(95.80)	157
383	(380.85)	594	(596.15)	977
31	(30.41)	47	(47.59)	78
140	(157.88)	265	(247.12)	405
730	(734.80)	1155	(1150.20)	1885
1424		2229		3653

$X^2 = 10.24$, $\chi^2_{6,0.95} = 12.59$.

TABLE 7.7 (*contd.*)

(x)

'Ireland' 1825		McCulloch		
19	(24.92)	43	(37.08)	62
38	(32.15)	42	(47.85)	80
71	(61.90)	83	(92.10)	154
427	(410.37)	594	(610.63)	1021
36	(33.36)	47	(49.64)	83
158	(170.02)	265	(252.98)	423
749	(765.28)	1155	(1138.72)	1904
1498		2229		3727

$X^2 = 9.84, \quad \chi^2_{6,\,0.95} = 12.59.$

(xi)

'Finance' 1823		McCulloch		
14	(19.70)	43	(37.30)	57
31	(25.23)	42	(47.77)	73
44	(43.89)	83	(83.11)	127
342	(323.45)	594	(612.55)	936
20	(23.15)	47	(43.85)	67
138	(139.26)	265	(263.74)	403
588	(602.32)	1155	(1140.68)	1743
1177		2229		3406

$X^2 = 7.36, \quad \chi^2_{6,\,0.95} = 12.59.$

(xii)

'Divided Allegiance'		McCulloch		
10	(11.40)	43	(41.60)	53
8	(10.76)	42	(39.24)	50
21	(22.37)	83	(81.63)	104
187	(168.02)	594	(612.97)	781
16	(13.55)	47	(49.45)	63
94	(77.24)	265	(281.76)	359
275	(307.65)	1155	(1122.35)	1430
611		2229		2840

$X^2 = 13.57, \quad \chi^2_{6,\,0.96} = 13.19.$

TABLE 7.7 (*contd.*)

(xiii) 'Ireland' 1825 pp. 360–8, 404–9		Remainder		
5	(5.16)	14	(13.84)	19
9	(10.32)	29	(27.68)	38
16	(19.29)	55	(51.71)	71
113	(116.01)	314	(310.99)	427
12	(9.78)	24	(26.22)	36
56	(42.93)	102	(115.07)	158
196	(203.50)	553	(545.50)	749
407		1091		1498

$X^2 = 7.65, \quad \chi^2_{6,\,0.95} = 12.59.$

classification (Table 7.6 rows 2 to 6), all of the computed χ^2 values being well below the 95 per cent critical value, with 6 degrees of freedom, of 12.59.[46] Again, it is clear that they were not all by the same hand – the computed χ^2 value of 32.61 exceeds even the 97.5 per cent critical value of 31.53. However, as with our tests of first word usage, it is also clear that the two papers on Ireland and that on Finance did proceed from the same hand – dropping the observations resulting from 'Divided Allegiance' reduces the computed χ^2 figure to 11.76, which is well below the 95 per cent critical value (with 12 degrees of freedom) of 21.03. Again, as with tests on first word usage, we find that McCulloch's works are consistent in their choice of collocations with 'the', with both of the articles on Ireland and the 1823 paper on Finance, while it is also clear that he was not responsible for 'Divided Allegiance'. The computed χ^2 values are 10.24, 9.84, 7.36 and 13.57 respectively. The 95 per cent critical value of 12.59 is exceeded only by the last of these figures.

This evidence may be interpreted as support for the view that McCulloch, and not Parnell, was the author of three of the disputed articles. For, using the collocation tables with seven rows, we are able to illustrate McCulloch's internal consistency, while failing (at a 6 per cent significance level) to find consistency in Parnell's work. But we have also found that each of the disputed papers is internally consistent. But if each of the disputed papers is internally consistent, whereas Parnell is inconsistent, this suggests that Parnell was not the author of any of the disputed papers. On the basis of his own observed *inconsistencies*, we should expect to find, were Parnell the author, the same degree of internal inconsistency within and between the disputed texts. Since, however, we find the disputed texts to be highly consistent internally, *and* also find three of them to be consistent with each other, it seems perfectly reasonable to conclude that Parnell was not the author of any of them. We are able to arrive at this conclusion on two grounds. On the one hand, we are not able to obtain consistency between Parnell's own works with these groups of collocations, yet we obtain consistency between three of the four disputed articles. On the other hand, there is the striking result, reported in Tables 7.13(i) to 7.13(iii) in the Appendix to this chapter, that it is remarkably hard to find consistency even within published works of Parnell taken on their own, a problem that we certainly did not experience with the disputed articles. Taken in conjunction with our results concerning McCulloch and the disputed texts, we arrive, as a result of our analysis of collocations with 'the', at the same result as we reached after analysing first word usage; the evidence is entirely consistent with McCulloch having been the author of the two articles on Ireland and the 1823 article on Finance; it is inconsistent with his having written 'Divided Allegiance', and it is inconsistent with Parnell having been responsible for *any* of these articles.

Of course, we cannot compare the work of Parnell and McCulloch using collocations with 'the', for the simple reason that we have no consistent pattern within Parnell's work. Thus it is that some of the rows of Table 7.6 are blank.

Some supplementary evidence may, however, be gathered by using a higher level of aggregation of data obtained from collocations with 'the'. The results of our tests on this basis are presented in Table 7.8 in summary form, which is based upon the contingency tables 7.9(i) to 7.9(xvii). For the construction of these tests, we used an amalgamation of collocations which produced five rows in the contingency tables. They were collocations with 'the' of: 'if' or 'which'; 'with' or 'from'; 'that' or 'by'; 'and' or 'as' or 'in' or 'to' or 'at' or 'for'; and 'all other collocations with the'.

With the data obtained from collocations with 'the' amalgamated to such an extent, we are able to make Parnell, as well as McCulloch, consistent. The computed χ^2 values are 6.71 and 9.77, both of which are well below the 95 per cent critical value of 15.51. Again, the four disputed texts exhibit internal consistency – with 4 degrees of freedom the 95 per cent critical value is 9.49, whereas the computed χ^2 values are 1.55 ('Ireland' 1822), 3.48 ('Ireland' 1825), 4.31 ('Finance' 1823) and 5.72 ('Divided Allegiance' 1825).[47] With these amalgamations of data we are able to obtain discrimination between the work of Parnell and McCulloch; the computed χ^2 is 9.13, which is significant at 6 per cent. This is a quite acceptable level of discrimination. These same amalgamations yield a result like that of our previous tests; the possibility that

TABLE 7.8 Collocations with 'the' – Parnell consistent

Texts analysed	X^2	d.f.	$\chi^2_{0.95}$	*Decision*	*Maximum type I error (where applicable)*	*Contingency table*
Penal Laws vs *Financial Reform* vs 'Finance' 1820	6.71	8	15.51	Accept the hypothesis of Parnell's internal consistency	–	7.9(i)
Principles vs 'Machinery' vs *Taxation*	9.77	8	15.51	Accept the hypothesis of McCulloch's internal consistency	–	7.9(ii)
'Ireland' 1822 internally	1.55	4	9.49	Accept the hypothesis of the internal consistency of 'Ireland' 1822	–	7.9(iii)
'Ireland' 1825 internally	3.48	4	9.49	Accept the hypothesis of the internal consistency of 'Ireland' 1825	–	7.9(iv) See also 7.9(xviii)
'Finance' 1823 internally	4.31	4	9.49	Accept the hypothesis of the internal consistency of 'Finance' 1823	–	7.9(v)
'Divided Allegiance' internally	5.72	4	9.49	Accept the hypothesis of the internal consistency of 'Divided Allegiance'	–	7.9(vi)
Parnell vs McCulloch	9.13	4	9.04*	Reject the hypothesis of consistency between Parnell and McCulloch	0.06	7.9(vii)
'Ireland' 1822 vs 'Ireland' 1825 vs 'Finance' 1823 vs 'Divided Allegiance'	34.00	12	21.03	Reject the hypothesis of overall consistency between the four disputed articles	0.005	7.9(viii)
'Ireland' 1822 vs 'Ireland' 1825 vs 'Finance' 1823	8.02	8	15.51	Accept the hypothesis of consistency between the three named articles	–	7.9(ix)

'Ireland' 1822 vs Parnell	10.22	4	9.49	Reject the hypothesis of consistency between Parnell and 'Ireland' 1822	0.04	7.9(x)
'Ireland' 1822 vs McCulloch	1.64	4	9.49	Accept the hypothesis of consistency between McCulloch and 'Ireland' 1822	–	7.9(xi)
'Ireland' 1825 vs Parnell	7.02	4	6.73**	Reject the hypothesis of consistency between Parnell and 'Ireland' 1825	0.14	7.9(xii)
'Ireland' 1825 vs McCulloch	5.61	4	9.49	Accept the hypothesis of consistency between McCulloch and 'Ireland' 1825	–	7.9(xiii)
'Finance' 1823 vs Parnell	6.18	4	5.99***	Reject the hypothesis. of consistency between Parnell and 'Finance' 1823	0.19	7.9(xiv)
'Finance' 1823 vs McCulloch	1.44	4	9.49	Accept the hypothesis of consistency between McCulloch and 'Finance' 1823	–	7.9(xv)
'Divided Allegiance' vs Parnell	15.73	4	9.49	Reject the hypothesis of consistency between Parnell and 'Divided Allegiance'	0.005	7.9(xvi)
'Divided Allegiance' vs McCulloch	20.76	4	9.49	Reject the hypothesis of consistency between McCulloch and 'Divided Allegiance'	0.005	7.9(xvii)

* 9.04 is the $\chi^2_{4,\,0.94}$ value.
** 6.73 is the $\chi^2_{4,\,0.85}$ value.
*** 5.99 is the $\chi^2_{4,\,0.80}$ value.

TABLE 7.9 Contingency tables – collocations with 'the' – Parnell consistent

(i) Parnell

Penal Laws		*Financial Reform*		'Finance' 1820		
12	(13.30)	19	(14.22)	9	(12.48)	40
17	(17.29)	16	(18.48)	19	(16.23)	52
47	(40.23)	35	(43.01)	39	(37.76)	121
118	(117.04)	129	(125.11)	105	(109.85)	352
343	(349.13)	375	(373.19)	332	(327.68)	1050
537		574		504		1615

$X^2 = 6.71, \quad \chi^2_{8,0.95} = 15.51.$

(ii) McCulloch

Principles		'Machinery'		*Taxation*		
10	(10.38)	16	(13.39)	17	(19.23)	43
13	(20.52)	28	(26.46)	44	(38.02)	85
44	(37.17)	46	(47.95)	64	(68.88)	154
153	(136.61)	169	(176.22)	244	(253.16)	566
318	(333.32)	435	(429.97)	628	(617.70)	1381
538		694		997		2229

$X^2 = 9.77, \quad \chi^2_{8,0.95} = 15.51.$

(iii) 'Ireland' 1822

pp. 79–87		Remainder		
6	(4.89)	23	(24.11)	29
10	(11.12)	56	(54.88)	66
13	(15.84)	81	(78.16)	94
57	(60.17)	300	(296.83)	357
154	(147.98)	724	(730.02)	878
240		1184		1424

$X^2 = 1.55, \quad \chi^2_{4,0.95} = 9.49.$

TABLE 7.9 (*contd.*)

(iv) 'Ireland' 1825

pp. 356–83		pp. 383–410		
11	(10.12)	12	(12.88)	23
25	(25.08)	32	(31.92)	57
34	(40.03)	57	(50.97)	91
143	(151.77)	202	(193.23)	345
446	(432.00)	536	(550.00)	982
659		839		1498

$X^2 = 3.48, \quad \chi^2_{4,0.95} = 9.49.$

(v) 'Finance' 1823

Material used in *Scotsman*		Remainder		
10	(8.40)	8	(9.60)	18
19	(20.99)	26	(24.01)	45
49	(41.05)	39	(46.95)	88
128	(133.87)	159	(153.13)	287
343	(344.70)	396	(394.30)	739
549		628		1177

$X^2 = 4.31, \quad \chi^2_{4,0.95} = 9.49.$

(vi) 'Divided Allegiance'

pp. 125–45		pp. 145–63		
5	(4.32)	3	(3.68)	8
7	(9.72)	11	(8.28)	18
39	(40.51)	36	(34.49)	75
85	(74.53)	53	(63.47)	138
194	(200.92)	178	(171.08)	372
330		281		611

$X^2 = 5.72, \quad \chi^2_{4,0.95} = 9.49.$

(vii)

Parnell		McCulloch		
40	(34.87)	43	(48.13)	83
52	(57.56)	85	(79.44)	137
121	(115.54)	154	(159.46)	275
352	(385.68)	566	(532.32)	918
1050	(1021.35)	1381	(1409.65)	2431
1615		2229		3844

$X^2 = 9.13, \quad \chi^2_{4,0.94} = 9.04.$

TABLE 7.9 (*contd.*)

(viii)

'Ireland' 1822		'Ireland' 1825		'Finance' 1823		'Divided Allegiance'		
29	(23.58)	23	(24.81)	18	(19.49)	8	(10.12)	78
66	(56.23)	57	(59.16)	45	(46.48)	18	(24.13)	186
94	(105.21)	91	(110.68)	88	(86.96)	75	(45.14)	348
357	(340.73)	345	(358.44)	287	(281.63)	138	(146.20)	1127
878	(898.24)	982	(944.92)	739	(742.43)	372	(385.41)	2971
1424		1498		1177		611		4710

$X^2 = 34.00$, $\chi^2_{12, 0.995} = 28.30$.

(ix)

'Ireland' 1822		'Ireland' 1825		'Divided Allegiance'		
29	(24.32)	23	(25.58)	18	(20.10)	70
66	(58.36)	57	(61.40)	45	(48.24)	168
94	(94.84)	91	(99.77)	88	(78.39)	273
357	(343.58)	345	(361.43)	287	(283.98)	989
878	(902.90)	982	(949.82)	739	(746.29)	2599
1424		1498		1177		4099

$X^2 = 8.02$, $\chi^2_{8, 0.95} = 15.51$.

(x)

'Ireland' 1822		Parnell		
29	(32.33)	40	(36.67)	69
66	(55.29)	52	(62.71)	118
94	(100.74)	121	(114.26)	215
357	(332.22)	352	(376.78)	709
878	(903.41)	1050	(1024.59)	1928
1424		1615		3039

$X^2 = 10.22$, $\chi^2_{4, 0.96} = 10.02$.

TABLE 7.9 (*contd.*)

(xi)

'Ireland' 1822		McCulloch		
29	(28.07)	43	(43.93)	72
66	(58.86)	85	(92.14)	151
94	(96.67)	154	(151.33)	248
357	(359.80)	566	(563.20)	923
878	(880.60)	1381	(1378.40)	2259
1424		2229		3653

$X^2 = 1.64, \quad \chi^2_{4,0.95} = 9.49.$

(xii)

'Ireland' 1825		Parnell		
23	(30.32)	40	(32.68)	63
57	(52.45)	52	(56.55)	109
91	(102.02)	121	(109.98)	212
345	(335.40)	352	(361.60)	697
982	(977.81)	1050	(1054.19)	2032
1498		1615		3113

$X^2 = 7.02, \quad \chi^2_{4,0.86} = 6.91.$

(xiii)

'Ireland' 1825		McCulloch		
23	(26.53)	43	(39.47)	66
57	(57.07)	85	(84.93)	142
91	(98.47)	154	(146.53)	245
345	(366.16)	566	(544.84)	911
982	(949.76)	1381	(1413.24)	2363
1498		2229		3727

$X^2 = 5.61, \quad \chi^2_{4,0.95} = 9.49.$

TABLE 7.9 (*contd.*)

(xiv)

'Finance' 1823		Parnell		
18	(24.45)	40	(33.55)	58
45	(40.89)	52	(56.11)	97
88	(88.11)	121	(120.89)	209
287	(269.38)	352	(369.62)	639
739	(754.17)	1050	(1034.83)	1789
1177		1615		2792

$X^2 = 6.18$, $\chi^2_{4,\,0.81} = 6.12$.

(xv)

'Finance' 1823		McCulloch		
18	(21.08)	43	(39.92)	61
45	(44.92)	85	(85.08)	130
88	(83.63)	154	(158.37)	242
287	(294.77)	566	(558.23)	853
739	(732.60)	1381	(1387.40)	2120
1177		2229		3406

$X^2 = 1.44$, $\chi^2_{4,\,0.95} = 9.49$.

(xvi)

'Divided Allegiance'		Parnell		
8	(13.18)	40	(34.82)	48
18	(19.21)	52	(50.79)	70
75	(53.80)	121	(142.20)	196
138	(134.50)	352	(355.50)	490
372	(390.32)	1050	(1031.68)	1422
611		1615		2226

$X^2 = 15.73$, $\chi^2_{4,\,0.995} = 14.86$.

TABLE 7.9 *(contd.)*

(xvii)

'Divided Allegiance'		McCulloch		
8	(10.97)	43	(40.03)	51
18	(22.16)	85	(80.84)	103
75	(49.27)	154	(179.73)	229
138	(151.46)	566	(552.54)	704
372	(377.14)	1381	(1375.86)	1753
611		2229		2840

$X^2 = 20.76, \quad \chi^2_{4,\,0.995} = 14.86.$

(xviii) 'Ireland' 1825

pp. 360–8, 404–9		Remainder		
5	(6.25)	18	(16.75)	23
14	(15.49)	43	(41.51)	57
32	(24.72)	59	(66.28)	91
87	(93.73)	258	(251.27)	345
269	(266.81)	713	(715.19)	982
407		1091		1498

$X^2 = 4.17, \quad \chi^2_{4,\,0.95} = 9.49.$

the four disputed texts were from the same pen is strongly rejected, with a computed χ^2 value of 34.00 which exceeds even the 99.5 per cent critical value of 28.30. It is again clear, however, that three of the disputed articles are consistent – the computed χ^2, once we drop the observations from 'Divided Allegiance', is only 8.02, well below the 95 per cent critical value of 15.51.

We can now test directly the possibility that Parnell wrote the disputed articles. Row 10 of Table 7.8 shows that his claim to have written the 1822 paper on Ireland may be rejected at a 4 per cent significance level, with a computed χ^2 value of 10.22. At the same time, it is clear, as it was with our previous tests, that we may accept that McCulloch wrote this piece, since the computed χ^2 value in his case is only 1.64. The result obtained from analysis of the data from the 1825 article on Ireland is less clear cut. A comparison with Parnell's work yields a computed χ^2 value of 7.02, while the corresponding figure for McCulloch's work is 5.61. While this evidence provides support for the hypothesis of McCulloch's authorship, the 86 per cent value of the relevant χ^2 distribution is 6.91, which means that there is a possibility of error of up to 14 per cent in rejecting Parnell as the author. This is an uncomfortably large type I error and the test would not, on its own, be very strong evidence. However, taken in conjunction with results of our other tests, this result is persuasive; and we may note that if, on the other hand, we were to reject the hypothesis of consistency between McCulloch's work and the 1825 article on Ireland, the probability of error would be 0.24, which is some 70 per cent greater than the corresponding figure for Parnell.

With this degree of amalgamation of the data, the evidence still clearly favours McCulloch as the author of the 1823 article on Finance. The computed χ^2 in his case is only 1.44, whereas in Parnell's case it is 6.18. Nevertheless, the rejection of Parnell is again not strong, with a maximum type I error of 0.19, which would, on its own, be only weakly persuasive. But taken in conjunction with our other evidence, with which it is entirely consistent, it seems quite clear that the article was McCulloch's and not Parnell's.

The results obtained from these tests for the article 'Divided Allegiance' are also consistent with our previous results. It seems clear that neither Parnell nor McCulloch wrote the article and, even with this degree of amalgamation, we may reject both possible authors with a type I error of only 0.5 per cent.

In this section of the chapter we have, then, approached the analysis of data from collocations with 'the' in two different ways. On the one hand, we are enabled to reject Parnell's claims to the authorship of any one of the disputed articles because each of them displays internal consistency on classification schemes for collocations with 'the' which serve also to demonstrate Parnell's own inconsistency, while three of them also show consistency with each other. At the same time, McCulloch's work, like the disputed articles, displays internal consistency and it is consistent with three of the texts under consideration, although not with 'Divided Allegiance'. This leads us to reject McCulloch as the author of the latter, but to accept the hypothesis that he was responsible for the two articles on Ireland and the one on Finance.

On the other hand, we have used a higher level of aggregation, which enables us to find some consistency within Parnell's published work – at least if we exclude his speeches – and to discriminate between his work and that of McCulloch. This same level of aggregation still enables us to reject the hypothesis that one hand was responsible for all four disputed texts, but to conclude that the statistical evidence is consistent with McCulloch having been responsible for three of them. We also conclude that Parnell wrote none of them, although, while we are able, at this level of aggregation, to reject his claim to authorship of the first 'Ireland' article and 'Divided Allegiance' with type I errors of, at most, 4 per cent and 0.5 per cent respectively, the high level of aggregation does not permit us to obtain such strong conclusions with respect to the second article on Ireland and the article on Finance. But the relative weakening of the results is due only to the extraordinary inconsistency of Parnell's own work, a matter which we are unable satisfactorily to explain. Even the weak results, however, point in the same direction as the strong results and we are simply not able to accept Parnell's claim to authorship of any of the disputed articles.

(c) Collocations with 'be'

Our analysis of collocations with 'be' proceeded along somewhat similar lines to those detailed in the previous section of this chapter. We used the following four sets of collocations with 'be': 'should' or 'would' or 'must'; 'to' or 'can' or 'may'; 'shall' or 'need' or 'noun'; 'could' or 'will' or 'might'. This is an exhaustive set of collocations with 'be'. From the data produced by this classification we obtained the results summarised in Table 7.10 which is based upon the detailed contingency tables 7.11(i) to 7.11(xii). Once again, we find that Parnell is internally *inconsistent*, while McCulloch is consistent, the computed χ^2 values being 14.78 and 10.09 respectively, while the 95 per cent critical value is 12.59. Once again, the rejection of consistent usage by Parnell is strong; the maximum type I error is only 2.5 per cent. This same classification also enables us to conclude that the four disputed texts are each internally consistent, with computed χ^2 values of 0.08 ('Ireland' 1822), 3.78 ('Ireland' 1825), 3.33 ('Finance' 1823) and 6.03 ('Divided Allegiance' 1825). Not one of these values exceeds the 95 per cent critical value of 7.81.[48] Analogously with the argument in the previous section, therefore, we feel able to interpret such consistency, taken in conjuction with consistency between three of the articles, as being itself *prima facie* inconsistent with the possibility that Parnell wrote the articles. Again, as in the case of collocations with 'the', it is a combination of consistency between three of the disputed articles (which we are unable to find parallelled in Parnell's own works) together with the internal consistency of *each* of the disputed pieces taken on its own (in contrast to Parnell's works taken on their own, as Tables 7.13(iv) to 7.13 (vi) in the Appendix to this chapter indicate) which lead to this conclusion.

As with our previous tests, it is clear that one hand was not responsible for all four articles (the computed χ^2 is 28.51, whereas the 99.5 per cent critical value is only 16.92); but it does again seem clear that one hand was

TABLE 7.10 Collocations with 'be' – Parnell inconsistent

Texts analysed	X^2	d.f.	$\chi^2_{0.95}$	*Decision*	*Maximum type I error (where applicable)*	*Contingency table*
Penal Laws vs *Financial Reform* vs 'Finance' 1820	14.78	6	12.59	Reject the hypothesis of Parnell's internal consistency	0.025	7.11(i)
Principles vs 'Machinery' vs *Taxation*	10.09	6	12.59	Accept the hypothesis of McCulloch's internal consistency	–	7.11(ii)
'Ireland' 1822 internally	0.08	3	7.81	Accept the hypothesis of the internal consistency of 'Ireland' 1822	–	7.11(iii)
'Ireland' 1825 internally	3.78	3	7.81	Accept the hypothesis of the internal consistency of 'Ireland' 1825	–	7.11(iv) See also 7.11(xiii)
'Finance' 1823 internally	3.33	3	7.81	Accept the hypothesis of the internal consistency of 'Finance' 1823	–	7.11(v)
'Divided Allegiance' internally	6.03	3	7.81	Accept the hypothesis of the internal consistency of 'Divided Allegiance'	–	7.11(vi)
Parnell vs McCulloch				N/A		
'Ireland' 1822 vs 'Ireland' 1825 vs 'Finance' 1823 vs 'Divided Allegiance'	28.51	9	16.92	Reject the hypothesis of overall consistency between the four disputed articles	0.005	7.11(vii)
'Ireland' 1822 vs 'Ireland' 1825 vs 'Finance' 1823	5.63	6	12.59	Accept the hypothesis of consistency between the three named disputed articles	–	7.11(viii)

'Ireland' 1822 vs Parnell				N/A		
'Ireland' 1822 vs McCulloch	1.87	3	7.81	Accept the hypothesis of consistency between McCulloch and 'Ireland' 1822	–	7.11(ix)
'Ireland' 1825 vs Parnell				N/A		
'Ireland' 1825 vs McCulloch	4.08	3	7.81	Accept the hypothesis of consistency between McCulloch and 'Ireland' 1825	–	7.11(x)
'Finance' 1823 vs Parnell				N/A		
'Finance' 1823 vs McCulloch	5.10	3	7.81	Accept the hypothesis of consistency between McCulloch and 'Finance' 1823	–	7.11(xi)
'Divided Allegiance' vs Parnell				N/A		
'Divided Allegiance' vs McCulloch	31.10	3	7.81	Reject the hypothesis of consistency between McCulloch and 'Divided Allegiance'	0.005	7.11(xii)

TABLE 7.11 Contingency tables – collocations with 'be' – Parnell inconsistent

(i) Parnell

Penal Laws		*Financial Reform*		'Finance' 1820		
15	(16.96)	38	(40.45)	39	(34.58)	92
21	(22.31)	61	(53.21)	39	(45.48)	121
10	(4.79)	4	(11.43)	12	(9.77)	26
6	(7.93)	21	(18.91)	16	(16.16)	43
52		124		106		282

$X^2 = 14.78, \quad \chi^2_{6,\,0.975} = 14.45.$

(ii) McCulloch

Principles		'Machinery'		*Taxation*		
64	(66.35)	96	(82.19)	75	(86.47)	235
52	(53.08)	56	(65.75)	80	(69.17)	188
16	(15.25)	14	(18.89)	24	(19.87)	54
23	(20.33)	26	(25.18)	23	(26.49)	72
155		192		202		549

$X^2 = 10.09, \quad \chi^2_{6,\,0.95} = 12.59.$

(iii) 'Ireland' 1822

pp. 79–87		Remainder		
14	(14.44)	66	(65.56)	80
15	(14.62)	66	(66.38)	81
3	(3.25)	15	(14.75)	18
5	(4.69)	21	(21.31)	26
37		168		205

$X^2 = 0.08, \quad \chi^2_{3,\,0.95} = 7.81.$

TABLE 7.11 (*contd.*)

(iv) 'Ireland' 1825

pp. 356–83		pp. 383–410		
57	(49.54)	49	(56.46)	106
43	(45.80)	55	(52.20)	98
10	(10.75)	13	(12.25)	23
19	(22.90)	30	(26.10)	49
129		147		276

$X^2 = 3.78, \quad \chi^2_{3,\,0.95} = 7.81.$

(v) 'Finance' 1823

Material used in *Scotsman*		Remainder		
20	(24.63)	43	(38.37)	63
30	(25.42)	35	(39.58)	65
4	(3.13)	4	(4.87)	8
7	(7.82)	13	(12.18)	20
61		95		156

$X^2 = 3.33, \quad \chi^2_{3,\,0.95} = 7.81.$

(vi) 'Divided Allegiance'

pp. 125–45		pp. 145–63		
6	(8.04)	7	(4.96)	13
34	(30.92)	16	(19.08)	50
3	(1.86)	0	(1.14)	3
4	(6.18)	6	(3.82)	10
47		29		76

$X^2 = 6.03, \quad \chi^2_{3,\,0.95} = 7.81.$

(vii)

'Ireland' 1822	'Ireland' 1825	'Finance' 1823	'Divided Allegiance'	
80 (75.33)	106 (101.42)	63 (57.32)	13 (27.93)	262
81 (84.53)	98 (113.81)	65 (64.33)	50 (31.34)	294
18 (14.95)	23 (20.13)	8 (11.38)	3 (5.54)	52
26 (30.19)	49 (40.65)	20 (22.97)	10 (11.19)	105
205	276	156	76	713

$X^2 = 28.51, \quad \chi^2_{9,\,0.995} = 23.95.$

TABLE 7.11 (*contd.*)

(viii)

'Ireland' 1822		'Ireland' 1825		'Finance' 1823		
80	(80.13)	106	(107.89)	63	(60.98)	249
81	(78.52)	98	(105.72)	65	(59.76)	244
18	(15.77)	23	(21.23)	8	(12.00)	49
26	(30.57)	49	(41.16)	20	(23.27)	95
205		276		156		637

$X^2 = 5.63, \quad \chi^2_{6,\,0.95} = 12.59.$

(ix)

'Ireland' 1822		McCulloch		
80	(85.64)	235	(229.36)	315
81	(73.14)	188	(195.86)	269
18	(19.58)	54	(52.42)	72
26	(26.64)	72	(71.36)	98
205		549		754

$X^2 = 1.87, \quad \chi^2_{3,\,0.95} = 7.81.$

(x)

'Ireland' 1825		McCulloch		
106	(114.08)	235	(226.92)	341
98	(95.68)	188	(190.32)	286
23	(25.76)	54	(51.24)	77
49	(40.48)	72	(80.52)	121
276		549		825

$X^2 = 4.08, \quad \chi^2_{3,\,0.95} = 7.81.$

(xi)

'Finance' 1823		McCulloch		
63	(65.94)	235	(232.06)	298
65	(55.98)	188	(197.02)	253
8	(13.72)	54	(48.28)	62
20	(20.36)	72	(71.64)	92
156		549		705

$X^2 = 5.10, \quad \chi^2_{3,\,0.95} = 7.81.$

TABLE 7.11 (*contd.*)

(xii) 'Divided Allegiance'		McCulloch		
13	(30.16)	235	(217.84)	248
50	(28.94)	188	(209.06)	238
3	(6.93)	54	(50.07)	57
10	(9.97)	72	(72.03)	82
76		549		625

$X^2 = 31.10, \quad \chi^2_{3,\,0.995} = 12.84.$

(xiii) 'Ireland' 1825 pp. 360–8, 404–9		Remainder		
13	(17.67)	93	(88.33)	106
20	(16.33)	78	(81.67)	98
2	(3.83)	21	(19.17)	23
11	(8.17)	38	(40.83)	49
46		230		276

$X^2 = 4.70, \quad \chi^2_{3,\,0.95} = 7.82.$

responsible for three of the articles, only 'Divided Allegiance' coming from another hand, for when we remove the observations relating to this article, the computed χ^2 value falls to 5.63 compared with a critical 95 per cent value of 12.59. Once again, we find that McCulloch's style in coupling words with 'be' is entirely consistent with that of the three papers which do seem to be from one pen, but it is wholly inconsistent with the style of 'Divided Allegiance', for the computed χ^2 values are 1.87, 4.08, 5.10 and no less than 31.10 respectively, and these values may be compared with a critical 95 per cent point of 7.81. Again the maximum probability of error in rejecting McCulloch as the author of 'Divided Allegiance' is only 0.5 per cent.

When we amalgamate the data sufficiently to produce consistency within the work of Parnell, it still leaves McCulloch consistent, but fails to discriminate between the work of the two authors. The results of our attempts to pursue this path are summarised in Table 7.12. The detailed contingency tables upon which this is based are not included as they provide little extra information in this particular case. The classification of collocations with 'be' is: 'would' or 'shall' or 'to' or 'must' or 'noun' or

TABLE 7.12 Collocations with 'be' – Parnell consistent

Texts analysed	X^2	d.f.	$\chi^2_{0.95}$	*Decision*	*Maximum type I error (where applicable)*
Penal Laws vs Financial Reform vs 'Finance' 1820	1.78	4	9.49	Accept the hypothesis of Parnell's internal consistency	–
Principles vs 'Machinery' vs *Taxation*	7.91	4	9.49	Accept the hypothesis of McCulloch's internal consistency	–
'Ireland' 1822 internally	4.17	2	5.99	Accept the hypothesis of the internal consistency of 'Ireland' 1822	–
'Ireland' 1825 internally	1.90	2	5.99	Accept the hypothesis of the internal consistency of 'Ireland' 1825	–
'Finance' 1823 internally	4.07	2	5.99	Accept the hypothesis of the internal consistency of 'Finance' 1823	–
'Divided Allegiance' internally	4.26	2	5.99	Accept the hypothesis of the internal consistency of 'Divided Allegiance'	–
Parnell vs McCulloch	0.92	2	5.99	Accept (fail to reject) the hypothesis of consistency between Parnell and McCulloch	–
'Ireland' 1822 vs 'Ireland' 1825 vs 'Finance' 1823 vs 'Divided Allegiance'	4.67	6	12.59	Accept the hypothesis of overall consistency between the four disputed articles	–
'Ireland' 1822 vs 'Ireland' 1825 vs 'Finance' 1823	4.14	4	9.49	Accept the hypothesis of consistency between the three named articles	–

'Ireland' 1822 vs Parnell	1.00	2	5.99	Accept the hypothesis of consistency between Parnell and 'Ireland' 1822	–
'Ireland' 1822 vs McCulloch	1.20	2	5.99	Accept the hypothesis of consistency between McCulloch and 'Ireland' 1822	–
'Ireland' 1825 vs Parnell	0.80	2	5.99	Accept the hypothesis of consistency between Parnell and 'Ireland' 1825	–
'Ireland' 1825 vs McCulloch	3,16	2	5.99	Accept the hypothesis of consistency between McCulloch and 'Ireland' 1825	–
'Finance' 1823 vs Parnell	0.62	2	5.99	Accept the hypothesis of consistency between Parnell and 'Finance' 1823	–
'Finance' 1823 vs McCulloch	0.62	2	5.99	Accept the hypothesis of consistency between McCulloch and 'Finance' 1823	–
'Divided Allegiance' vs Parnell	0.40	2	5.99	Accept the hypothesis of consistency between Parnell and 'Divided Allegiance'	–
'Divided Allegiance' vs McCulloch	0.03	2	5.99	Accept the hypothesis of consistency between McCulloch and 'Divided Allegiance'	–

'need'; 'should' or 'can' or 'may'; 'could' or 'will' or 'might'. As is apparent from Table 7.12, we have had to aggregate so highly in order to produce consistency within the work to which Parnell's name is attached that we have lost all power of discrimination. We are unable to discriminate between the work of Parnell and of McCulloch and we are unable to reject the claim of either of them to have written any of the disputed articles. Statistical analysis at this level of amalgamation has not helped. But it is important to record one fact. In our search for a suitable classification scheme we have *never* found a set of amalgamations of collocations which both exhibited consistency within the work of McCulloch, consistency within the disputed pieces, *and* let to a rejection of his claims to have written either of the articles on Ireland or that on Finance. Thus we have not encountered any evidence either with collocations with 'be' or with collocations with 'the' which casts any doubt whatever upon the conclusions of this chapter.

III. CONCLUSION

The statistical analysis in this chapter leads us to conclude that the habits of style in choice of first words and in collocations with 'the' and 'be' exhibited in the two articles on Ireland of 1822 and 1825 and the article on Finance of 1823 are wholly compatible with those exhibited in the work of McCulloch. The habits exhibited within the article 'Divided Allegiance' are not, however, compatible with his work. Nor, however, are they consistent with the work of Parnell, in so far as we have been able to find any consistency within the latter. Parnell's habits, *when consistent*, are not compatible with any one of the four disputed texts except at a level of aggregation so high that all discrimination is lost, and when their inconsistency is made clear, and not glossed over by a high level of amalgamation, his literary habits are not consistent with any of the disputed articles, which display not only considerable internal consistency but, in the case of three of them, remarkable consistency with each other. The statistical evidence is, thus, itself inconsistent with Parnell's claim to authorship of any of the articles. It is entirely consistent with McCulloch's claims to the authorship of those three of the four articles which he did, in fact, claim. On the authorship of the fourth article, 'Divided Allegiance', we can throw little light. The Copinger list is clearly at fault; and we simply do not know who wrote the article.

APPENDIX

The difficulties which we encountered in obtaining any consistency between different works appearing from the pen of Sir Henry Parnell, led us to investigate the internal consistency of samples of *single* works appearing under his name. The results of this investigation are presented in Tables 7.13(i) to 7.13(vi). As will be apparent from the discussion in Chapter 7, the inconsistency of texts attributed to Parnell is chiefly manifested in the use of collocations with 'the' and with 'be'. Our primary aim in examining the internal consistency of samples of single works by Parnell, was to attempt to discover whether there was any contrast between the very high level of internal consistency exhibited by the four disputed articles discussed in this chapter and Parnell's own work. As will be apparent from the discussion above, the results of such a comparison provide support for the view that Parnell could not have written any of the disputed articles. But the very process of investigating Parnell's internal consistency *within* one work also gives particular interest to the question of Parnell's methods of composition.

For it is clear that Parnell's work, even when we take single pieces, exhibits clear signs of inconsistency. Thus, when we examine collocations with 'the', it would appear that *Penal Laws* is, if we are prepared to admit a type I error of 17 per cent, internally inconsistent. This represents quite a large type I error; but it does suggest that obtaining consistency within this particular work of Parnell is not easy. The section from *Financial Reform* is internally consistent but the *Edinburgh Review* article of 1820 'Finance' is also inconsistent in the use of collocations with 'the'. Table 7.13(iii) exhibits, however, low expected values for four of its 14 cells. If we amalgamate rows 1 and 5 to eliminate this problem (in which case only 2 of 12 cells would have low expected values, which is an acceptable proportion), the computed χ^2 rises to 11.80, which is to be compared with a $\chi^2_{5,\,0.95}$ of 11.07. We are thus enabled to reject the hypothesis of internal consistency in this particular case with a type I error no large than 5 per cent.

Further indications of inconsistency can be obtained from an examination of collocations with 'be'. *Penal Laws* once again suggests some internal inconsistency; the computed χ^2 of 10.10 exceeds the 97.5 per cent critical value of 9.35. The evidence of inconsistency here seems really very strong. However, 4 of the 8 cells in the contingency Table 7.13(iv) have low expected values. We can correct this by amalgamating rows 3 and 4 of the table. We then obtain a computed χ^2 of 9.26 which may be compared with the 99 per cent critical value of the χ^2 distribution,

TABLE 7.13 Contingency tables

(i) Collocations with 'the' – Parnell, *Penal Laws*

pp. 1–21		pp. 21–61		
4	(2.27)	1	(2.73)	5
3	(5.45)	9	(6.55)	12
9	(9.54)	12	(11.46)	21
64	(57.25)	62	(68.75)	126
5	(8.18)	13	(9.82)	18
28	(32.26)	43	(38.74)	71
131	(129.04)	153	(154.96)	284
244		293		537

$X^2 = 9.30, \quad \chi^2_{6,\,0.83} = 9.21.$

(ii) Collocations with 'the' – Parnell, *Financial Reform*

pp. 71–94		pp. 94–109		
3	(4.70)	6	(4.30)	9
2	(3.66)	5	(3.34)	7
8	(10.45)	12	(9.55)	20
87	(82.06)	70	(74.94)	157
10	(9.41)	8	(8.59)	18
36	(32.40)	26	(29.60)	62
154	(157.32)	147	(143.68)	301
300		274		574

$X^2 = 5.76, \quad \chi^2_{6,\,0.95} = 12.59.$

(iii) Collocations with 'the' – Parnell, 'Finance' 1820

pp. 55–61		pp. 61–9		
0	(0.85)	2	(1.15)	2
10	(7.18)	7	(9.82)	17
7	(8.88)	14	(12.12)	21
61	(51.56)	61	(70.44)	122
0	(2.11)	5	(2.89)	5
25	(24.09)	32	(32.91)	57
110	(118.33)	170	(161.67)	280
213		291		504

$X^2 = 11.79, \quad \chi^2_{6,\,0.92} = 11.44.$

TABLE 7.13 (*contd.*)

(iv) Collocations with 'be' – Parnell, *Penal Laws*

pp. 1–21		pp. 21–61		
9	(4.90)	6	(10.10)	15
6	(6.87)	15	(14.13)	21
0	(3.27)	10	(6.73)	10
2	(1.96)	4	(4.04)	6
17		35		52

$X^2 = 10.10, \quad \chi^2_{3,\,0.975} = 9.35.$

(v) Collocations with 'be' – Parnell, *Financial Reform*

pp. 71–94		pp. 94–109		
15	(14.71)	23	(23.29)	38
22	(23.61)	39	(37.39)	61
2	(1.55)	2	(2.45)	4
9	(8.13)	12	(12.87)	21
48		76		124

$X^2 = 0.56, \quad \chi^2_{3,\,0.95} = 7.81.$

(vi) Collocations with 'be' – Parnell, 'Finance' 1820

pp. 55–61		pp. 61–9		
8	(10.67)	31	(28.33)	39
14	(10.67)	25	(28.33)	39
2	(3.28)	10	(8.72)	12
5	(4.38)	11	(11.62)	16
29		77		106

$X^2 = 3.16, \quad \chi^2_{3,\,0.95} = 7.81.$

with 2 degrees of freedom, which is 9.21. However, the other two Parnell pieces are each internally consistent in the use of collocations with 'be'.

In summary, then, *Penal Laws* is internally inconsistent using both sets of collocations with type I errors of 17 per cent and $2\frac{1}{2}$ per cent respectively. While *Financial Reform* is internally consistent on both tests, 'Finance' 1820 exhibits signs of inconsistency in the use of collocations with 'the'.

Thus, at least on the basis of this limited investigation, there are questions about the internal consistency of each of Parnell's works examined individually. Taken in conjunction with the pronounced difficulty in finding consistency between his works, we should like, tentatively, to advance the following hypothesis. We would suggest that Parnell was in the habit of accumulating material for a publication or a speech and then entrusting the process of writing to another hand, subsequently correcting and amending the draft presented to him. If this were his habitual method of working, it might explain how it was that he came to claim authorship of articles which it is quite clear he did not write but for which he may have supplied some (in these particular cases rather limited) material to McCulloch. It would also explain how the inconsistency noted above between the references to the Catholic Association in Parliament by Parnell, and those in the *Edinburgh Review*, arose. Such a hypothesis is the only one consistent with all the evidence available to us in connection with Parnell's claims and published works. We have no direct evidence beyond that detailed in this chapter and it is possible (although we do not think it is likely) that a larger scale investigation of the statistical characteristics of Parnell's works might lead to different conclusions. We can advance our hypothesis about Parnell's method of working only tentatively; but on the evidence so far available it does seem to be at least plausible.

8 William Huskisson and the Authorship of the *Essays on Political Economy*, 1830

I. HISTORICAL BACKGROUND

In 1830 Longman's published a volume entitled *Essays on Political Economy: in which are illustrated The Principal Causes of the Present National Distress; with Appropriate Remedies*. There are fifteen essays in all, as well as a preliminary discussion and a conclusion. They are:

1. On the motives to industry
2. On security of property
3. On improvements in the productive powers of labour
4. On currency in general, and particularly coin
5. On paper currency
6. On the importation and exportation of gold and silver
7. On variations in the value of gold and silver
8. On the origin and increase of capital
9. On the employment of capital generally, its division and value
10. On the different employments of capital
11. On the employment of capital in agriculture, mines, and fisheries
12. On the employment of capital in manufactures
13. On the employment of capital in commerce
14. On mercantile shipping
15. On supply and demand

The *Essays* have been republished[1] with an admirable introduction by Professor G. S. L. Tucker who re-discovered the work in about 1953.[2] Tucker provided excellent summaries of the contents of the essays and, as a result of detective work over a long period, produced a convincing case concerning the probable authorship.

The analytical apparatus used in the essays is basically that of Adam Smith. In particular, a reader will notice the emphasis on the generation of an agricultural surplus, as in Adam Smith's 'natural order of development';[3] the idea that the comforts of the mass of the people measure wealth;[4] the idea that economic development takes place alongside water in the first instance, as in Smith;[5] the fact that the material on self-interest and the allocation of capital reads very much like Smith;[6] that the advantages of trade are in the form of an opportunity cost statement but of *absolute* advantage;[7] the presence of the Smithian welfare judgement that the interests of (less numerous) producers are outweighed by the interests of (more numerous) consumers;[8] the fact that the free trade case is Smithian,[9] although it is exceedingly well done; and the general innocence of the Ricardian preconceptions and apparatus which the author of these *Essays* manifests. It is true that Adam Smith's sectoral ranking of investment, with agriculture at the top, is rejected,[10] but this was quite normal in post-Smithian writers who otherwise adhered to his apparatus.

Another noticeable feature is the very strong and repeated condemnation of the Corn Laws.[11] Tucker sees this as one of the keys to the putative author's desire for anonymity, as the same person had been much more ambiguous about the Corn Laws in Parliament.

There are some strange contrasts within the *Essays*. On the one hand, the author seems to have been influenced remarkably little by post-Smithian writing and, indeed, to be hostile to some of it. Thus, for instance, we find a condemnation of the Ricardian idea that wages adjust to taxation.[12] Similarly, although this was published in 1830, the author is either ignorant of, or resistant to, the principle of 'metallic' fluctuation of a mixed paper and metallic currency and instead appears to favour[13] a *fixed* amount of paper currency, determined by Parliament. Yet, despite this lack of reliance on the work of other writers, the range and grasp of the essays, particularly in dealing with monetary matters, is remarkable. In particular, Essay VII shows a detailed, and at times subtle, knowledge of the working of the foreign exchange markets and of the internal and external markets for the precious metals. Essays VI and VII contain an outstanding account, for the period, of the operation of the Gold Standard in practice. There is also an excellent discussion[14] of internal and external economies of scale, with particular emphasis on the development of entrepreneurial and manufacturing skills.

It is true that the analytical grasp sometimes seems to be of varying strength. One comment by the author[15] suggests that he himself had an imperfect understanding of the transfer mechanism in international trade. Yet elsewhere, notably in Essay VIII,[16] he seems to understand it perfectly well.

In fact, one of the most interesting things about this book of essays is that it shows how a highly intelligent and observant man, well-grounded in Adam Smith but who otherwise, despite detailed knowledge of the Bullion and Resumption Committees of 1810 and 1819,[17] shows little sign of extensive reading in the subject – indeed most of his references are to evidence before parliamentary committees, and he refers once to McCulloch, once to Malthus (but only about Scottish agriculture) and once to Ricardo (the determination of natural price), with Tooke the only person referred to frequently (five times), while Torrens is not referred to at all – could deal with major economic problems and produce significant advance through the interaction of a knowledge of Smithian economics, *and* a mass of detailed knowledge of the working of the economic system. In this connection, it is particularly interesting to observe that Hume is not referred to; and, although it is clear, from Essay V, that the author understood the price-specie-flow mechanism, it seems that he had worked it out for himself, and in a rather clumsy manner. This is particularly interesting because Thornton is not referred to – any material concerning velocity the author also apparently worked out for himself – and he shows no sign of understanding Hume's inflationary mechanism. Yet the result was a book on economic growth – which is what these essays are – that would have been regarded as a major contribution had it been widely known. The role of aggregate demand in growth is a constant theme, and the essays are full of aperçus.

Perhaps this independence of the post-Smithian classical literature helps to explain one interesting aspect of the essays – an attack on landlords who, in order to increase their political influence, either let farms at high rents and make abatements according to their own generosity, or let farms at rents below the real annual value, to tenants at will. Both these measures, by increasing the dependence of the tenant upon the landlord, increase the influence of the latter.[18] This state of affairs is unfavourably contrasted with that in manufacturing, and it is asserted that:

> no capitalists of consideration will ever commence the business of farming upon the condition of expected abatements in rent, or

> expected permission to continue on the farm. To be placed in a state of dependance [sic]; to subject their capitals, when laid out in improvements, to the caprice of a landlord; are terms to which no affluent capitalists will ever voluntarily submit.[19]

This point of view, which could certainly have been derived from the putative author's own experience in Sussex – he lived at Eartham, near Chichester – is very striking because it runs counter to the later Classical stereotype of efficient English capitalist agriculture contrasted with inefficient Irish agriculture, the poor state of which was due in part to the role of the landlords.[20] This evil aspect of English agriculture was rendered worse, in the author's view, by the Speenhamland system which, by increasing the level of the poor rates, made it easier for the tenants to press for, or retain, low rents.[21]

We share Tucker's view of the importance of the *Essays*. If they were written by the important political figure to whom Tucker attributed them, they show how deeply analytical considerations lay behind the thinking of a practical statesman. This is significant counter-evidence to the arguments of those who believe that a mixture of ignorance and the exigencies of party politics explain economic policy in the first part of the 19th century.

Of course, the author could fall into traps. Thus, at one point,[22] we find one of the first uses of the 'we are not maintaining our share of world trade' argument which has been so popular with post World War II commentators but which is actually fallacious because, with new countries becoming industrialised and diversifying in the course of growth, we could not hope to. But, at times, the analysis is really significant. This is particularly true of the trade cycle analysis which includes (before J. S. Mill's *Unsettled Questions*) excess demand for money in the downswing of the trade cycle.

So who wrote the *Essays*? Tucker, in a piece of detective work extending over about a dozen years, found that the author had originally been called George Robertson, and that this was the name in Longman's accounts but that the firm had no address for him. On the basis of internal evidence, Tucker compiled the following list of characteristics which could be attributed to the author.

1. The author's economics came from Adam Smith, using short chains with frequent illustrations.
2. He may have been a member of parliament and even of government.
3. He had detailed knowledge of parliamentary reports, especially those

of the Bullion and Resumption committees, and may have been a member of these committees.

4. He agreed with the conclusions of the committees and sought monetary stability.
5. He possessed 'a quite extraordinary factual knowledge' of trade and currency.
6. He was particularly interested in Central and South America, notably in Brazil.
7. He seemed most knowledgeable of all about London and Liverpool.
8. He was a free trader and supported the tariff reforms of the 1820s.[23]

On the basis of this list, Tucker's Research Assistant, Helen Bridge, identified William Huskisson as by far the most likely candidate. Particularly important was contemporary evidence from people like Alexander Baring and Henry Brougham of the extent of Huskisson's practical knowledge.[24] He was also free to write the essays at the date in question (1829), having resigned in 1828 from the post of Colonial Secretary after a disagreement with Wellington; and there is a parallel with his use of leisure to compose, in 1810, *The Question Concerning the Depreciation of our Currency*[25] after his resignation in 1809 from the post of Secretary to the Treasury. Huskisson was also sensitive and depressed by criticism, and this would explain the anonymity of the *Essays*. Indeed, in one of his speeches, he referred to 'the vituperation, to the endless obloquy, to the calumny' to which he was exposed because of his support for free trade.[26]

Tucker and Helen Bridge also found a number of parallels between Huskisson's published speeches and the contents of the essays. These include the insistence that tariff protection was illusory and did not deserve to be called 'protection';[27] the elementary and detailed style of exposition;[28] the emphasis on monetary history and especially Lord Liverpool's *Treatise on the Coins of the Realm*;[29] the importance attached to the circulation of bills of exchange in Lancashire and chartered banks in Scotland;[30] the classification of wealth;[31] and the treatment of the trade balance.[32] A final point, first noticed by Helen Bridge, was that although a number of important statesmen of the period are mentioned in the essays, Huskisson is not. Tucker and his assistant also point to some inconsistencies between the speeches and the essays, particularly over the state of the British shipping interest, the Corn Laws, and the suppression of small notes, which they attribute to the pressures of Huskisson's parliamentary position.

All this, so far, seems persuasive in sum (although not all the grounds are equally so), but hardly conclusive. Towards the end of his investigation, however, Tucker succeeded in obtaining two pieces of much more firm evidence. Firstly, he located amongst the Huskisson papers a manuscript from one Don Juan Garcia del Rie which contained a passage reproduced in the *Essays* as 'one account', without giving the source of this account. In addition, he found that the ledger record at Longman's has been closed *after* Huskisson's death and that the account had been signed 'Geo Robertson'. With the help of the New South Wales police, the fragment of handwriting has been identified as that of Huskisson's half-brother, who was also a trusted confidant of the statesman.[33] Unfortunately, the Huskisson Papers do not help us here; the letters of 1828–9 from Captain Thomas Huskisson to William Huskisson[34] are concerned with embezzlement in the Navy Pay Office.

Apart from the intriguing detail of this twelve-year hunt, the matter is of interest to us because the evidence is still only circumstantial. There are at least two other candidates for authorship who would fit the profile which Tucker obtained from the internal evidence: James Deacon Hume, whom Tucker mentions,[35] and William Jacob. The former, who was Secretary to the Board of Trade 1828–40, played, in his previous capacity as Comptroller of Customs, a central administrative role in the implementation of the free trade policy with which Huskisson was associated in the 1820s. The latter, suggested to us by Professor Barry Gordon, fits the profile particularly well. He was a merchant trading to South America, and an MP, he published *Travels in Spain*, he was an expert on both the corn trade and the precious metals[36] and he was in the Board of Trade 1822–42. To confuse the picture further, *both* J. D. Hume and Jacob were associates of Huskisson. Jacob's own account of his connection with the latter is so striking in the context of trying to establish authorship from internal evidence that, had Professor Tucker not had the two items of 'hard' evidence referred to above, Jacob would have started *almost* equal favourite with Huskisson – almost, because Jacob published in 1831 under his own name and because what he published was a substantial work, the preparation of which would almost certainly have ruled out simultaneous preparation of the *Essays* (although the bulk of either could well have been prepared in earlier years). At all events, Jacob wrote in the preface to his *Precious Metals*: 'The following sheets owe their composition to the friendship with which, during more than twenty-five years, I had been honoured by the late Mr. Huskisson',[37] and it is apparent that Huskisson had an important formative influence on the studies leading to Jacob's book.

Tucker made a number of attempts to trace the original manuscript of the *Essays*, since Huskisson apparently produced three manuscripts of any one piece, but without success.[38] We had no more success in this respect. Apart from the South American material referred to by Tucker, no further evidence has been gleaned from the Huskisson papers. There is a volume of official papers 1828–30[39] which is particularly concerned with economic fluctuations; but there does not seem to be any material in it relating to the essays. Most interestingly of all, to us, he apparently tried the Mosteller and Wallace technique of statistical identification of authorship discussed earlier in this study, without success.[40] Since we are interested in the use of statistical techniques in such a context, it seems obvious that we should try on this problem the techniques that we are using, firstly, because we know from other contexts that they do work, and, secondly, because it will be interesting to see if they confirm the hard evidence.

We used the following as texts. From the three volumes of Huskisson's *Speeches*,[41] we used his speech of 11 June 1822 on Mr Western's Motion on the Resumption of Cash Payments[42] which is around 10,700 words. Secondly, we used his speech on the State of the Country 16 March 1830,[43] which is over 11,000 words. Thirdly, we used the whole of his pamphlet *The Question Concerning the Depreciation of our Currency* of 1810,[44] which is around 37,000 words. From the *Essays* themselves we took Essays IV, V and VI,[45] giving nearly 28,000 words. Since we also have to show that the tests discriminate, we included for comparison a work by James Deacon Hume *Thoughts on the Corn Laws*,[46] and a lengthy section[47] of Jacob's *Precious Metals*.

II. STATISTICAL ANALYSIS

We have noted above that there are three writers in particular who seem plausible candidates for authorship of the *Essays*: Huskisson, J. D. Hume and W. Jacob. Our sample of Huskisson material consists, as indicated above, of three distinct works. We have only one work *each* to represent Hume and Jacob, and so the work of both these authors has been divided into two parts to test for internal consistency. The same is true of the material from the *Essays*.

(a) First word usage

The analysis of first word usage produced the results summarised in Table 8.1. This is derived from the contingency tables 8.2(i) to 8.2(x). The

TABLE 8.1 First word usage

Texts analysed	X^2	d.f.	$\chi^2_{0.95}$	*Decision*	*Maximum type I error (where applicable)*	*Contingency table*
Resumption vs *State of the Country* vs *Depreciation*	11.23	8	15.51	Accept the hypothesis of internal consistency of Huskisson	–	8.2(i)
Essays internally	8.22	4	9.49	Accept the hypothesis of internal consistency of *Essays*	–	8.2(ii)
Corn Laws internally	2.51	4	9.49	Accept the hypothesis of internal consistency of Hume	–	8.2(iii)
Precious Metals internally	2.40	4	9.49	Accept the hypothesis of internal consistency of Jacob	–	8.2(iv)
Huskisson vs Hume	28.05	4	9.49	Reject the hypothesis of consistency between Huskisson and Hume	0.005	8.2(v)
Huskisson vs Jacob	18.77	4	9.49	Reject the hypothesis of consistency between Huskisson and Jacob	0.005	8.2(vi)
Hume vs Jacob	30.96	4	9.49	Reject the hypothesis of consistency between Hume and Jacob	0.005	8.2(vii)
Hume vs *Essays*	10.01	4	9.49	Reject the hypothesis of consistency between Hume and *Essays*	0.05	8.2(viii)
Jacob vs *Essays*	16.48	4	9.49	Reject the hypothesis of consistency between Jacob and *Essays*	0.005	8.2(ix)
Huskisson vs *Essays*	9.39	4	9.49	Accept the hypothesis of consistency between Huskisson and *Essays*	–	8.2(x)

TABLE 8.2 Contingency tables – first word usage

(i) Huskisson

Resumption		*State of the Country*		*Depreciation*		
22	(30.49)	51	(42.18)	98	(98.32)	171
16	(18.90)	28	(26.15)	62	(60.95)	106
12	(10.52)	10	(14.55)	37	(33.92)	59
26	(18.72)	20	(25.90)	59	(60.37)	105
31	(28.35)	39	(39.22)	89	(91.42)	159
107		148		345		600

$X^2 = 11.23, \quad \chi^2_{8,\,0.95} = 15.51.$

(ii) *Essays on Political Economy*

pp. 80–147		pp. 147–205		
61	(63.65)	61	(58.35)	122
27	(30.78)	32	(28.22)	59
14	(9.39)	4	(8.61)	18
37	(31.83)	24	(29.17)	61
41	(44.35)	44	(40.65)	85
180		165		345

$X^2 = 8.22, \quad \chi^2_{4,\,0.95} = 9.49.$

(iii) Hume, *Corn Laws*

pp. 1–40		pp. 40–78		
43	(40.55)	41	(43.45)	84
16	(18.34)	22	(19.66)	38
3	(1.93)	1	(2.07)	4
22	(21.24)	22	(22.76)	44
14	(15.93)	19	(17.07)	33
98		105		203

$X^2 = 2.51, \quad \chi^2_{4,\,0.95} = 9.49.$

TABLE 8.2 (*contd.*)

(iv) Jacob, *Precious Metals*

pp. v–ix, 270–95		pp. 295–323		
42	(37.99)	25	(29.01)	67
17	(16.45)	12	(12.55)	29
8	(9.07)	8	(6.93)	16
4	(5.10)	5	(3.90)	9
22	(24.38)	21	(18.62)	43
93		71		164

$X^2 = 2.40, \quad \chi^2_{4,\,0.95} = 9.49.$

(v)

Huskisson		Hume		
171	(190.54)	84	(64.46)	255
106	(107.60)	38	(36.40)	144
59	(47.07)	4	(15.93)	63
105	(111.33)	44	(37.67)	149
159	(143.46)	33	(48.54)	192
600		203		803

$X^2 = 28.05, \quad \chi^2_{4,\,0.995} = 14.86.$

(vi)

Huskisson		Jacob		
171	(186.91)	67	(51.09)	238
106	(106.02)	29	(28.98)	135
59	(58.90)	16	(16.10)	75
105	(89.53)	9	(24.47)	114
159	(158.64)	43	(43.36)	202
600		164		764

$X^2 = 18.77, \quad \chi^2_{4,\,0.995} = 14.86.$

(vii)

Hume		Jacob		
84	(83.52)	67	(67.48)	151
38	(37.06)	29	(29.94)	67
4	(11.06)	16	(8.94)	20
44	(29.32)	9	(23.68)	53
33	(42.04)	43	(33.96)	76
203		164		367

$X^2 = 30.96, \quad \chi^2_{4,\,0.995} = 14.86.$

(viii)

Essays		Hume		
122	(129.69)	84	(76.31)	206
59	(61.07)	38	(35.93)	97
18	(13.85)	4	(8.15)	22
61	(66.10)	44	(38.90)	105
85	(74.29)	33	(43.71)	118
345		203		548

$X^2 = 10.01, \quad \chi^2_{4,\,0.95} = 9.49.$

(ix)

Essays		Jacob		
122	(128.10)	67	(60.90)	189
59	(59.65)	29	(28.35)	88
18	(23.05)	16	(10.95)	34
61	(47.45)	9	(22.55)	70
85	(86.76)	43	(41.24)	128
345		164		509

$X^2 = 16.48, \quad \chi^2_{4,\,0.995} = 14.86.$

(x)

Essays		Huskisson		
122	(106.97)	171	(186.03)	293
59	(60.24)	106	(104.76)	165
18	(28.11)	59	(48.89)	77
61	(60.60)	105	(105.40)	166
85	(89.08)	159	(154.92)	244
345		600		945

$X^2 = 9.39, \quad \chi^2_{4,\,0.95} = 9.49.$

five rows of the contingency tables correspond to the following first words: 'the'; 'it'; 'this'; 'but' or 'a'; 'if' or 'in'. It is clear that the work of Huskisson exhibits internal consistency when analysed on this basis; the computed χ^2 value is 11.23, while the critical 95 per cent point for 8 degrees of freedom (since we have three works) is 15.51. The *Essays*, the work of J. D. Hume, and that of Jacob, also exhibit internal consistency, producing computed χ^2 values of 8.22, 2.51 and 2.40 respectively. These may be compared with the 95 per cent point of 9.49 for 4 degrees of freedom (since we are considering two parts of one work in each case). In the comparison of the work of Huskisson and J. D. Hume, the differences in first word usage are marked and are statistically significant. The computed χ^2 value is 28.05, which would only be achieved by chance with a probability of less than 0.005. It seems clear that the two authors exhibit marked differences in style and that examination of habits of first word usage enables us to discriminate clearly between them. Similarly, we find that Huskisson's first word usage is very different from that of Jacob (with a computed χ^2 of 18.77), and J. D. Hume and Jacob are also clearly distinguished (with a computed χ^2 of 30.96).

First word tests, then, show internal consistency and successfully discriminate between authors. The next stage of the analysis is to compare the work of each individual author with the whole of the anonymous material. We find that there is a marked, and statistically significant, difference in style measured in this way, between Hume and the anonymous writer, for the computed χ^2 is 10.01, which exceeds the 95 per cent point of 9.49. We obtain similar discrimination between Jacob and the anonymous writer (with a computed χ^2 of 16.48). It is, therefore, reasonable to conclude that the evidence of this test indicates clearly that neither J. D. Hume nor Jacob was responsible for the *Essays*. The style of Huskisson, on the other hand, *is* consistent with that of the author of the *Essays*, comparison of a sample of his work with the *Essays* yielding a χ^2 value of 9.39, which lies below the critical value of 9.49. Clearly, there are differences between the sample and the *Essays*, but these occur in only two of the five rows of Table 8.2(x), and do not produce a statistically significant difference. In contrast, the discrepancy between J. D. Hume's habits and those of the anonymous hand occur in all but one row and cumulate to a statistically significant difference.

Analysis of first word usage enables us to conclude, therefore, that Huskisson was the author of the *Essays* and to reject the hypotheses that either Hume or Jacob was responsible.

(b) Collocations with 'the'

From an analysis of habitual couplings with 'the', similar conclusions emerge. Again, we find that the evidence is consistent with the hypothesis that Huskisson was the author of the *Essays*, while it is inconsistent with the possibility that either of the other two candidates for authorship was responsible. The results of tests on collocations with 'the' are summarised in Table 8.3 and the details are to be found in the contingency tables 8.4(i) to 8.4(x). Each contingency table has seven rows, cor-

TABLE 8.3 Collocations with 'the'

Texts analysed	X^2	d.f.	$\chi^2_{0.95}$	*Decision*	*Maximum type I error (where applicable)*	*Contingency table*
Resumption vs *State of the Country* vs *Depreciation*	11.44	12	21.03	Accept the hypothesis of internal consistency of Huskisson	–	8.4(i)
Essays internally	6.87	6	12.59	Accept the hypothesis of internal consistency of *Essays*	–	8.4(ii)
Corn Laws internally	7.80	6	12.59	Accept the hypothesis of internal consistency of Hume	–	8.4(iii)
Precious Metals internally	9.56	6	12.59	Accept the hypothesis of internal consistency of Jacob	–	8.4(iv)
Huskisson vs Hume	31.58	6	12.59	Reject the hypothesis of consistency between Huskisson and Hume	0.005	8.4(v)
Huskisson vs Jacob	22.65	6	12.59	Reject the hypothesis of consistency between Huskisson and Jacob	0.005	8.4(vi)
Hume vs Jacob	43.81	6	12.59	Reject the hypothesis of consistency between Huskisson and Jacob	0.005	8.4(vii)
Hume vs *Essays*	25.09	6	12.59	Reject the hypothesis of consistency between Hume and *Essays*	0.005	8.4(viii)
Jacob vs *Essays*	21.50	6	12.59	Reject the Hypothesis of consistency between Jacob and *Essays*	0.005	8.4(ix)
Huskisson vs *Essays*	5.02	6	12.59	Accept the hypothesis of consistency between Huskisson and *Essays*	–	8.4(x)

TABLE 8.4 Contingency tables – collocations with 'the'

(i) Huskisson

Resumption		*State of the Country*		*Depreciation*		
34	(29.74)	28	(25.73)	73	(79.52)	135
13	(9.91)	10	(8.58)	22	(26.51)	45
40	(40.98)	37	(35.46)	109	(109.57)	186
63	(65.43)	63	(56.62)	171	(174.95)	297
71	(76.23)	64	(65.96)	211	(203.82)	346
19	(23.35)	22	(20.21)	65	(62.44)	106
42	(36.35)	20	(31.45)	103	(97.20)	165
282		244		754		1280

$X^2 = 11.44$, $\chi^2_{12,\,0.95} = 21.03$.

(ii) *Essays on Political Economy*

pp. 84–147		pp. 147–205		
39	(35.93)	27	(30.07)	66
8	(7.62)	6	(6.38)	14
53	(47.90)	35	(40.10)	88
78	(90.36)	88	(75.64)	166
104	(102.88)	85	(86.12)	189
30	(26.13)	18	(21.87)	48
44	(45.18)	39	(37.82)	83
356		298		654

$X^2 = 6.87$, $\chi^2_{6,\,0.95} = 12.59$.

(iii) Hume, *Corn Laws*

pp. 1–40		pp. 40–78		
47	(39.75)	31	(38.25)	78
3	(6.63)	10	(6.37)	13
20	(17.84)	15	(17.16)	35
56	(57.08)	56	(54.92)	112
56	(58.61)	59	(56.39)	115
15	(16.31)	17	(15.69)	32
41	(41.79)	41	(40.21)	82
238		229		467

$X^2 = 7.80$, $\chi^2_{6,\,0.95} = 12.59$.

TABLE 8.4 (*contd.*)

(iv) Jacob, *Precious Metals*

pp. v–ix, 270–95		pp. 295–323		
22	(23.85)	27	(25.15)	49
1	(0.97)	1	(1.03)	2
33	(33.09)	35	(34.91)	68
39	(35.04)	33	(36.96)	72
47	(39.91)	35	(42.09)	82
10	(16.55)	24	(17.45)	34
12	(14.60)	18	(15.40)	30
164		173		337

$X^2 = 9.56, \quad \chi^2_{6,\,0.95} = 12.59.$

(v)

Huskisson		Hume		
135	(156.06)	78	(56.94)	213
45	(42.50)	13	(15.50)	58
186	(161.92)	35	(59.08)	221
297	(299.67)	112	(109.33)	409
346	(337.77)	115	(123.23)	461
106	(101.11)	32	(36.89)	138
165	(180.97)	82	(66.03)	247
1280		467		1747

$X^2 = 31.58, \quad \chi^2_{6,\,0.995} = 18.55.$

(vi)

Huskisson		Jacob		
135	(145.65)	49	(38.35)	184
45	(37.20)	2	(9.80)	47
186	(201.06)	68	(52.94)	254
297	(292.10)	72	(76.90)	369
346	(338.80)	82	(89.20)	428
106	(110.82)	34	(29.18)	140
165	(154.36)	30	(40.64)	195
1280		337		1617

$X^2 = 22.65, \quad \chi^2_{6,\,0.995} = 18.55.$

TABLE 8.4 (*contd.*)

(vii)

Hume		Jacob		
78	(73.77)	49	(53.23)	127
13	(8.71)	2	(6.29)	15
35	(59.83)	68	(43.17)	103
112	(106.88)	72	(77.12)	184
115	(114.43)	82	(82.57)	197
32	(38.34)	34	(27.66)	66
82	(65.05)	30	(46.95)	112
467		337		804

$X^2 = 43.81, \quad \chi^2_{6,\,0.995} = 18.55.$

(viii)

Essays		Hume		
66	(84.01)	78	(59.99)	144
14	(15.75)	13	(11.25)	27
88	(71.76)	35	(51.24)	123
166	(162.19)	112	(115.81)	278
189	(177.36)	115	(126.64)	304
48	(46.67)	32	(33.33)	80
83	(96.26)	82	(68.74)	165
654		467		1121

$X^2 = 25.09, \quad \chi^2_{6,\,0.995} = 18.55.$

(ix)

Essays		Jacob		
66	(75.89)	49	(39.11)	115
14	(10.56)	2	(5.44)	16
88	(102.95)	68	(53.05)	156
166	(157.07)	72	(80.93)	238
189	(178.84)	82	(92.16)	271
48	(54.12)	34	(27.88)	82
83	(74.57)	30	(38.43)	113
654		337		991

$X^2 = 21.50, \quad \chi^2_{6,\,0.995} = 18.55.$

TABLE 8.4 (*contd.*)

(x) *Essays*		Huskisson		
66	(67.97)	135	(133.03)	201
14	(19.95)	45	(39.05)	59
88	(92.66)	186	(181.34)	274
166	(156.57)	297	(306.43)	463
189	(180.92)	346	(354.08)	535
48	(52.08)	106	(101.92)	154
83	(83.86)	165	(164.14)	248
654		1280		1934

$X^2 = 5.02, \quad \chi^2_{6,\,0.95} = 12.59.$

responding to the following collocations with 'the': 'and'; 'be'; 'with' or 'from'; 'on' or 'upon' or 'by'; 'to' or 'into'; 'after' or 'or' or 'as'; 'which' or 'at' or 'but'. Using these collocations in the seven groups listed, we find clear consistency at the same points as our analysis of first word lead one to expect it, and equally clear discrimination where expected. The computed χ^2 values in the four tests of consistency are 11.44, 6.87, 7.80 and 9.56, which correspond respectively to the figures calculated from data from the samples of the writings of Huskisson, from the *Essays*, from the work of Hume, and from that of Jacob. The first figure is to be compared with a critical value of 21.03 (the χ^2 95 per cent point with 12 degrees of freedom), and the remaining three are to be compared with 12.59. (There are six degrees of freedom only in these tests as we are comparing a work divided into two parts, data from each of which has seven classifications.) These results lead to the acceptance of the hypothesis that the three named authors and the anonymous author are all internally consistent in their usage of collocations with 'the' as classified. The pairwise comparisons of the three authors reveal significant differences. The computed χ^2 figures in comparing Huskisson with Hume, Huskisson with Jacob, and Hume with Jacob, are 31.58, 22.65, and 43.81 respectively. The 99.5 per cent point of the χ^2 distribution with 6 degrees of freedom is only 18.55, and thus we are able to conclude that our classification discriminates successfully between authors. The final comparisons are between the work of each possible author in turn and the *Essays*. The writings of both Hume and Jacob are very different in style to the anonymous *Essays*, and comparison by means of tests on collocations with 'the' yields χ^2 values of 25.09 and 21.50 respectively. It seems reasonable to reject firmly the possibility that either Hume or Jacob wrote the *Essays*. Huskisson's style is, however, wholly compatible with the unknown author, comparison yielding a computed χ^2 of just 5.02 when the 95 per cent critical point is 12.59.

The evidence obtained from analysis of collocations with 'the' is, then, about as conclusive as statistical analysis of this sort can be, and is wholly consistent with the evidence obtained in the previous section from analysis of first word usage. It is, however, even stronger, and lends considerable weight to the hypothesis that Huskisson, not Hume or Jacob, wrote the *Essays*.

(c) Collocations with 'be'

Our last set of tests examines the data provided by collocations with 'be'. A summary of the results is presented in Table 8.5 and the details are presented in the contingency tables 8.6(i) to 8.6(x). The contingency tables each have six rows, which correspond to the collocations of 'be' with: 'would'; 'will'; 'could' or 'should' or 'must' or 'may'; 'shall' or 'can' or 'might'; 'to' or 'need'; 'noun'. It is interesting to note that these rows are exhaustive of the collocations; hence the column totals represent the total number of occurrences of 'be' in the works under examination. This is in contrast to the analyses of first words and of collocations with 'the' where, in each case, we examined only a subset of the total. Thus, in the examination of first words, the column totals do not represent the total number of sentences. It is important to be clear about the reason for this contrast between our tests. The classifications presented are those most suited to the purposes of producing internal consistency within the known work of one author and discrimination between his work and the known work of another author. 'be' is preceded by any one of twelve words, which facilitates an exhaustive classification; by contrast, J. D. Hume, for example, uses about 20 distinct first words in every 100 sentences.

The results obtained with 'be' are as strong as those with 'the', and once again indicate that Huskisson was the author of the *Essays*. On the tests of internal consistency, Huskisson's work yields a computed χ^2 of 3.89, which is to be compared with 18.31 (the 95 per cent point of the χ^2 distribution with 10 degrees of freedom), while the *Essays*, Hume's *Corn Laws*, and Jacob's *Precious Metals* yield χ^2 values of 8.25, 5.74 and 2.92 respectively. The 95 per cent point of the χ^2 distribution with 5 degrees of freedom is 11.07 and thus, in each of the four cases under consideration, there is no difficulty in accepting that the works exhibit internal consistency. The pairwise comparisons yield χ^2 values which show clear discrimination. The lowest of them is 24.13 (the work of Huskisson

TABLE 8.5 Collocations with 'be'

Texts analysed	X^2	d.f.	$\chi^2_{0.95}$	*Decision*	*Maximum type I error (where applicable)*	*Contingency table*
Resumption vs *State of the Country* vs *Depreciation*	3.89	10	18.31	Accept the hypothesis of internal consistency of Huskisson	–	8.6(i)
Essays internally	8.25	5	11.07	Accept the hypothesis of internal consistency of *Essays*	–	8.6(ii)
Corn Laws internally	5.74	5	11.07	Accept the hypothesis of internal consistency of Hume	–	8.6(iii)
Precious Metals internally	2.92	5	11.07	Accept the hypothesis of internal consistency of Jacob	–	8.6(iv)
Huskisson vs Hume	43.24	5	11.07	Reject the hypothesis of consistency between Huskisson and Hume	0.005	8.6(v)
Huskisson vs Jacob	24.13	5	11.07	Reject the hypothesis of consistency between Huskisson and Jacob	0.005	8.6(vi)
Hume vs Jacob	27.04	5	11.07	Reject the hypothesis of consistency between Hume and Jacob	0.005	8.6(vii)
Hume vs *Essays*	23.89	5	11.07	Reject the hypothesis of consistency between Hume and *Essays*	0.005	8.6(viii)
Jacob vs *Essays*	22.24	5	11.07	Reject the hypothesis of consistency between Jacob and *Essays*	0.005	8.6(ix)
Huskisson vs *Essays*	5.88	5	11.07	Accept the hypothesis of consistency between Huskisson and *Essays*	–	8.6(x)

TABLE 8.6 Contingency tables – collocations with 'be'

(i) Huskisson

Resumption		*State of the Country*		*Depreciation*		
22	(19.19)	25	(26.20)	79	(80.61)	126
5	(6.55)	11	(8.94)	27	(27.51)	43
32	(34.12)	45	(46.58)	147	(143.30)	224
17	(20.11)	30	(27.45)	85	(84.45)	132
27	(24.52)	35	(33.48)	99	(103.00)	161
12	(10.51)	11	(14.35)	46	(44.14)	69
115		157		483		755

$X^2 = 3.89, \quad \chi^2_{10,\,0.95} = 18.31.$

(ii) *Essays on Political Economy*

pp. 84–147		pp. 147–205		
28	(28.29)	28	(27.71)	56
12	(15.66)	19	(15.34)	31
56	(52.03)	47	(50.97)	103
26	(31.32)	36	(30.68)	62
58	(49.51)	40	(48.49)	98
15	(18.19)	21	(17.81)	36
195		191		386

$X^2 = 8.25, \quad \chi^2_{5,\,0.95} = 11.07.$

(iii) Hume, *Corn Laws*

pp. 1–40		pp. 40–78		
15	(12.80)	14	(16.20)	29
20	(23.83)	34	(30.17)	54
54	(48.10)	55	(60.90)	109
27	(24.27)	28	(30.73)	55
21	(26.03)	38	(32.97)	59
17	(18.97)	26	(24.03)	43
154		195		349

$X^2 = 5.74, \quad \chi^2_{5,\,0.95} = 11.07.$

TABLE 8.6 (*contd.*)

(iv) Jacob, *Precious Metals*

pp. v–ix, 270–95		pp. 295–323		
2	(1.80)*	1	(1.20)	3
5	(4.20)*	2	(2.80)	7
29	(27.60)	17	(18.40)	46
16	(15.60)	10	(10.40)	26
19	(20.40)	15	(13.60)	34
1	(2.40)	3	(1.60)	4
72		48		120

$X^2 = 2.92, \quad \chi^2_{5,\,0.95} = 11.07.$

* If we amalgamate these two rows to eliminate the low expected values, we obtain $X^2 = 2.90, \quad \chi^2_{4,\,0.95} = 9.49.$

(v)

Huskisson		Hume		
126	(106.00)	29	(49.00)	155
43	(66.34)	54	(30.66)	97
224	(227.73)	109	(105.27)	333
132	(127.88)	55	(59.12)	187
161	(150.45)	59	(69.55)	220
69	(76.59)	43	(35.41)	112
755		349		1104

$X^2 = 43.24, \quad \chi^2_{5,\,0.995} = 16.75.$

(vi)

Huskisson		Jacob		
126	(111.31)	3	(17.69)	129
43	(43.14)	7	(6.86)	50
224	(232.97)	46	(37.03)	270
132	(136.33)	26	(21.67)	158
161	(168.26)	34	(26.74)	195
69	(62.99)	4	(10.01)	73
755		120		875

$X^2 = 24.13, \quad \chi^2_{5,\,0.995} = 16.75.$

TABLE 8.6 (*contd.*)

(vii)

Hume		Jacob		
29	(23.81)	3	(8.19)	32
54	(45.39)	7	(15.61)	61
109	(115.34)	46	(39.66)	155
55	(60.28)	26	(20.72)	81
59	(69.20)	34	(23.80)	93
43	(34.97)	4	(12.03)	47
349		120		469

$X^2 = 27.04, \quad \chi^2_{5,\,0.995} = 16.75.$

(viii)

Essays		Hume		
56	(44.64)	29	(40.36)	85
31	(44.64)	54	(40.36)	85
103	(111.34)	109	(100.66)	212
62	(61.44)	55	(55.56)	117
98	(82.45)	59	(74.55)	157
36	(41.49)	43	(37.51)	79
386		349		735

$X^2 = 23.89, \quad \chi^2_{5,\,0.995} = 16.75.$

(ix)

Essays		Jacob		
56	(45.01)	3	(13.99)	59
31	(28.99)	7	(9.01)	38
103	(113.66)	46	(35.34)	149
62	(67.13)	26	(20.87)	88
98	(100.70)	34	(31.30)	132
36	(30.51)	4	(9.49)	40
386		120		506

$X^2 = 22.24, \quad \chi^2_{5,\,0.995} = 16.75.$

TABLE 8.6 (*contd.*)

(x)

Essays		Huskisson		
56	(61.57)	126	(120.43)	182
31	(25.03)	43	(48.97)	74
103	(110.62)	224	(216.38)	327
62	(65.63)	132	(128.37)	194
98	(87.62)	161	(171.38)	259
36	(35.52)	69	(69.48)	105
386		755		1141

$X^2 = 5.88$, $\chi^2_{5,\,0.95} = 11.07$.

compared with that of Jacob), and this may be compared with the 99.5 per cent point of the relevant χ^2 distribution, which is only 16.75. Our classification system thus produces both the required discrimination between authors, and the consistency within the work of one author, which we require.

Comparison of the work of J. D. Hume with the *Essays* yields a χ^2 value of 23.89, while Jacob's yields 22.24. We can thus reject the possibility that either J. D. Hume or Jacob wrote the *Essays*, for a third time. Having obtained a computed χ^2 of 5.88, when comparing Huskisson's work with the *Essays*, in this third set of tests, we accept the hypothesis that Huskisson was indeed the author.

III. CONCLUSION

Each of the three sets of tests discussed above leads us to the conclusion that we reject the possibility that Hume or Jacob could have been the author of the *Essays*. They also lead us to accept the hypothesis that Huskisson was the author. These results are, statistically speaking, strong. The type I errors in rejecting the hypotheses of consistency between Hume and the *Essays* and between Jacob and the *Essays* are, in particular, very low.

9 Summary and Conclusions

In this study we have attacked an age-old problem, that of authorship identification, taking as our particular concern some of the outstanding puzzles in the field of economic literature.

Attempts to discriminate between authors through the gathering of numerical characteristics of a text and, subsequently, the application of statistical techniques to the numbers thus obtained, are about a century old. The statistical approaches employed have tended to rely upon parametric methods; and for long they concentrated on variables such as word length and sentence length, although more recently attention has been diverted towards the frequency of either common or uncommon words. As Chapter 2 shows, however, we have not followed these precedents; the statistical technique employed in this study is non-parametric, and the variables chosen relate to the relative frequency (either at the head of a sentence or in couplings with other words) of the different uses of a few common words.

We have also accepted as a basic premise that statistical analysis, in this field, can never be satisfactory on its own; it can be employed only as a supplement to a background of literary and historical detection. Each of our chapters has thus set out the background, in the history of economic literature, of the disputed pieces, and has made clear the various clues which have enabled us to narrow the field of possible authors. At the same time, although statistical analysis has to be employed in conjunction with historical work, we believe that the actual performance of the statistical tests should be kept separate from any subjectively-formed relative probabilities which may have originated in the course of the detective work – apart, that is, from the unavoidable short-listing of candidates for authorship. Accordingly, we have not used a Bayesian technique, which would involve reliance on 'priors' which would be generated in a subjective way.

The general approach which we have employed, and in particular the statistical methodology used, has proved remarkably satisfactory in solving problems of authorship attribution, even in such difficult areas as 17th century economic pamphlets. Although the problem of the authorship of the 17the century 'Philopatris' pamphlet concerning the East India trade, discussed in Chapter 3, proved difficult of solution, we were able to conclude that this was indeed the work of Sir Josiah Child. The subsidiary 17th century problems which we discussed in Chapter 3 also proved rewarding. We were able to satisfy ourselves that Robert Ferguson, who wrote on commission for the East India Company, was indeed the notorious plotter; we believe that Child wrote another pamphlet which has occasionally been attributed to him, though rather uncertainly; and we also believe that Child may have had a hand in a third pamphlet. Moreover, the method adopted proved able to indicate those works which it would be dangerous to attribute to any *one* author – the perennial problem of *substantially* altered drafts.

The 17th century literature proved particularly difficult, both because of peculiarities in the use of English, which are discussed in Chapter 2, and because of the small size of some of the texts with which we dealt. However, the 19th century literature – with one rather strange, indeed intriguing, exception, retailed in Chapter 7 – proved very much more amenable. The first 19th century problem investigated is discussed in Chapter 4. We examined the question of the authorship of an *Edinburgh Review* article of October 1819 which has been attributed to both Robert Torrens and J. R. McCulloch – the latter being implicated largely, it would seem, by the presence in the article of a discussion of the work of Sismondi. On the basis of the statistical results we obtained, we had no hesitation in concluding that the entire article was the work of Torrens. This was an example of the successful employment of the statistical technique in a situation where there seemed to be not so much a conflict of evidence as a conflict of interpretations of the available literary and historical background.

In Chapter 5, by contrast, there was not so much a conflict of interpretation of evidence as a lack of substantial evidence. Two anonymous pamphlets, *Observations on Certain Verbal Disputes* and *Inquiry into . . . Demand* have been attributed to Samuel Bailey; but the basis of this attribution lay, very largely, in apparent similarities between material in the pamphlets and other published material known to be by Bailey. Nevertheless, the preliminary historical evidence suggested that the attribution of one of these pamphlets to Bailey was wrong – in that Bailey flatly denied having even seen the work until he read it some years after publication. This, in itself, is not necessarily conclusive; certainly our investigations in Chapter 7 show that unambiguous *claims* to authorship, found in primary sources, may not always be reliable. But in this case our statistical tests indicated that the denial was correct; Bailey, we are quite clear, did not write the *Observations*. The question naturally arises as to who was the real author. Attention to the text of the work produced one tiny literary clue which led to Henry Brougham; and statistical analysis then confirmed the likelihood that he was, indeed, the author. The available background evidence concerning the *Inquiry* is even more scanty, although there certainly is internal evidence which could be interpreted as pointing in the direction of what is known of Bailey. It is gratifying, therefore, to be able to report that our statistical results do, indeed, indicate that the literary characteristics of the *Inquiry* are compatible with the known work of Bailey himself, and we have thus concluded that he did write the pamphlet.

Bailey again features in Chapter 6, in which we addressed ourselves to two questions: the authorship of a famous (and corrosive) attack upon him, which appeared in the *Westminster Review* in 1826, and the authorship of the textbook *Elements of Political Economy* which appeared under the name of James Mill.

This may appear, at first sight, an odd coupling of problems. But the two most likely candidates to have written the cutting assault on Bailey were the two Mills, father and son; and it has also been suggested that J. S. Mill was, through his preparation of notes following lessons in economics from his father, responsible for the text of the *Elements*. Thus we needed samples of the writings of both these authors to enable us to draw any conclusions about the authorship of the *Westminster Review* attack; and, provided with this material, we were in a position to deal with the question of the authorship of the *Elements* at the same time.

James Mill does, indeed, turn out to be the author of the harsh review – not surprisingly, since both historical and internal evidence to support his authorship were strong. Nevertheless, some distinguished authorities, lacking, it is true, the most recent historical evidence, had attributed the essay to J. S. Mill on the basis of the internal evidence; and it was thus worth investigating the matter statistically. The large samples of the writings of J. S. and James Mill which we employed then enabled us to conclude quite firmly that James Mill wrote his own *Elements* – the chances of J. S. Mill having been responsible are, statistically speaking, tiny.

Chapter 7, as we have hinted above, posed some of the most difficult and intriguing problems with which we have had to deal. For here we had a clear *conflict*, in the evidence available from primary sources, on the authorship of several *Edinburgh Review* articles. Our investigation started with two articles on Ireland, of 1822 and 1825, which had always been attributed to J. R. McCulloch, and had been claimed by him, but which, as Professor F. W. Fetter discovered, were also claimed by Sir Henry Parnell in a letter to MacVey Napier which is in the British Museum. Further investigation led however to the discovery of other – and at least equally surprising – claims by Parnell. Here, then, there was not a lack of evidence, or a conflict of interpretation, but a flat contradiction between *primary* sources.

In investigating this problem, we encountered a difficulty which we met nowhere else in our study. For we could find little statistical consistency in the work of Sir Henry Parnell, who had made such remarkable claims to the authorship of *Edinburgh Review* articles. We had, at an early stage of our study, to discard from our samples of his writings, Parliamentary speeches by him; but at that stage we felt that the difficulties we had encountered with the speeches might be something which could be explained through the employment, in the 19th century, of a speech writer, similar to those common in the 20th century. But we found that we were plagued with the problem of inconsistency with the remainder of Parnell's work; and at times we could produce consistency within his work only by a degree of amalgamation of literary habits which made it impossible to distinguish at all between the work of different writers. We were ultimately forced to the conclusion that Parnell must have been in the habit of supplying material for others to work into the form of an article, and that this practice led him, in the course of time, to claim authorship of articles to which he had made only a minimal contribution through the supply of a small amount of the raw material used. This would explain both the inconsistency within the works which appeared under the name of Parnell, and also his quite unambiguous claims to have been the author of material which certainly bears all the hallmarks of being from the robust fist of J. R. McCulloch, material which indeed contained elements inconsistent with Parnell's position as expressed in Parliament.

But the problem of inconsistency between works appearing under the name of Henry Parnell ultimately provided a solution to our difficulty; for while his work was inconsistent when different pieces were compared, and also, to some extent, exhibited inconsistency within the same piece, the disputed articles – not only the two on Ireland which originally drew us to this matter, but also a third on Ireland and one on Public Finance which had been drawn into our enquiry by the discovery of the greater extent of Parnell's claims – were internally consistent. Moreover, three of the four articles were completely consistent with each other. This very consistency indicated that Parnell, whose own work displayed no such consistency, could not be the author of the disputed articles.

Chapter 7 posed some very special problems; but we feel that it is an indication of the robustness of the methodology that it withstood this very severe test and enabled us to arrive at conclusions in what was, at first sight, a very intractable case.

No such difficulties confronted us in the investigations reported in Chapter 8. Indeed, we would suggest that if anyone wishes to study the method at its best – and certainly at its most uncomplicated – they should start with Chapter 8, which is at the end of the book only for reasons of chronology. In this chapter, we deal with the problem of assigning authorship of some remarkable *Essays on Political Economy* of 1830, which appeared under the name of an author who almost certainly never existed. As a result of some almost equally remarkable detective work, by the late Professor G. S. L. Tucker, the name of the statesman William Huskisson had emerged as a front runner amongst the candidates for authorship. But there were two other strong candidates: J. D. Hume of the Board of Trade, and William Jacob the celebrated writer on the corn trade and on precious metals; and, to complicate the historical background further, *both* men were close associates of Huskisson.

However, the statistical results were remarkably clear cut; they show, about as unambiguously as this can possibly be done, that the late Professor Tucker's surmise is correct – that Huskisson was indeed the author of this quite outstanding work. It is, indeed, a matter to us of some regret that Tucker should have died before we obtained this result.

In sum, then, we hope that there is enough in this volume to interest a wide range of readers. To the economist, as historian of economic thought, the questions discussed here should certainly be of direct interest. But we hope that historians, as well as those concerned with the application of statistical techniques to literary problems, and, in particular, those who, like the authors of the great *Wellesley Index to Victorian Periodicals*, have worked tirelessly on the identification of the authorship of anonymous 19th century articles, will all find material of interest in this volume. We hope too that others will take up the matter where we have left off, develop the method further, and employ it to solve the sort of problems of authorship attribution discussed in this volume.

Notes

Notes to Chapter One: Introduction

1. See the references to the work of W. C. Wake and of G. Udney Yule below.
2. See the references to the work of Mendenhall below.
3. It is not immediately obvious that word length is at the mercy of the printer; it was Yule, to whose discussion we refer below, who first drew attention to this problem.
4. This is particularly evident in the difficulties experienced in one investigation dealing with dialogue in a novel by Sir Walter Scott. See S. M. Michaelson, A. Q. Morton and N. Hamilton-Smith, *To Couple is the Custom* (University of Edinburgh, Dept. of Computer Science, 1977) p. 37.
5. E. Ellegard, *Who was Junius*? (Stockholm: Almqvist and Wiksell, 1962).
6. See F. Mosteller and D. L. Wallace, *Inference and Disputed Authorship: The Federalist* (Reading, Mass.: Addison-Wesley, 1964) ch. 1.
7. Michaelson *et al.*, op. cit.
8. E. R. Houghton (ed.), *The Wellesley Index to Victorian Periodicals*, vol. I (Toronto: Toronto University Press, 1966).
9. See D. Ricardo, *Works and Correspondence*, ed. P. Sraffa (Cambridge: Cambridge University Press, 1951–73) vol. III, pp. 427–34; vol. IV, pp. 99, 112n, 279, 415–16. In the case of Parish, in particular, the investigation, while exemplary, remains tantalisingly inconclusive. The witness was described as 'a Continental Merchant' and Cannan conjectured that this might be N. M. Rothschild. However, Sraffa found the style and content of the mysterious evidence different from evidence given by Rothschild in 1819 and 1832; and he also pointed out that since there was nothing compromising in the evidence given, the 'very fact of the witness being in London at all must have been the cause of discretion – yet Rothschild's residence in London was no secret'. Moreover, two *Hansard* references indicated that the witness was abroad. Sraffa noted that the witness was asked particularly about Hamburg, while other (identified) merchants were asked about the currency of their particular country. Hamburg had been occupied by the French since 1806 and under the Berlin and Milan decrees a visit to England constituted a serious offence. Seven British firms continued in Hamburg under French occupation, and one of them, Thornton & Power, Parish & Co., is listed in the Bullion Report as transmitting subsidies, a matter referred to in the anonymous evidence. By linking all this with evidence in the Public Record Office and Hamburg archives, a strong circumstantial case is presented that Parish was the anonymous witness.
10. T. C. Mendenhall, 'The Characteristic Curves of Composition', *Science*, IX, no. 214 (11 March 1887) pp. 237–49, and 'A Mechanical Solution of a

Literary Problem', *Popular Science Monthly*, 9 (1901) pp. 97–105. Mendenhall's work is discussed in C. B. Williams, 'A Note on an Early Statistical Study of Literary Style', in E. S. Pearson and M. G. Kendall (eds), *Studies in the History of Statistics and Probability*, vol. I (London: Griffin, 1970) pp. 241–9. De Morgan's initial idea is related in R. D. Lord, 'De Morgan and the Statistical Study of Literary Style', ibid., p. 251.

11. Williams, op. cit., p. 249.
12. Williams refers to his early, unsuccessful, work in 'A Note on the Statistical Analysis of Sentence-Length as a Criterion of Literary Style', *Biometrika*, 31 (1940) pp. 356–61.
13. G. Udney Yule, 'On Sentence-Length as a Statistical Characteristic of Style in Prose; with Application to Two Cases of Disputed Authorship', *Biometrika*, 30 (1938) pp. 363–90.
14. Ibid., p. 371. Yule appears, however, to have made an error in the calculations on which he based this view – see Wake, 1957 (note 26 below), at p. 334.
15. Yule, op. cit., pp. 363–5.
16. Ibid. pp. 365–6.
17. Ibid., p. 382.
18. Williams, 1940, note 12 above.
19. H. S. Sichel, 'On a Distribution Representing Sentence-length in Written Prose', *Journal of the Royal Statistical Society*, Series A, vol. 137 (1974) pp. 25–34.
20. E. Ellegard, *A Statistical Method for Determining Authorship: The Junius Letters 1769–1772* (Gothenburg: Elander, 1962).
21. Ibid., p. 10.
22. G. Udney Yule, *The Statistical Study of Literary Vocabulary* (Cambridge: Cambridge University Press, 1944).
23. Ellegard, *A Statistical Method*, p. 10.
24. See note 6 above; and F. Mosteller and D. L. Wallace, 'Inference in an Authorship Problem', *Journal of the American Statistical Association*, 58 (1963) pp. 275–309.
25. Ibid., p. 278.
26. See especially W. C. Wake, 'Sentence-Length Distributions of Greek Authors', *Journal of the Royal Statistical Society*, Series A, vol. 120 (1957) pp. 331–46.
27. S. M. Michaelson and A. Q. Morton, 'Positional Stylometry', in A. J. Aitken, R. W. Bailey and N. Hamilton-Smith (eds), *The Computer and Literary Studies* (Edinburgh: Edinburgh University Press, 1973) pp. 69–83 at p. 70.
28. Michaelson *et al.* (note 4 above) p. 16.
29. Yule, op. cit., pp. 364–7, 373, 374.
30. Ibid., pp. 381–2.
31. Sir Henry Parnell, Baron Congleton, *A History of the Penal Laws against the Irish Catholics from the year 1689 to the Union*, 4th edn (London: Longman, 1825).
32. Ellegard, *A Statistical Method*, pp. 12–13.

Notes to Chapter Two: Statistical Background

1. Distributions of literary variables such as individual word distributions, word length distributions and sentence length distributions, are all skewed to the right and are characterised, therefore, by having a mean which is markedly less than the variance. Their skewed nature prohibits their description by a Normal distributon (which is symmetric), and the relationship between the mean and variance prohibits the use of both the Binomial and Poisson distributions (the former has a mean greater than its variance and the latter has equality of the two). The Negative-Binomial distribution was examined in G. U. Yule, *The Statistical Study of Literary Vocabulary* (Cambridge: Cambridge University Press, 1944), but Yule concluded: 'I made one or two attempts to see whether this expression [the Negative Binomial distribution formula] could be made to describe a word-distribution with any accuracy . . . but they were all complete failures' (p. 55). The observed characteristics of the distributions of literary variables have led investigators to use a log-normal form. See for example C. B. Williams, 'A Note on the Statistical Analysis of Sentence Length as a Criterion of Literary Style', *Biometrika*, 31 (1940) pp. 356–61, and W. C. Wake, 'Sentence Length Distributions of Greek Authors', *Journal of the Royal Statistical Society* (cited hereafter as *JRSS*), Series A, 120 (1957) pp. 331–46. However, its applicability has not been examined using statistical tests of goodness of fit. We have experimented with this distribution for use with sentence-length and word distributions, but unfortunately our χ^2 tests of goodness of fit have constantly rejected its applicability.
2. See H. S. Sichel, 'On a Distribution Representing Sentence-length in Written Prose', *JRSS*, Series A, 137 (1974) pp. 25–34, in which a compound Poisson distribution is proposed and utilised with some degree of success.
3. For an excellent exposition of non-parametric techniques see S. Siegel, *Nonparametric Statistics for the Behavioural Sciences* (London: McGraw-Hill Kogakusha, 1956), and for a selective introduction to such methods see, for example, W. W. Daniel and J. C. Terrell, *Business Statistics: Basic Concepts and Methodology*, 2nd edn (London: Houghton-Mifflin, 1979) ch. 12.
4. F. Mosteller and D. L. Wallace, 'Inference in an Authorship Problem', *Journal of the American Statistical Association* (cited hereafter as *JASA*), 58 (1963) pp. 275–309, and *Inference and Disputed Authorship. The Federalist* (London: Addison-Wesley, 1964).
5. *JASA*, loc. cit., p. 291.
6. *JASA*, loc. cit., p. 302.
7. De Morgan to Heald, 18 August 1851, reprinted in R. D. Lord, 'De Morgan and the Statistical Study of Literary Style', *Biometrika*, 45 (1958) p. 282.
8. Ibid.
9. S. Michaelson and A. Q. Morton, 'Positional Stylometry', in A. J. Aitken, R. W. Bailey and N. Hamilton-Smith (eds), *The Computer and Literary Studies* (Edinburgh: Edinburgh University Press, 1973) pp. 69–83.
10. Ibid., pp. 75, 76.
11. Ibid., p. 83.

12. The words examined were: 'and', 'as', 'at', 'but', 'by', 'for', 'in', 'it', 'of', 'that', 'the', 'to', and 'upon'.
13. The set of frequently occurring first words comprises: 'a', 'and', 'but', 'if', 'in', 'it', 'now', 'suppose', 'the', 'there', 'this', and 'we'.
14. This specific problem was noted at an early stage of the development of statistical techniques by Yule, 'On Sentence-Length as a Statistical Characteristic of Style in Prose: With Application to Two Cases of Disputed Authorship', *Biometrika*, 30 (1938) pp. 363–90. Yule quotes (p. 364) from R. B. McKerrow, *An Introduction to Bibliography for Literary Students* (Oxford: Clarendon Press, 1928): 'So far as punctuation is concerned there seems very little evidence that many authors exercised any care about it whatsoever. . . . Such punctuation as is found in ordinary Mss. of the sixteenth and seventeenth centuries is indeed most erratic' (ibid. p. 250).
15. That is, other than by the positioning of a word as a first word.
16. See notes 26 and 42 to Chapter 8.
17. We need no longer be concerned with the vocabulary and word totals since they do not affect scaling but only the origin of the graph. This is because $\ln(n_i/V) = \ln(n_i) - \ln(V)$ and $\ln(x_i/W) = \ln(x_i) - \ln(W)$.
18. See note 55 to chapter 3.
19. An expression such as 'should he be' is *not* a coupling with 'should', for that requires the expression 'should be'; rather, it is treated as a coupling with 'noun'. Similarly, expressions like 'would they be' and 'will it be' are both treated as couplings with 'noun'.
20. For a full statement of the distribution of X^2 see, for example, A. M. Mood, F. A. Graybill and D. C. Boes, *Introduction to the Theory of Statistics*, 3rd edn (London: McGraw-Hill Kogakusha, 1974) ch. IX, Section 5, especially at p. 459.
21. S. Michaelson, A. Q. Morton and N. Hamilton-Smith, *To Couple is the Custom* (see Chapter 1, note 4).

Notes to Chapter Three: Sir Josiah Child's Economic Writings

1. We are grateful to Professor David Collard for drawing to our attention the problem of the authorship of the 'Philopatris' pamphlet discussed in this chapter.
2. *A Treatise wherein is demonstrated I. That the East India Trade is the most National of all Foreign Trades. II. That the Clamors, Aspersions, and Objections made against the present East India Company, are Sinister, Selfish, or Groundless. III. That since the discovery of the East Indies, the Dominion of the Sea depends much upon the Wane or Increase of that Trade, and consequently the Security of the Liberty, Property, and Protestant Religion of this Kingdom. IV. That the Trade of the East Indies cannot be carried on to National advantage, in any other way than by a General Joynt-Stock. V. That the East India Trade is more profitable and necessary to the Kingdom of England, than to any other Kingdom or Nation in Europe.* (London: T. J. for Robert Boulter, and J. R. for the Honourable East-India Company, 1681.)
3. On Child's dominance, see Sir W. W. Hunter, *A History of British India*, vol. II (London: Longman, 1900), especially ch. 8, pp. 275–323. Child's rise

seems all the more remarkable when one examines the records of the East India Company. Prior to Child becoming Governor, Papillon, though Deputy Governor, seems to have been in *de facto* control, chairing 53 of 85 meetings of the Directors between 20 August 1680 and 12 April 1681, when Child was elected Governor. His predecessor, Sir William Thomson, attended somewhat spasmodically and seems to have been in poor health.

4. Charles King, *The British Merchant or Commerce Preserv'd* (London: Darby, 1721; reprinted New York: Kelley, 1968) vol. I, p. 182. King, however, was not certain of the pamphlet's authorship. He referred to 'a Pamphlet wrote by Sir *Josiah Child*, or at least by his Direction' – loc. cit. He does not even give the title of the pamphlet but it can be identified by a reference he makes to material on p. 19 of it.
5. J. R. McCulloch, *The Literature of Political Economy: A Classified Catalogue of Select Publications in the Different Departments of that Science, with Historical, Critical, and Biographical Notices* (London: Longman, 1845). McCulloch cites the *British Merchant* attribution and comments: 'whoever compares it with his "Discourse of Trade" . . . will be satisfied that Sir Josiah was its author' (p. 99).
6. W. R. Scott, *The Constitution and Finance of English, Scottish and Irish Joint-Stock Companies to 1720*, vol. II. *Companies for Foreign Trade, Colonisation, Fishing and Mining* (Cambridge: Cambridge University Press, 1910). See p. 144, note 3 (which refers back to p. 142, note 1) where Scott cites the 'Philopatris' pamphlet as evidence of Child's view on the possibility of issuing a new East India stock; he also cites Somers' *Tracts* as evidence of Papillon's support for such a stock. But inspection of *A Collection of Scarce and Valuable Tracts on the Most Interesting and Entertaining Subjects: but Chiefly such as Relate to the History and Constitution of these Kingdoms. Selected from . . . Libraries; Particularly that of the late Lord Somers*, 2nd edn rev. Walter Scott (London: Cadell, 1812) VIII, pp. 455ff, reveals that the citation is again the 'Philopatris' work.
7. J. Viner, *Studies in the Theory of International Trade* (1937; reprinted London: Allen and Unwin, 1964) p. 603.
8. K. N. Chaudhuri, *The Trading World of Asia and the English East India Company 1660–1760* (London: Cambridge University Press, 1978) pp. 427, 611.
9. Hunter, op. cit., p. 275.
10. On Child's virtuosity in this respect, see, in particular, Hunter, op. cit., ch. 8, especially p. 310.
11. On Child's holding of East India Company stock, see W. O. Letwin, *The Origins of Scientific Economics. English Economic Thought 1660–1776* (London: Methuen, 1963) pp. 25–6n and p. 37n.
12. On these pamphlets, see Letwin, op. cit., especially ch. 1. On the joint pamphlet, see ibid., p. 31, and the East India Company Court Book (cited hereafter as CB) 19 August 1681, 32, f. 140a, quoted in note 39 below. The joint pamphlet is analysed later in this chapter. The identification of Ferguson is from CB, 30, f. 187, 7 February 1677, IOR B/34, which records that he was paid 'twenty Guinies [sic.] for his pains' in writing a pamphlet for the Company. Letwin (op. cit., p. 33) suggests that Ferguson was the celebrated religious controversialist and plotter of that name.

13. Letwin, op. cit., p. 235.
14. *Brief Observations* (note 49 below) p. 3.
15. 'Philopatris', p. 2.
16. Letwin, op. cit., pp. 235–6.
17. 'Philopatris', p. 4.
18. *New Discourse of Trade* (note 55 below) Preface [p. 20].
19. Letwin, op. cit., pp. 34–5, 236.
20. CB, 32, f. 162b, 30 September 1681, IOR B/36.
21. CB, 32, f. 164b, 5 October 1681, IOR B/36.
22. T. B. Macauley, *The History of England from the Accession of James II* 1849 (London: Dent, Everyman edition, 1906) vol. 3, pp. 20–31 at p. 22.
23. CB, 32, f. 165b, 7 October 1681, IOR B/36.
24. CB, 32, f. 173b, 11 November 1681, IOR B/36.
25. A. W. F. Papillon, *Memoirs of Thomas Papillon, of London, Merchant, 1623–1702* (Reading: Joseph J. Beechcroft, Printer, 1887) pp. 82–3.
26. Hunter, op. cit., pp. 283–7; Letwin, op. cit., pp. 34–5.
27. The manuscript is in the Papillon papers now held at County Hall, Maidstone. The reference is U1015 015/4. We are grateful to staff of Kent Record Office for assistance in locating the document and for giving us access to the Papillon papers.
28. See note 6 above.
29. Letwin, op. cit., p. 235 note 1.
30. 'Philopatris', p. 10.
31. Chaudhuri, op. cit., p. 427.
32. 'Philopatris', pp. 21–2.
33. Chaudhuri, op. cit., pp. 611–12.
34. However, a search of the Court Book from 20 August 1680 to 7 November 1681 did not reveal a record of any such debate.
35. See note 20 above.
36. *Answer of the said East India Company* in *Allegations of the Turkey Company . . . against the East-India Company . . . to the Privy Council* . . . , 1681.
37. Letwin, op. cit., p. 238.
38. S. A. Khan, *East India Trade in the XVIIth Century* (Oxford: Oxford University Press, 1923; reprinted New Delhi: Chand, n.d.) p. 195.
39. Court Book, 32, f. 140a, 19 August 1681. 'Two papers delivered by the Turkey Merchants . . . were now read in Court; and also a paper drawn-up in answer into the same; which upon debate was referred to the Governo^r Deputy & Com^tees, to make such amendm^ts therein as they shall think fit.'
40. 'Philopatris' (note 2 above) p. 21.
41. Ibid., pp. 12–15.
42. Ibid., pp. 8, 18.
43. *The Humble Answer of the Governor, Deputy Governor, and Court of Committees of the East-India Company, to a Paper of Propositions for Regulation of the East-India Company, received from the Right Honourable the Earl of Nottingham, their Majesties principal Secretary of State*, 1692, in Somers, *Tracts*, III (1751) p. 181.
44. Letwin, op. cit., pp. 238–9.

45. *Humble Answer*, p. 626, '*Seventhly*, If it be thought by any, that envy the company's good fortune, that some few of the company are too rich and powerful in the committee, the company answer, that to cure that, if it be a fault, there needs no new laws nor articles in any charter, for a very few years will cure that without such preternatural force; for that the sons of such men were never known to succeed their fathers in the painful fatigue of the company's affairs, but did always settle themselves upon an easier course of life by a revenue in land.'
46. *Humble Answer*, p. 622; 'Philopatris', pp. 21–2.
47. *The Great Honour and Advantage of the East India Trade to the Kingdom, Asserted* (London: T. Speed, 1697).
48. Letwin, op. cit., p. 239.
49. Sir Josiah Child, *Brief Observations Concerning Trade, and Interest of Money* (London: Elizabeth Calvert and Henry Mortlock, 1668).
50. *An Essay on Wool, and Woollen Manufacture, for the Improvement of Trade to the Benefit of Land, Feeders of Sheep, Clothiers, and Merchants* (London: J. Bonwicke, 1693).
51. Letwin, op. cit., p. 237.
52. It could, perhaps, be argued that Letwin's particular points of contrast are not, in themselves, unassailable. For Child was not concerned with keeping *trade* free from merchant companies; and all that he said about freedom of *manufacture* was that it should be retained but with a public seal of approval made available.
53. *A Discourse of the Nature, Use and Advantages of Trade. Proposing some Considerations for the Promotion and Advancement thereof, By a Registry of Lands. Preventing the Exportation of Coyn. Lowering the Interest of money. Inviting Foreign Families into England* (London: Randal Taylor, 1694).
54. Letwin, op. cit., pp. 237–8.
55. Sir Josiah Child, *A New Discourse of Trade, Wherein is Recommended several weighty Points relating to Companies of Merchants* (London: John Everingham, 1693) pp. 143–4.
56. See note 49 above.
57. See note 55 above.
58. See note 2 above.
59. *The East-India-Trade a most profitable trade to the Kingdom, and Best Secured and Improved by A Company and a Joint-Stock* (London: 1677). See note 12 above.
60. pp. 200–33, 276–97 of Robert Ferguson, *The Interest of Reason in Religion; with the Import and Use of Scripture – metaphors; and the Nature of the Union betwixt Christ and Believers* (London: D. Newman, 1675).
61. Sir Thomas Culpepper (the Elder), *A Tract against Usurie*, 1621, reprinted as 'A Small Treatise Against Usury', pp. 205–30 of Child's *New Discourse of Trade*.
62. The distribution involved has on the horizontal axis the number of times a word is used as a proportion of total number of words in a piece; on the vertical axis we measure the number of words in each category as a proportion of vocabulary.

Notes to Chapter Four: Torrens, McCulloch, and the *Edinburgh Review*, 1819

1. 'Mr Owen's Plans for Relieving the National Distress', *Edinburgh Review*, 32 (October 1819) pp. 453–77.
2. 'On Mr Owen's Plan, and the Causes of the Present Distress', *Scotsman*, 21 August 1819, pp. 265–6.
3. Especially *Edinburgh Review*, loc. cit., pp. 455 and 459.
4. The critical disputed section is p. 469 (lower half) to p. 475 (upper half).
5. Lord Robbins, *Robert Torrens and the Evolution of Classical Economics* (London: Macmillan, 1958); F. W. Fetter, 'The Authorship of Economic Articles in the *Edinburgh Review*, 1802–47', *Journal of Political Economy*, 61 (1953) pp. 232–5. For Sraffa, see text and note 13 below. Other references may be found in W. O. Thweatt, 'The Digression on Sismondi: By Torrens or McCulloch?', *History of Political Economy*, 6 (1974) pp. 435–53 at pp. 438–9 note 18.
6. J. S. Chipman, 'A Survey of the Theory of International Trade: Part 2', *Econometrica*, 33 (1965) pp. 710–12.
7. T. Sowell, *Say's Law* (Princeton, N.J.: Princeton University Press, 1972) pp. 11–12.
8. D. Ricardo, *Works and Correspondence*, ed. P. Sraffa (Cambridge: Cambridge University Press, 1951–73) vol. 8, p. 159.
9. R. Torrens, *An Essay on the Production of Wealth* (London: Longman, 1821; reprinted New York: A. M. Kelley, 1965) pp. 378–89.
10. Ricardo, *Works*, vol. 8, p. 376.
11. J. Viner, *Studies in the Theory of International Trade* (1937; reprinted London: Allen and Unwin, 1964) p. 194 note and p. 621.
12. See note 5 above.
13. The Viner papers are not available for public inspection, and we are very grateful to Professor Winch for making this information available to us privately and to Professor Viner's family for giving us permission to refer to the papers.
14. The reference is at p. 473 of the disputed article.
15. Thweatt, 'Digression', pp. 440–3. The reference is to 'Effects of Machinery and Accumulation', *Edinburgh Review*, 35 (March 1821) pp. 102–23.
16. Thweatt, 'Digression', pp. 443–4, 452.
17. Ibid., pp. 448–9.
18. Ibid., p. 450.
19. Ricardo, *Works*, vol. 8, pp. 159, 165. See also ibid., pp. 82, 227, 376. The article was 'Taxation and the Corn Laws', *Edinburgh Review*, 33 (January 1820) pp. 155–87.
20. 'Throughout all McCulloch's changes of attitude to population problems and to the Poor Law one factor remained fairly constant – his advocacy of emigration.' – D. P. O'Brien, *J. R. McCulloch: A Study in Classical Economics* (London: Allen and Unwin, 1970) p. 331.
21. *Essay on the Production of Wealth*, p. 385.
22. Ibid., p. 397.
23. Ibid., p. 400.
24. See Lord Robbins, *Robert Torrens*, especially chapters IV and V, and D. P.

O'Brien, 'The Transition in Torrens' Monetary Thought', *Economica*, N.S. 32 (1965) pp. 269–301.

25. It is not true that, as one commentator believed, McCulloch was 'a notorious plagiariser' – Chipman, op. cit. To our knowledge, the only person who ever accused McCulloch of plagiarism was Samuel Read; and he was mistaken. McCulloch was a self-plagiarist; but that is a different matter. He habitually used footnote citation and quotation marks; indeed, his work is at times so loaded down with references that removal of the quoted matter reduces quite perceptibly the amount for computer analysis.
26. Especially between pp. 371–83 of the *Essay* and pp. 471–3 of the *Review*. This had earlier been indicated by Lord Robbins (*Robert Torrens*, p. 177).
27. The three references are: (i) the *Edinburgh* article, 'Effects of Machinery and Accumulation' (note 15 above); (ii) McCulloch's review of Sismondi, *Nouveaux Principes*, in the *Scotsman*, 24 April 1819, p. 134; and the section in McCulloch, *Principles of Political Economy*, 1st edn (Edinburgh, 1825) pp. 165–92. All these date from the same period, and they all deal with the same subject as the 'Digression'.
28. McCulloch's own list of his contributions was published in a number of places, mainly through the agency of his son-in-law, H. G. Reid. See in particular his *Biographical Notice of John Ramsey McCulloch* (privately printed, London 1865) and *Notes and Queries*, 5 ser., vol. x, 5 October 1878, pp. 262–3. This list is in agreement, as Professor Fetter has pointed out, with McCulloch's own bound three volume set of his contributions to which he refers in his *Catalogue* (1862) and which is in his library at Reading University. It also corresponds with the contents of the bound set of McCulloch's articles in the Goldsmith Library, University of London.
29. On Jeffrey's control of McCulloch, see O'Brien, *J. R. McCulloch*, p. 35.
30. Ibid., p. 34.
31. On the Copinger list, see E. R. Houghton (ed.), *The Wellesley Index to Victorian Periodicals 1824–1900*, vol. I (Toronto: Toronto University Press, 1966) pp. 426–7. The case for the association with Longman's is discussed in F. W. Fetter, 'A Probable Source of Copinger's "On the Authorship of the First Hundred Numbers of the *Edinburgh Review*" ', *The Library*, 5 ser., IX (1954) pp. 49–53.
32. J. R. McCulloch, *A Treatise on the Principles and Practical Influence of Taxation and the Funding System* (1845), reprinted ed. D. P. O'Brien (Edinburgh: Scottish Academic Press, 1975).
33. J. R. McCulloch, *The Principles of Political Economy, with Some Inquiries Respecting their Application*, 5th edn (Edinburgh: A. and C. Black, 1864).
34. *Edinburgh Review*, March 1821 – see note 15 above.
35. *Edinburgh Review*, October 1819 – see note 1 above.
36. R. Torrens, *An Essay on the External Corn Trade with an Appendix on the Means of Improving the Condition of the Labouring Classes*, 5th edn (London: Longman, 1829).
37. See note 2 above.
38. See note 9 above.
39. D. P. O'Brien and A. C. Darnell, 'Torrens, McCulloch, and the "Digression on Sismondi": whose digression?', *History of Political Economy*, 12 (1980) pp. 383–95.

Notes to Chapter Five: Samuel Bailey and Two Anonymous Pamphlets

1. D. Ricardo, *Works and Correspondence*, ed. P. Sraffa (Cambridge: Cambridge University Press, 1951–73) vol. IX, pp. 27, 38.
2. New York: A. M. Kelley, 1967.
3. [S. Bailey], *A Critical Dissertation on the Nature, Measure and Causes of Value; Chiefly in Reference to the Writings of Mr. Ricardo and his followers* (London: R. Hunter, 1825).
4. K. Marx, *Theories of Surplus Value* (London: Lawrence and Wishart, 1972) vol. III, p. 110.
5. Ibid., pp. 124–5, 144.
6. Ibid., p. 162.
7. Ibid., p. 117.
8. J. A. Schumpeter, *History of Economic Analysis* (London: Allen and Unwin, 1954) p. 599 note 22.
9. E. R. A. Seligman, 'On Some Neglected British Economists' part I, *Economic Journal*, XIII (1903) pp. 335–63 at p. 351.
10. R. M. Rauner, *Samuel Bailey and the Classical Theory of Value* (London: Bell, 1961) p. 89.
11. T. Sowell, 'Samuel Bailey Revisited', *Economica*, 37 (1970) pp. 402–8.
12. Rauner, loc. cit.
13. T. De Quincy, *Collected Writings*, ed. Masson (London: Black, 1897) vol. IX, p. 49.
14. T. Sowell, *Say's Law* (Princeton, N.J.: Princeton University Press, 1972).
15. Ibid., pp. 54, 91, 92, 94, 131–4.
16. For a list of Bailey's publications, compiled by his friend Alexander Ireland, see *Notes and Queries*, 5 ser., IX (March 1878) pp. 182–5.
17. Samuel Halkett and James Laing, *Dictionary of Anonymous and Pseudonymous English Literature*, new ed. by J. Kennedy, W. A. Smith and A. F. Johnson (Edinburgh: Oliver and Boyd, 1926–34).
18. Our thanks are due to Mr Douglas Matthews of the London Library for providing us with copies of the inscriptions.
19. We must thank in particular staff of Yale, Northwestern, Edinburgh and Columbia University Libraries and of the Library of Congress and the British Museum, for dealing with enquiries about the two pamphlets discussed in this chapter.
20. We are grateful to Mr Atkins of Sheffield City Libraries for informing us of the existence of Bailey's copies of these pamphlets, which are held in the Arts and Humanities Library at Sheffield.
21. K. Dennis, 'The Bailey Notebooks and Authorship of "Verbal Disputes"', *History of Economic Thought Newsletter*, no. 11 (Autumn 1973) pp. 17–18.
22. R. M. Rauner failed to discover the presence of the Bailey papers in Edinburgh, despite an exhaustive search. See R. M. Rauner, 'Samuel Bailey and Classical Economics', Ph.D. thesis, University of London 1956, App. D, p. 713. The papers are not mentioned either in the excellent standard guide by R. P. Sturges, *Economists' Papers 1750–1950* (Durham, N.C.: Duke University Press, 1975). We are grateful to Dr Hall of Edinburgh University Library for his help in connection with these papers.
23. *Observations*, pp. 27–8.

24. *Observations*, p. 37.
25. Edinburgh University Library, Mss. Gen. 69[7]; Notebook I, pp. 106–7.
26. For example, Edinburgh, Mss. Gen. 69[12], p. 162.
27. Edinburgh, Mss. Gen. 69[7]; Notebook I, pp. 108–9.
28. Ibid., pp. 114–17.
29. Ibid., pp. 82–3.
30. Only p. 122 of Notebook I is blank.
31. Notebook I, pp. 124–6.
32. *Observations*, p. 35.
33. [H. Brougham], 'Lord Lauderdale on Public Wealth', *Edinburgh Review*, IV (1804) pp. 343–77.
34. W. E. Houghton (ed.), *The Wellesley Index to Victorian Periodicals*, vol. I (Toronto: Toronto University Press, 1966) p. 435.
35. *Dictionary of National Biography*, vol. VI, (1886) pp. 448–58 at p. 449.
36. We must thank Mrs J. Percival of University College London Library for supplying us with a sample of Brougham's handwriting.
37. We refer to the material on shipping on pp. 11–12 and the reference to Brazil on p. 15.
38. *Inquiry*, p. 8.
39. *Inquiry*, p. 109.
40. *Dictionary of National Biography*, vol. II (1885) p. 409. On Bailey's visit to America, which may have occurred in 1817, see Rauner's Ph.D. thesis (note 22 above), pp. 535–6.
41. We are extremely indebted to Professor Barry Gordon, who responded to our inquiry about possible authorship of the two pamphlets. In reply, Professor Gordon made out an excellent *a priori* case that Brougham was the author of the *Inquiry*. His case rested on internal evidence that the author was neither Tory nor radical, neither land owner nor commercial man. This led him to the possibility of a Whig lawyer and to certain parallels between material in the pamphlet and positions advanced elsewhere by Brougham. Several months ensued between our original letter and Professor Gordon's considered reply; by the time we received the latter we were convinced, as a result of our statistical tests, that Brougham was responsible for the *Observations*. But apart from Professor Gordon and ourselves, no one seems to have connected *either* of the anonymous pamphlets with Brougham.
42. [S. Bailey], *A Letter to a Political Economist; occasioned by an article in the Westminster Review on the Subject of Value. By the Author of the Critical Dissertation on Value Therein Reviewed* (London: R. Hunter, 1826).
43. C. F. Cotterill, *An Examination of the Doctrines of Value as set forth by Adam Smith, Ricardo, M'Culloch, Mill, the Author of 'A Critical Dissertation, &c.', Torrens, Malthus, Say &c. &c. being a Reply to those Distinguished Authors* (London: Simkin and Marshall, 1831).

Notes to Chapter Six: James Mill, J. S. Mill, and Samuel Bailey

1. S. Bailey, *A Critical Dissertation on the Nature, Measure, and Causes of Value; Chiefly in Reference to the Writings of Mr. Ricardo and his Followers. By the Author of Essays on the Formation and Publication of Opinions, &c.*

&c. (London: R. Hunter, 1825). There does not seem to be any dispute about the authorship of this work. R. M. Rauner, in his Ph.D. thesis, 'Samuel Bailey and Classical Economics' (University of London, 1956) notes (p. 713) that Bailey's signature appears on the title page of the copy of the *Critical Dissertation* in the Department of Local History, Sheffield City Library.

2. *Westminster Review*, v (January 1826) pp. 157–72, 'On the Nature, Measures, and Causes of Value'.
3. *A Catalogue of Books, the Property of a Political Economist; with Critical and Bibliographical Notices* (London: privately printed, 1862) p. 284.
4. F. W. Fetter, 'Economic Articles in the *Westminster Review* and their Authors, 1824–51', *Journal of Political Economy*, 70 (1962) pp. 570–96 at pp. 570–1.
5. R. M. Rauner, *Samuel Bailey and the Classical Theory of Value* (London: Bell, 1961) (hereafter cited as *Value*) pp. 149–57.
6. J. Mill, *Analysis of the Phenomena of the Human Mind* (London: Baldwin and Cradock, 1835).
7. Ibid., I, 83–145.
8. Rauner, *Value*, p. 152.
9. Ibid., p. 153.
10. Ibid., p. 153. On this, see D. P. O'Brien, *J. R. McCulloch: A Study in Classical Economics* (London: Allen and Unwin, 1970) pp. 130–6.
11. Rauner, *Value*, pp. 153–4.
12. Ibid., p. 154; *Westminster Review*, loc. cit., pp. 168–71.
13. Ibid., p. 154. See *Westminster Review*, VI (July 1826) pp. 1–23. Mill's authorship of this article is accepted by the *Wellesley Index* (III, p. 564), on the strength of two sources: Place's diary and a marked set of *Westminster Review* in Somerville College, Oxford. The latter is discussed further below.
14. Rauner, *Value*, p. 155. The attack was in James Mill, *A Fragment on Mackintosh; being Strictures on Some Passages in the Dissertation by Sir James Mackintosh prefixed to the Encylopaedia Britannica* (London: for Baldwin and Cradock, 1835).
15. See the diary of J. L. Mallet in *Political Economy Club Centenary Volume* (London: Macmillan, 1921) p. 224.
16. On James Mill as the man 'behind' Ricardo, see T. W. Hutchison, 'Some Questions about Ricardo', *Economica*, N.S. 19 (1952) pp. 415–32 at pp. 431–2.
17. E. Halevy, *The Growth of Philosophic Radicalism*, trans. M. Morris (London: Faber, 1928) p. 445.
18. Ibid., pp. 19–68, 'Sir James on Hobbes'.
19. J. S. Mill, *Autobiography*, 8th edn (London: Longman, 1886) p. 122.
20. For example, I, pp. 31–2n, II p. 1.
21. A. Bain, *James Mill. A Biography* (London: Longman, 1882; reprinted New York: A. M. Kelley, 1967) pp. 27–9, 156–7, 162.
22. Ibid., p. 424.
23. Op. cit., p. 150.
24. Op. cit., p. 262.
25. J. S. Mill, op. cit., pp. 68–9.
26. Ibid., p. 18.

27. Ibid., p. 29.
28. J. S. Mill, *A System of Logic Ratiocinative and Inductive Being a Connected View of the Principles of Evidence and the Methods of Scientific Investigation* (1843), reprinted ed. J. M. Robson and R. F. McCrae (Toronto: Toronto University Press, 1973).
29. Ibid., p. 112n.
30. Ibid., p. 175.
31. Ibid., p. 827.
32. Ibid., p. 889.
33. *Autobiography*, p. 133. See also M. St J. Packe, *The Life of John Stuart Mill* (London: Secker and Warburg, 1954) p. 74.
34. Ibid., p. 17.
35. *Logic*, pp. 879–86.
36. S. Bailey, *A Letter to a Political Economist Occasioned by an Article in the Westminster Review on the Subject of Value. By the Author of the Critical Dissertation on Value Therein Reviewed* (London: R. Hunter, 1826).
37. *Letter*, p. 79; J. Mill, *Elements of Political Economy* 2nd edn (London: Baldwin, Cradock and Joy, 1826) p. 98.
38. *Westminster Review*, loc. cit., p. 158.
39. The paper was apparently sent to Mill, for it was found amongst the Mill–Ricardo papers, but must have been considered by him to be unsuitable for publication – see Ricardo, *Works*, ed. Sraffa (Cambridge: Cambridge University Press, 1951–73) IV, pp. 358–9.
40. 'While the knowledge of the science [of Political Economy] is still confined to a comparatively small number, it has two powerful classes of enemies, the interested and the ignorant; who, we daily see, assume to themselves a merit in decrying it.' *Westminster Review*, loc. cit., p. 172. See also Professor D. Winch's comments in *James Mill: Selected Economic Writings* (Edinburgh: Oliver and Boyd, 1966) p. 192.
41. *A New English Dictionary on Historical Principles*, ed. J. A. H. Murray vol. II (Oxford: Clarendon Press, 1889) p. 892.
42. See especially *Letter*, pp. 19–20, 33–5.
43. Ibid., p. 35.
44. *Letter*, p. 79.
45. Ibid., p. 80. See also ibid., p. 89.
46. *Westminster Review*, III (January 1825) pp. 213–32, 'Periodical Literature – Quarterly Review: Political Economy'. The source for the attribution is the standard work N. MacMinn, J. R. Hainds and J. M. McCrimmon, *Bibliography of the Published Writings of John Stuart Mill* (Evanston, Ill.: Northwestern University, 1943), which is based upon Mill's own list.
47. J. S. Mill, *Principles of Political Economy with some of their Applications to Social Philosophy* (1848), reprinted ed. J. M. Robson, 2 volumes (Toronto: Toronto University Press, 1965). See, in particular, the discussion of causes of changes in value (I, pp. 159–60), and of the impossibility of a general rise in value (I, pp. 166–7).
48. Ibid., pp. 466–8.
49. Ibid., p. 469.
50. J. M. Robson, 'A Note on Mill bibliography', *University of Toronto Quarterly*, 34 (October 1964) pp. 93–7. We have checked the Somerville set

against what is known from other sources, and it appears to be accurate, though not comprehensive.

51. Ibid., p. 94. For the MacMinn bibliography, see note 46 above.
52. Pp. 254–303 of the Winch edition (note 40 above).
53. Pp. 455–501 of the Toronto edition (note 47 above).
54. Note 46 above.
55. Pp. 19–68 (note 14 above).
56. Rauner, *Value*, p. 155. Bailey made notes on this work and concluded: 'On the whole I found this an acute but very peevish rude and unmannerly work, showing nothing of the spirit of the gentleman or the true philosopher.' Index Rerum, vol. I, Gen. 69[4], Bailey Papers, Edinburgh University Library.
57. Pp. 91–168 (note 6 above).
58. *Autobiography*, p. 28.
59. Ibid., p. 62.
60. Mill to Ricardo, 28 December 1820, *Works*, VIII, pp. 326–9.

Notes to Chapter Seven: McCulloch, Parnell, and the *Edinburgh Review*

1. 'Ireland', *Edinburgh Review*, 37 (1822) pp. 60–109; ibid., 41 (1825) pp. 356–410.
2. *A Catalogue of Books, the Property of a Political Economist* (London: privately printed, 1862) p. 147.
3. Ibid., p. 202.
4. *A Dictionary, Practical, Theoretical, and Historical of Commerce and Commercial Navigation*, ed. H. G. Reid (London: Longman, 1869) pp. xxxi–xxxii.
5. *Notes and Queries*, 5th series, vol. 10, 5 October 1878, pp. 262–3.
6. See R. D. C. Black, *Economic Thought and the Irish Question 1817–1870* (Cambridge: Cambridge University Press, 1960) pp. 73, 74.
7. British Museum, Add. Mss. 34622, ff. 438–9.
8. 'Catholic Emancipation – Power of the Pope – Divided Allegiance of the Catholics', *Edinburgh Review*, 43 (November 1825) pp. 125–63. For a discussion of Copinger's list, and the possibility that it is based on Longman's records, see *The Wellesley Index to Victorian Periodicals*, ed. W. E. Houghton, vol. I (Toronto: University of Toronto Press, 1966) pp. 426–8, and F. W. Fetter, 'A Probable Source . . .', *The Library*, 5th Series, IX (1954) pp. 49–53.
9. The list given by Parnell contains, apart from the two articles on Ireland discussed here, an article on Finance (vol. 39, 1823, pp. 1–43), discussed below, another on this subject (vol. 33, 1820, pp. 54–69), two more on Ireland (vol. 43, 1825, pp. 125–63 as in note 8 above, and vol. 43, 1826, pp. 461–96), and two late articles, 'Customs Duties' (vol. 72, 1841, pp. 418–55) and 'Financial Measures' (vol. 74, 1842, pp. 506–37).
10. McCulloch to Parnell, 17 June 1825, Parnell papers.
11. The three speeches were: (i) that on the Irish Insurrection Bill, 24 June 1823 (*Hansard*, N. S., IX, cols 1148–85, the report in *Hansard* being taken from the version of the speech published by Ridgway); (ii) *The Speech of Sir Henry Parnell, . . . upon Lord Althorp's motion for a Committee on the State*

of Ireland (London: Ridgway, 1824), delivered 11 May 1824; (iii) that on the Unlawful Societies in Ireland Bill, 10 February 1825 (*Hansard*, N. S., XII, cols 204–33, the report being again taken from a version published by Ridgway).

12. On this last matter, see the third of Parnell's speeches referred to in the previous note.
13. See D. P. O'Brien, *J. R. McCulloch* (London: Allen and Unwin, 1970) p. 349.
14. Note 11 above.
15. *Edinburgh Review*, January 1825, loc. cit., at p. 361.
16. *Edinburgh Review*, June 1822, loc. cit., at p. 81.
17. Ibid., p. 89.
18. *Edinburgh Review*, January 1825, loc. cit., at p. 380.
19. In Mss. AL187 in the University of London Library, there is a letter of 17 August 1827 from one Dugald Bannatyne to McCulloch. It contains the phrase: 'I am glad that I am to see you here on your way, from Ireland.'
20. *Edinburgh Review*, loc. cit., pp. 380–1.
21. See O'Brien, op. cit., pp. 91–6.
22. D. Ricardo, *Works and Correspondence*, ed. P. Sraffa (Cambridge: Cambridge University Press, 1951–73) IX, pp. 160, 186.
23. 'Civil Affairs of Ireland', *Edinburgh Review*, 43 (February 1826) pp. 461–96.
24. Ibid., pp. 463, 480, 482.
25. *Edinburgh Review*, January 1825, loc. cit., pp. 368–76.
26. See O'Brien, op. cit., pp. 22–34, on McCulloch's links with the *Scotsman*.
27. *Edinburgh Review*, June 1822, loc. cit., p. 109; ibid., 1825, loc. cit., p. 410. Italics in both originals.
28. J. R. McCulloch, *A Treatise on the Principles and Practical Influence of Taxation and the Funding System*, 1845, 1852, 1863, new edition, ed. D. P. O'Brien (Edinburgh: Scottish Academic Press, 1975) p. 341.
29. Ricardo, *Works*, loc. cit.
30. *Edinburgh Review*, June 1822, loc. cit., pp. 96–7.
31. Ricardo, *Works*, IX, pp. 185–6.
32. *Edinburgh Review*, January 1825, loc. cit., pp. 366–7.
33. See note 11 above.
34. *Edinburgh Review*, January 1825, loc. cit., pp. 385–6.
35. Ibid., pp. 390ff.; cf. O'Brien, op. cit., pp. 288–9, 374–8.
36. Ibid., pp. 399–400; cf. O'Brien, op. cit., pp. 349–50.
37. Sir H. Parnell, *A History of the Penal Laws against the Irish Catholics; from the Year 1689, to the Union* (London: Longman, 1825). The sections were pp. 1–5, 12–23, 27–32, 56–61.
38. Sir H. Parnell, *On Financial Reform*, 3rd edn (London: Murray, 1831). We used pp. 71–109 of this work.
39. See note 8 above.
40. Vol. 39, pp. 1–43.
41. *Treatise on Taxation*, ed. O'Brien, p. 425.
42. Pp. 1–21 of the *Review* correspond with pp. 401–15 of the *Treatise*; pp. 22–30 correspond with pp. 419–28, and pp. 31–37 correspond with pp. 451–59.
43. *Hansard*, 1st ser., XL (1819), cols 1429–38, 1 July 1819.
44. 'Finance', *Edinburgh Review*, 33 (January 1820), pp. 54–69.

45. In the case of 'Ireland' 1822, we tested pp. 79–87, 'Government and Magistracy', the only section not containing material reproduced from the *Scotsman*, against the remainder of the article. For 'Ireland' 1825, we tested pp. 356–83 (Introduction and Part I of the article, dealing with causes of political and religious discontent) against pp. 383–410 (Part II, dealing with causes of Irish poverty, and conclusion). As a subsidiary check, we tested those parts of the article containing material reproduced from the *Scotsman* (see Table 7.1) against the rest of the article. The result of this subsidiary test is reported in Table 7.5 (xviii). The article proves to be internally consistent, however divided.
46. As with tests on first word usage we used two different divisions of the 1825 'Ireland' article – see note 45 above. The supplementary test is reported in Table 7.7(xiii).
47. A supplementary test of consistency in the case of 'Ireland' 1825 (see note 45 above) is reported in Table 7.9(xviii).
48. A supplementary test of consistency in the case of 'Ireland' 1825 (see note 45 above) is reported in Table 7.11(xiii).

Notes to Chapter Eight: Huskisson and the *Essays on Political Economy*

1. Canberra: Australian National University, 1976.
2. Tucker's introduction to *Essays*, p. xvii.
3. *Essays*, pp. 14ff.
4. Ibid., p. 17.
5. Ibid., pp. 78–9.
6. Ibid., p. 291.
7. Ibid., pp. 336–7, 362.
8. Ibid., p. 370 and *passim*.
9. For example, ibid., p. 406.
10. Ibid., pp. 287, 403–5.
11. Ibid., pp. 39, 63, 239, 255 (a parallel with the East India monopoly), 275–6, 305–7, 427–30).
12. Ibid., p. 64.
13. Ibid., pp. 149–50. The concept of 'metallic fluctuation' dated from 1825–6.
14. Ibid., pp. 343–53.
15. Ibid., p. 226. The author seems to deny that a transfer of hoarded precious metals involves a capital movement.
16. See also ibid., p. 383.
17. Huskisson was a member of both Committees. See *Report from the Select Committee appointed to inquire into the Cause of the High Price of Bullion, Parliamentary Papers*, 1810 (349), III, p. 1, and *First and Second Reports from the Committee of Secrecy appointed to consider of the state of the Bank of England, with reference to . . . the Resumption of Cash Payments*, ibid., 1819 (202, 282), III, p. 1.
18. *Essays*, pp. 308–16.
19. Ibid., p. 310.
20. See R. D. C. Black, *Economic Thought and the Irish Question 1817–1870* (Cambridge: Cambridge University Press, 1960) ch. 2.
21. *Essays*, pp. 322–3.

22. Ibid., pp. 433–4.
23. Tucker's introduction to *Essays*, pp. xix–xx.
24. Tucker's introduction to *Essays*, p. xxi.
25. Ibid., p. xxiii. The pamphlet was *The Question concerning the Depreciation of our Currency stated and examined* (London: Murray, 1810).
26. See *The Speeches of the Right Honourable William Huskisson, with a biographical memoir*, 3 volumes (London: Murray, 1831) III, pp. 418–9. See also ibid., p. 421.
27. Ibid., p. xxiii.
28. Ibid., p. xxiv.
29. Ibid., p. xxv.
30. Ibid., p. xxvi.
31. Ibid., pp. xxvii–xxix.
32. Ibid., pp. xxix–xxx.
33. Ibid., pp. xxxiii–xxxv. It should, however, be said that to the untrained eye there appears to be no resemblance between the signature 'Geo Robertson' and the handwriting of Captain Thomas Huskisson contained in Add. Mss. 38045, ff. 367–71.
34. British Museum, Add. Mss. 38757, ff. 112, 118, 133, 211.
35. Ibid., p. xxxii n. See C. Badham, *The Life of James Deacon Hume* (London: Smith Elder, 1859) ch. II.
36. Jacob was particularly well-known as an expert on the corn trade. For an example of his work in this area see his *Report on the Trade in Foreign Corn, and on the Agriculture of the North of Europe* (London: Ridgway, 1826), which was one of a number of publications by Jacob on the corn trade.
37. W. Jacob, *An Historical Inquiry into the Production and Consumption of the Precious Metals*, 2 volumes (London: Murray, 1831; reprinted New York: A. M. Kelley, 1968) p. v.
38. Tucker's introduction to *Essays*, p. xxxii. Tucker's source for the belief in several manuscript copies was C. R. Fay.
39. Add. Mss. 38762.
40. Tucker, loc. cit.
41. See note 26 above.
42. Ibid., II, pp. 130–66.
43. Ibid., III, pp. 514–51.
44. See note 25 above.
45. *Essays*, pp. 81–205.
46. J. D. Hume, *Thoughts on the Corn-Laws as connected with Agriculture, Commerce and Finance* (London: Rivington, 1815).
47. Jacob, op. cit. (note 37 above), vol. I, pp. v–ix, 270–323.

Index